THE
SPECIAL
FORCES

PETER MACDONALD

THE SPECIAL FORCES

PETER MACDONALD

CHARTWELL BOOKS, INC.

PHOTOGRAPHIC ACKNOWLEDGMENTS

Australian Army 249, 250, 251 top, 251 bottom; Belgian Army 172, 173, 174, 175 top, 175 bottom, 176; Bundesgrenschutz 200, 201; Canadian Armed Forces 177, 178 top, 178 bottom, 179, 180; Central Press 67, 77; Defence 79, 242; Edward Stanford/PMA 119 top, 134, 135, 136; Imperial War Museum 68, 69, 86, 99, 119 bottom, 120, 121, 182–3, 203; Italian Navy 207, 208; Keystone Press Agency 21 top, 147 bottom, 225, 226, 227, 228, 229, 230, 232; Norwegian Armed Forces 218, 219, 220–221, 222–223; Paolo Valpolini 202, 204, 205, 206; Parachute Regiment 123, 125, 137; Paul Hogan 139; Peter Macdonald 73, 85, 88, 89, 91, 109, 110, 115 top, 115 bottom, 118, 126, 127, 128, 130–131, 131 top, 132–133, 137 top, 137 bottom, 138 top, 138 bottom, 140, 141, 142–143, 144 top, 144 bottom, 145 top, 145 bottom, 171, 181, 184 top, 184 bottom, 185, 189 top, 189 bottom, 190–191, 192 top, 192 bottom, 193, 194, 195 top, 195 bottom, 196 top, 196 bottom, 197, 198–199, 239, 243, 245; PMA Pictures 71, 74, 80 top, 149, 159, 168, 247; Rex Features 169, 231, 233, 241, 244; Royal Marines 76, 87, 92, 94, 95, 96–97, 98, 100–101, 102, 103, 104, 105, 106, 107, 111, 112 top, 112 bottom, 113, 116, 117, 209; Royal Netherlands Marine Corps 210, 212, 213, 214–215, 216–217; SAS Regimental Association 75, 80 bottom, 81, 83, 84; Swedish Armed Forces 237; Tass 147 top, 150, 151, 152, 154, 155, 157, 160, 161, 165, 166, 167; TRH Picture Library 38, 153, 163, 164, 235, 248; US Department of Defense/82nd Airborne/1st SOCOM 7, 8, 9, 10, 11, 12, 13, 15, 16, 17, 19, 20, 20–21, 22, 24, 25, 26, 27, 28, 29 top, 29 bottom, 30, 31, 33, 34, 35 top, 35 bottom, 36, 37, 39 top, 39 bottom, 41, 42, 43, 44, 45, 46, 47, 48 top, 48 bottom, 49, 50, 51, 52, 53, 54, 55, 56, 57, 58 top, 58 bottom, 60, 61, 62, 63, 64, 65, 240.

Front cover: The archetypal image of the US Army Special Forces Soldier. (US Department of Defense)

Back cover: A marine on the mountain leader (ML2) course run by the Mountain and Arctic Warfare Cadre. (Richard Cooke)

Title spread: Forces from the 82nd Airborne Division arriving in Europe as part of Reforger 1986, an annual exercise in rapid deployment. (TRH/USAF)

Other Acknowledgments
The author wishes to thank the following units, organizations and individuals: 82nd Airborne Division PAO, Major Doug Sams and Lieutenant Phil Parker; HQ 1st SOCOM PAO, Captain Bill Gerhards; DOD Washington, Bettie Sprigg and Ed Michalski; Luftlandebrigade 27, Oberstleutnant H-A Schoen and Hauptmann Bach; Royal Marines, Captain Joe Gordon, Captain Rob Need and Sergeant Peter Williams; RHQ The Parachute Regiment, Captain Tom Smith; SIRPA Paris, Captain Richard Lacoste; INFOSERM Brussels, A Braechmans, Adjutant Chef; Regiment Para-Commando Etat-Major, Belgium; and the officers and men of 539 Assault Squadron and the M & AW Cadre, Royal Marines.

The author would also like to thank Leslie McDonnell, Dr T R White, Edward Stanford and Brigadier P G Macdonald for their contributions to this book.

For copyright reasons this edition is for sale only within the U.S.A.

This edition published 1987 by Chartwell Books, Inc.
A division of Book Sales, Inc.
110 Enterprise Avenue
Secaucus, New Jersey 07094

Prepared by
The Hamlyn Publishing Group Limited
Bridge House, London Road, Twickenham, Middlesex, England

Copyright © 1987 The Hamlyn Publishing Group Limited
ISBN 1-55521-112-7

Printed in Spain

CONTENTS

UNITED STATES ARMY SPECIAL FORCES

The United States Army Special Forces, commonly known as the 'Green Berets', are the US Army's primary elite formation. Highly trained in the art of guerrilla warfare, Special Forces are capable of carrying out a variety of missions behind enemy lines. The primary role of the 'Green Berets', which they share with other specialist units such as Britain's Special Air Service Regiment (SAS), is strategic raiding and counter-insurgency operations. The basic fighting unit of the 'Green Berets' is the Special Forces Operational Detachment A (SFOD A), which is more popularly known as the 'A Team'. Each A Team consists of 12 men, with each man having been trained in one particular speciality such as communications, medicine, heavy weapons or engineering. In addition to these individual skills all members of the US Army Special Forces are trained in parachuting, amphibious operations and mountain and arctic warfare. The A Teams are capable of operating independently or as part of a larger group. Four A Teams are led by a 'B Team' which provides the command and control element, and consists of five officers and 18 enlisted men.

The US Army Special Forces were formed by the activation of the 10th Special Forces Group (Airborne) at Fort Bragg on 20 June 1952. Under the command of Colonel Aaron Bank who had set up the US Army's Psychological Division, the 10th Special Forces Group was to pioneer United States unconventional warfare (UW) operational concepts. Brigadier General Robert A McClure, Chief of the Army Psychological Warfare Staff Section of the Pentagon, had seen the need to set up a unit trained in guerrilla warfare to counter Communist-backed revolutionary forces in the third world. The concept of Special Forces was not new to the United States, and to understand the reasons for their formation it is necessary to go back to the Second World War and the covert operations of the Office of Strategic Ser-

vices (OSS) to which modern-day US Army Special Forces owe lineage. Incorporating some of the previous US Intelligence Departments, the OSS was formed in late 1941 by General William 'Wild Bill' Donovan. A 'civilian' general, Donovan had practised corporate law after leaving the US Army at the end of the First World War, having been awarded America's three highest military decorations. With energy and resourcefulness Donovan set about creating an organization capable of undertaking a wide variety of special operations.

In many ways the OSS was similar to the British Special Operations Executive (SOE), with which it was to carry out a number of combined missions. The primary role for the OSS was the gathering, collation and evaluation of strategic information, but it also undertook specialist espionage and sabotage missions behind enemy lines. Initially Donovan recruited a number of army officers, industrialists and academics, and these men were then divided into various detachments. Some of the largest subdivisions within the OSS were the operational groups. These groups, or OSS Detachments, were composed of 34-man teams and were infiltrated into enemy-occupied countries to organize resistance and to train guerrilla groups. During the war over 80 OSS Detachments parachuted into France, Italy, Greece, Yugoslavia and South-East Asia, operating in many cases with considerable success. One such group, Detachment 101, operated in Burma. This Detachment trained and equipped over 9,000 Kachin tribesmen, who became known as 'Kachin Rangers', and was commanded by OSS Major Carl Eifler. Apart from being a former Chief Inspector of the Mexican Border Patrol, Eifler was a martial arts master and an old acquaintance of General Joseph Stilwell, the commander of American Forces in China, Burma and India. By the end of the war, Detachment

The archetypal image of the US Army Special Forces soldier.

101 had conducted some of the most successful irregular military operations against the enemy, and was credited with having killed over 5,500 Japanese and wounding a further 10,000, with the loss of only 15 OSS lives. Another group, Detachment 202, operated in China where it carried out a number of important and successful strategic reconnaissance missions against the Japanese.

After the Allied invasion of Normandy in 1944 the OSS operated a number of 'Jedburgh' teams, or 'Jed' teams as they were known in Overlord vernacular. Under the control of the Special Operations Branch, these three-man teams parachuted behind enemy lines to organize and arm resistance groups, to harass enemy reinforcements and to cut lines of communication. The Jedburgh teams comprised two officers, one from the OSS or SOE and the other either a French or other Allied national, and an American or British serviceman. Jed teams also acted as liaison between the guerrillas and Allied Headquarters and were responsible for co-ordinating strategic attacks.

Another department that was linked with the OSS was MIS-X, which was responsible for aiding evaders and escapers from occupied Europe. Like its British equivalent, MI 9, MIS-X was responsible for exfiltrating thousands of Allied aircrew from enemy territory. Other OSS groups also became involved in this type of work; Detachment 101 rescued 215 airmen in Burma alone.

The OSS area of operations extended throughout the world with the exceptions of South America, which was under the control of the Federal Bureau of Investigation, and of the Pacific theatre, which was covered by another branch of Military Intelligence. There is no doubt that the OSS contributed greatly to the Allied war effort and was a major factor in bringing about the final defeat of the Axis powers. Together, the SOE and the OSS were pioneers in the field of irregular and guerrilla warfare. They proved that small parties of highly trained personnel in uniform can operate behind enemy lines, supplying vital strategic information and organizing resistance movements and guerrilla armies to strike the enemy where he is most vulnerable – the rear. This role has now been taken over by Special Forces.

After the end of the Second World War the OSS was disbanded along with other elite wartime formations, such as the Rangers, and the British Special Air Service and Special Operations Executive. The United States eventually reactivated the US Army Rangers and the British reformed the SAS, which was able to carry out a number of missions previously undertaken by the SOE. Military planners in the United States realized the need for the formation of a unit that would be capable of undertaking similar missions to those carried out by the Office of Stragegic Services. This led to the creation of the US Army Special Forces.

In 1951 the Korean War was raging, and the United States, together with other member countries of the United Nations, were supporting the southern Republic of Korea against the North Korean Army invasion. The North Korean Army was backed by the Communist Chinese, and had mounted a surprise offensive against South Korea in June of the previous year. Apart from the Korean War there were other smaller Communist-supported civil wars in progress throughout the world, as well as the constant threat posed to Western Europe by massed Soviet forces on its borders.

Also in 1951 the US Army Psychological Warfare Staff had set up a Special Operations Section. This Section was responsible for looking into the feasibility of forming a military group that was capable of carrying out guerrilla warfare to counter the Communist threat.

The Special Operations Section was commanded by Colonel Wendell Fertig who, with his Planning Officer, Colonel Russell W Volckman, had commanded

Most Special Forces' personnel are Ranger-trained. Although there were no Ranger battalions active during the Vietnam War, many SF personnel underwent Ranger training in the USA.

Special Forces' soldiers practise unarmed combat at Fort Bragg, North Carolina.

guerrilla units in the Philippines during the Second World War. The Section's Operations Officer was Colonel Aaron Bank who was a former member of the OSS and had served with the Jedburgh teams in France and Indo-China. These three officers pooled together their experiences and came up with a number of proposals. Their basic concept owed much to the training, organization and operations of the OSS.

The proposals put forward by the Special Operations Section met with resistance from a variety of quarters. The US Army saw the formation of such a unit as a drain on the manpower of other, 'more important combat', units, and many failed to realize the impact that small special operations units could have on the overall outcome of a war. The newly formed Central Intelligence Agency (CIA) was also a major opponent for they felt that they themselves were capable of carrying out missions in enemy territory.

FORMATION

In 1952 proposals to create a unit specializing in unconventional warfare were accepted. Colonel Bank selected a site for the future Psychological Warfare School at Fort Bragg, North Carolina, and in June 1952 the unit, named the 10th Special Forces Group (Airborne), was activated.

Colonel Bank looked for a particular type of volunteer for this new organization. Initial recruiting had begun in April, and by May the volunteers had started to arrive at Fort Bragg. Bank selected a number of men with previous experience, soldiers who had served with the Rangers and the Airborne, and men who had formally served with special operations units during the Second World War. Bank was looking for skilled professionals, mature men who would be prepared to take risks and who would be able to think and act individually as well as being able to operate as part of a team. Bank was also able to recruit a number of foreign nationals, displaced persons from Communist-occupied countries, who were able to join the US Army because of the Lodge Act. (This was an Act that allowed foreigners to gain US citizenship after serving a period in the Army.) This gave the Special Forces a number of men fluent in a variety of languages.

After selection, the men underwent a rigorous training programme. Initial training was done at an individual level. As in all special forces training, much emphasis was placed on the individual, and apart from being highly trained in basic infantry-type skills, the recruits underwent intensive specialist training. These new skills included such specialities as communications, demolitions, operational intelligence and medicine. At the same time recruits were cross-trained in a second speciality. This special forces trait allows groups to be broken down into smaller subsections while retaining the same high level of expertise and also compensates, to some extent, for the loss of any member of a group who might become a casualty as it allows the group to continue its mission without losing its only expert.

Unconventional warfare techniques also took up much of the training schedule, and the men were trained in such aspects as sabotage, escape and evasion (E&E), and

The use of small craft such as this is a proven method of infiltrating raiding and reconnaissance parties.

resistance to interrogation (RTI). Training started at team level and by the time the Psychological Warfare Center and School opened at Fort Bragg in October 1952, the 10th Special Forces Group (Airborne) were ready to have their skills tested. Several exercises were staged, and a tradition of involving the civilian population in guerrilla warfare exercises was established. The local civilian population would provide support for the Special Forces teams in the form of gathering intelligence and providing 'safe houses', while the local police and National Guard units tried to hunt them down. These exercises are continued today in one form or another.

Advanced training was also undertaken. The Group learned the techniques of mountain and arctic warfare in Colorado

and practised amphibious operations in Florida. Throughout this period great emphasis was placed on initiative and leadership skills. Not only were the men trained in their individual and team skills, but they were also taught how to instruct and so were capable of passing their skills onto others. By the end of 1952 the 10th Special Forces Group had finished its training and was ready to deploy.

EARLY DEPLOYMENT

The years between 1953 to 1961 brought about few changes to the US Army Special Forces. In early 1953 the 10th Special Forces Group sent a detachment to Korea where they acted as advisors to Far East Command. Later in the year conflict in East Berlin between Communist forces and the East German workers made the US Army realize the importance of having Special Forces permanently deployed in Europe; as a result, half of the Group moved to Bad Tölz in West Germany. The remainder stayed at Fort Bragg and were reformed as 77th Special Forces Group (Airborne).

In 1956 77th Group sent two special training teams to Japan whence they conducted a number of training missions throughout South-East Asia. In 1957 these teams formed the nucleus for the 1st Special Forces Group which was activated in Okinawa. As the new Group expanded, teams were deployed in Thailand, Nationalist China and Vietnam. From July 1957 until October 1962 both 1st and 77th (redesignated the 7th in 1960) Special

US Army Special Forces must be able to operate in a variety of terrains and climates. Here SF personnel undergo training in mountain and arctic warfare.

Forces Groups deployed training teams in Laos to train the Royal Laotian Army. These teams, later designated 'White Star' Mobile Training Teams, gained much experience which was to be of use to the US Army during the conflict in Vietnam.

Towards the end of the 1950s it became apparent that there would be a continued increase in guerrilla warfare in South-East Asia, especially in Vietnam. It was, therefore, more than likely that the Special Forces would become involved in a more complex aspect of unconventional warfare, that of counter-insurgency.

The year 1961 brought change to the US Army Special Forces and marked the beginning of their expansion. In October President John F Kennedy visited Fort Bragg to see the Special Warfare Center and the 7th Special Forces Group. Up until this time the Special Forces comprised a little-known formation even inside military circles and its function and capabilities were even less understood. President Kennedy, aware of the increasing threat of Communist-backed revolutions and guerrilla warfare, recognized the need for a US counter-insurgency force. The 7th Special Forces Group and the Special Warfare Center went all out to demonstrate their varied capabilities, techniques and equipment. Kennedy was impressed — he had found his force — and shortly after his visit he ordered an expansion programme for the Special Forces. (Kennedy was also the one who authorized the wearing of the

Rappelling skills are an important part of all special forces' training. Here two men demonstrate the evacuation of a casualty.

green beret, although it had unofficially been adopted some time before.) Thus 1st, 7th and 10th Special Forces Groups were brought up to strength. A 5th Special Forces Group was activated at the end of 1961 and deployed in support of the training missions in South-East Asia, and in 1963 three more Groups (3rd, 6th and 8th SFGA) were formed.

Rapid expansion brought with it a number of inherent problems. Although a Special Forces Training Center had been formed and extra funds allocated for training, reorganization and new equipment, there were diffculties in getting the right calibre of recruit in the quantity required. However, in spite of a lowering in the standards of training and selection, the Special Forces managed to produce a higher quality soldier than the remainder of the US Army. Although expansion created problems, it brought with it a number of benefits. The increased budget allowed better equipment to be tested and introduced, and with more funds, both individual and team training were improved, and the cross-training programme with Allied armies was increased.

Training teams from the various Groups were deployed throughout the world and undertook a variety of different missions. Teams acted as military advisors to foreign governments and trained their security forces in counter-insurgency operational techniques. They also provided teams to aid a number of civic action programmes, often helping local populations in remote, rural areas with construction projects. The experience gained by these teams was invaluable. Skills such as medicine and engineering were practised and much of what was learned was soon being taught at the Special Warfare Training Center.

During this period each Special Forces Group was assigned its own area of operations. The 1st SF Group was deployed in South-East Asia and had teams operating in Laos, the Philippines, South Vietnam, South Korea, Taiwan and Thailand. The 3rd SF Group operated throughout Africa and had teams in the Congo, Ethiopia, Guinea and Kenya. The 5th SF Group supported the 1st in South-East Asia. The 6th SF Group was responsible for the Middle East and trained the special forces of Iran, Jordan, Pakistan, Saudi Arabia and Turkey. Both the 7th and 8th SF Groups operated in Central and South America which, because of their geographic positions in relation to the United States and the complexity of Latin American politics, were considered of great strategic importance. But it was in the area of South-East Asia that the US Army Special Forces were to be involved in their most controversial series of operations.

Leadership skills are stressed in all aspects of SF training. Here students take turns in planning training missions while being assessed by an SF instructor.

VIETNAM

Vietnam had been part of French Indo-China, which consisted of Laos, Cambodia and Vietnam. In 1930 the Indo-Chinese Communist Party had been formed by Ho Chi Minh with the express aim of securing independence from French colonial rule. Guerrilla warfare began in 1941 but was halted by the Japanese occupation of the area. Then, in 1944, the Viet Minh were reactivated and fought, first, the Japanese and, after their defeat, the French. Most of these operations were conducted in the north of Vietnam with the Viet Minh being led by General Vo Nguyen Giap who was Ho Chi Minh's principal military commander. Both men had been trained in the guerrilla warfare doctrines of Mao Tse-tung and their strategy followed three basic principles: first, a period of clandestine preparation and organization; second, open guerrilla warfare; and finally, the move to conventional warfare for the last, decisive battle.

The French military forces were finally defeated at Dien Bien Phu in 1954 and in the same year the Geneva Agreement divided Vietnam into two countries, north and south of the 17th parallel. The government of South Vietnam, led by Ngo Dinh Diem, was faced with an increasing insurgency problem as the Viet Minh stepped up clandestine activities in the South. There was a steady increase in these operations which, by the end of the 1950s, had moved into the phase of open guerrilla warfare. The South Vietnamese Army, known as the Army of the Republic of Vietnam (ARVN), was a conventional force and incapable of countering this type of threat. The United States, under the Eisenhower administration, supported Diem *and* had men trained in counter-insurgency operations — the Special Forces.

The United States Military Assistance Advisory Group for Indo-China had been in Vietnam since 1950. It had provided the government of South Vietnam with advisors and had helped create a force that was capable of combating a conventional attack from the North. The ARVN was not, however, capable of countering the Viet Minh threat, and in late 1957 the first teams from the 1st Special Forces Group arrived in South Vietnam.

The South Vietnamese had established a Commando Training Center at Nha Trang, and it was here that the teams from 1st Special Forces Group started to train the men who would form the cadre of the Vietnamese SF. Both the 1st and 77th (later 7th) Special Forces Groups trained the ARVN in unconventional warfare techniques and special operations, with the 77th SF Group concentrating on training the first Vietnamese Rangers.

In 1960 the guerrilla war in the South was still escalating. In the rural areas village chiefs were being assassinated or kidnapped at a rate of 15 per week, others were defecting, and some villages were actively supporting groups of guerrillas. There were also an estimated 7,000 active guerrillas operating in South Vietnam, and in December 1960 the National Front for the Liberation of South Vietnam was formed. This organization, known as the Viet Cong, was composed of the Viet Minh and villagers recruited from the rural areas of South Vietnam itself. A state of emergency was declared by President Diem in October 1961, and by 1962 the US Military presence in Vietnam numbered about 4,000. The total Viet Cong force, however, was estimated to be 50,000 strong. The political situation worsened, and after President Diem's assassination in November 1963, the country had a number of different leaders and fell into increasing political confusion. The United States continued to support the ARVN and the Viet Cong grew in numbers and effectiveness while being supported by the North Vietnamese Army (NVA).

Civil Irregular Defence Group While the situation in South Vietnam worsened, the US Army Special Forces became increasingly involved with a programme which was to become their longest and most important contribution to the war effort. It began as the Area Development programme in 1961 and was redesignated the Civil Irregular Defence Group (CIDG) programme the following year.

The Central Highlands of South Vietnam were of vital strategic importance because the region represented an area where the borders of Laos, Cambodia and South Vietnam met. A rugged, mountainous region, ideal for enemy infiltration, it was an area over which the South Vietnamese government had little control. The Central Highlands were inhabited by various small groups of natives. A small minority of the Vietnamese population, these groups had been neglected, and at times even persecuted, by the national government. These tribes knew the region better than anyone else. Many were discontented with the old establishment and ripe for exploitation by the Viet Cong guerrillas.

The CIDG programme was initially aimed at the Montagnard tribes who were of a completely different racial origin to the Vietnamese and were despised by the vast majority of them. This made the SF teams ideal for this type of deployment, and the Montagnard groups came under the control of the US Army rather than the ARVN.

The Montagnards quickly grew to

A member of the Lac
Luong Dac Biet (LLDB),
together with a Special
Forces' NCO, on board a
river-craft in South
Vietnam. The relations
between the two countries'
special forces were often
difficult and they tended to
operate independently in
most areas.

paid civilian employees of the US Army, and were trained and equipped by the SF.

The programme was successful from the outset. By the end of 1962 there were over 200 villages and 12,000 armed Rhade Montagnards involved in the programme. The CIDG moved from being a self-defence force to one capable of carrying out reconnaissance and fighting patrols. A number of other programmes were incorporated into CIDG and specialist training centres, such as the Mountain Commando Training Center, were established. The village self-defence programme was expanded to incorporate other areas of South Vietnam and by 1964 this force numbered 43,000. Meanwhile the CIDG

Rappelling from hovering helicopters is a useful technique for inserting teams, especially when a tree canopy precludes the opportunity to land.

accept the SF personnel and a close relationship soon developed between the two groups, so close in some cases that members of SF teams were made honorary members of the tribe. Despite the fact that there was no common language between the individual tribes, and only two of the tribes (the Rhade and the Jarai) had any form of written language, there was little problem in communicating. The SF team practised what had been known by the British SAS in Malaya and Borneo as a 'hearts and minds' campaign. This involved living and working with the indigenous population, sharing food and accommodation, and using SF skills, such as medicine, to better the lives of the locals. Once they had won over the Montagnards, the SF teams organized them into local defence units. The CIDG became strike force numbered over 18,000 and was constantly involved in border surveillance and reconnaissance missions. Other ethnic minorities such as the Khmers and Nungs were soon being included in the CIDG programme.

In late 1964 the 5th Special Forces Group was relocated to Vietnam in stages and put in charge of the overall operation. There were, at this time, 40-odd CIDG camps that had been run by teams from the 1st, 5th and 7th Special Forces Groups. These teams spent six months at their assigned camp before handing over to a relieving team. This had the obvious drawback of loss of continuity as the fresh team would have to learn the area as well as any peculiarities from scratch. A new system was introduced in 1964 whereby team members spent a year in the camps before being rotated out as individuals. This system worked well; the Montagnards felt more secure with familiar faces, there was no adverse effect on the training cycle and the teams were able to maintain a higher level of operations.

Studies and Observation Group As the war escalated, both sides continued to increase support to their troops in the field. The US supplied advisors and equipment to the ARVN and SF personnel to run the CIDG programme. At the same time the North Vietnamese continued to increase the supply of weapons and equip-

Special Forces on a combat survival course. The ability to live off the land and survive with the minimum amount of equipment is one of the most important basic skills of the special forces' soldier.

Ranger units are primarily lightly equipped, fast-moving groups capable of operating in a variety of terrains.

ment to the growing number of Viet Cong guerrillas operating inside South Vietnam. Most of these supplies were being infiltrated into South Vietnam across its borders from Laos and Cambodia.

In 1964 a secret unit was formed to counter the cross-border infiltration of supplies. It was called the Studies and Observation Group (SOG), and later became known simply as C & C (Command and Control). The new force was to carry out clandestine operations inside Laos and Cambodia, two countries which were officially 'off-limits' to US forces.

The actual operations conducted inside Laos, Thailand and Cambodia were, and still are, classified 'secret'. The type of mission, however, is typical of that undertaken by Special Forces. The operations were conducted in such a way as to maintain secrecy and were concealed from all but the highest command. Missions included sabotage, subversion and psychological operations, which were intended to cause the enemy the maximum amount of physical damage and to influence enemy strategy to the advantage of the United States and its allies.

The SOG cross-border patrols were known as Spike Teams or Recon Teams (RTs) and were composed of Montagnards or Nung tribesmen led by SF personnel. These teams usually consisted of 12 men and operated mainly in Cambodia (codename 'Daniel Boone') and Laos (codename 'Prairie Fire'). Because of the sensitive nature of these missions, those involved wore no unit insignia and carried no identification. Many of the SF personnel wore locally made camouflage uniforms and, on covert operations, both they and the Montagnards wore black-dyed jungle suits, similar to those worn by the Viet Cong.

The weapons that were used by the Spike Teams varied, depending on personal choice. The 5.56 mm M-16 rifle was the US standard-issue weapon, but many carried the shorter CAR-15, which fired the same ammunition but had a shorter barrel and a telescopic butt. Captured enemy weapons such as the Soviet AK-47 were often used, as were enemy shotguns and grenade launchers. The method of infiltration across the border varied, depending on the mission, but usually the Teams were infiltrated and extracted by UH-1 helicopters (Hueys). They were also capable of calling in air strikes should they be pinned down by a superior enemy force.

The Studies and Observation Group carried out a number of successful operations. It also provided much-needed intelligence on the strength, organization and disposition of enemy forces outside South Vietnam. Supply lines in the tri-border area

were constantly harassed by the Spike Teams, and the intelligence they provided on the network of cross-border trails (known collectively as the Ho Chi Minh Trail) was invaluable to US strategies.

Mobile Strike Force The Mobile Strike Force concept grew out of the need for the Special Forces to be able to reinforce its various camps. Locally raised reaction forces were not strong enough to counter the increasing threat of siege to the CIDG and Strike Force camps, and the SOG Spike Teams could do little but harass the NVA units that were coming across the border in greater strength. In 1965 each SF 'C Team' deployed in one of the four Corps areas was authorized to raise a battalion-sized Mobile Strike Force. The 5th SF Group also raised its own Strike Force which was capable of providing reinforcement throughout South Vietnam. Each 'Mike Force', as the Mobile Strike Forces were called, was under the direct command of a Special Forces A Team. By

late 1966 the strength of the Mike Forces had increased to between two to three battalions each, with an additional reconnaissance company and an ARVN Special Forces team. The South Vietnamese Army's SF was known as the LLDB (Lac Luong Dac Biet), and there was usually an LLDB team attached to each Strike Force. More often than not the LLDB ran the administration and organization of the camp while the US SF team commanded the combat operations.

In late 1967 each Mike Force was controlled by a SF B Team, and an additional Strike Force was created by the CIDG. The CIDG groups, known as the Mobile Guerrilla Forces, differed from Mike Forces in that their basic mission was to conduct ambushes and raids in enemy-controlled areas. The role of the Mike Forces was more offensive, and, in addition to their basic missions, they also carried out four successful battalion-sized airborne assaults between 1967 and 1969.

The organization and composition of the Mike Force and the Camp Strike Force varied throughout the war. Both groups were controlled and led by personnel from Special Forces A or B Teams. Their areas of operation depended on the terrain, but each camp usually controlled an area of between 100 to 200 sq km (40 to 75 sq miles). They usually operated independently but occasionally took part in joint operations with US or ARVN units. The training that they received was somewhat

Static-line parachuting from a C-130 aircraft. Bad weather and high wind speeds at ground level are the most common restrictions in airborne operations.

*Above: American-trained
South Vietnamese special
forces rest after capturing
a hill from the Viet Cong,
near the Cambodian
border.*

*Left: HALO/HAHO
parachuting is one of the
more sophisticated but
effective methods of
deploying small groups
behind enemy lines.*

Operation Eagle Claw 1980. RH-53D helicopters of Delta Force on board USS Nimitz *before the ill-fated rescue attempt.*

limited and they were lightly equipped. In spite of these limitations they were ideal troops for carrying out operations against the Viet Cong.

The US Army Special Forces Teams were used extensively during the Vietnam War. As well as being involved with a number of programmes such as CIDG, SOG and the Mobile Strike Force, they also trained Cambodians and Thais. The United States began to withdraw its troops in 1970 and, although some SF programmes were dissolved and others taken over by the LLDB and ARVN, Special Forces' personnel continued to be active in various capacities until 1975.

Following the US withdrawal, fighting became more fierce, especially in the strategic Central Highlands area which had been controlled by the SF teams. Supplies came across the border via the Ho Chi Minh Trail, unhindered by the no longer existing Spike Teams. The De-Militarized Zone between North and South Vietnam fell shortly after the withdrawal of the US Marine Corps and Army. Saigon, the capital, was taken by the North Vietnamese Army and the Viet Cong in April 1975.

During their near decade of combat operations in South-East Asia, the Special Forces were awarded 17 Medals of Honor, 80 Distinguished Service Crosses, 8,369 Bronze Stars, 765 Silver Stars and 2,559 Purple Hearts. Added to this impressive total, a number of SF personnel also received awards for gallantry from their Allies. The US Special Forces emerged from Vietnam as the most highly decorated unit of its size in the history of the United States Army.

POST VIETNAM

The US Army Special Forces underwent a number of changes following the beginning of the US withdrawal from Vietnam. In 1969 there were 2,300 SF personnel involved in the CIDG programme alone; thus when this and other programmes terminated in 1970 there were larger numbers of SF personnel surplus to requirements. There were also elements of the Army's senior command structure who did not realize the Special Forces' valuable contribution to the war effort in South-East Asia. Some even considered that the SF was a secret 'private army' over which they had too little control.

There were a number of cutbacks through the US Army, with some units being reduced in strength, and others being disbanded. The Special Forces were no exception. At the end of 1969 the 3rd Special Forces Group was deactivated and the 10th Group returned from Germany leaving only one element at Bad Tölz. The 6th Group was deactivated in 1971 and the Africa and Middle East operational areas were taken over by the 5th and 7th SF Groups; the latter also took over the Latin American area when 8th SF Group was disbanded in 1972. The 1st SF Group, in 1974, was the final major deactivation, but there were other changes in manpower and training.

During the 1970s the Special Forces kept a low profile. Apart from sending a few Teams to Europe and Africa, the main emphasis was on supplying military assistance, in the form of advisors, to Latin America. Another threat that increased during the 1970s was international terrorism, and to counter this menace, the 1st

Special Forces Operational Detachment-Delta was formed. 'Delta Force' was established in July 1978. Initially commanded by Colonel Charles Beckwith, Delta Force was involved in the ill-fated Operation Eagle Claw, the US attempt to rescue hostages held by Iranian revolutionaries at the US Embassy in Teheran.

SPECIAL FORCES TODAY

Although the US Army Special Forces have undergone some changes since their formation, they have basically remained the same. Their roles today place more emphasis on strategic reconnaissance, intelligence and clandestine missions. They have, however, retained their ability to conduct counter-insurgency operations, while increasing their capability for counter-terrorist missions with the formation of Operational Detachment – Delta.

The organization of the SF Group has been modified in the light of experience gained in Vietnam. An SF Service Company equipped with much-needed UH-1 helicopters (Hueys) has been formed. This gives the SF Groups their own aircraft for logistic and team support without having to rely on other units. The Groups' Headquarters and Headquarters Company has been reduced in size, and is now responsible only for command and control. Communications equipment has been greatly improved and each Group has its own SF Signal Company. Combat Intelligence Companies were introduced in the late 1970s and are now being reorganized into Combat Electronic Warfare Intelligence (CEWI) Companies, capable of conducting psychological operations.

Each SF Group consists of three battalions, each with its own headquarters element or C Team. Each SF Operational Detachment C controls three SF Companies, each consisting of one B Team which provides the command and control element, and six A Teams, each comprising 12 men with the following specialities:

Detachment Commander	Captain
Executive Officer	1st Lieutenant/ WO
Operations Sergeant	E8
Heavy Weapons Leader	E7
Assistant Operations Sergeant	E7
Light Weapons Leader	E7
Medical NCO	E7
Radio Operator Supervisor	E7
SF Engineer Sergeant	E7
Assistant Medical NCO	E6
Chief Radio Operator	E5
SF Engineer	E5

Training The selection criteria for personnel volunteering for the Special Forces are very high. They must be eligible for a secret security clearance because of the training they will receive. They must be airborne-qualified (or willing to become so) and good swimmers, capable of swimming over 50 m (55 yd) in boots and clothing. Only those who have graduated from High School are accepted into the Special Forces, and they must have passed their advanced physical readiness test, advanced individual military training and junior NCOs (Non-Commissioned Officer) school (E4-E7).

Special Forces training takes place at Fort Bragg, Camp Mackall, Key West, Fort Sam Houston and Western North Carolina. There are six basic qualification courses for SF military occupation speciality (MOS), and all SF personnel must be proficient in at least one of the following six skills.

Signals The basic course lasts 25 weeks. It covers the operation of all radios in use by Special Forces and the types of procedures employed, and includes instruction in encoding and decoding. Morse code (CW or continuous wave as it is known in the military) is used extensively in SF operations and by the end of the course the students must be able to send and receive at eight words per minute. There is an advanced signals course, which teaches subjects such as radio repair, and to pass this course a speed of 15 words per minute must be attained.

Medicine This course is the most intensive and is recognized by other special

Signalling is another important SF skill. Sophisticated communications equipment with 'burst' morse transmission reduces the likelihood of Teams being located by enemy direction-finding units.

forces as being the best SF medical course in the world. It is divided into three phases. The first 18 weeks are spent at Fort Sam Houston in Texas where the students are instructed in basic medicine. After this they return to Fort Bragg for the advanced phase. Here they are taught preventive medicine as well as the treatment of disease and missile wounds. They spend 21 weeks at Fort Bragg before practising their new-found skills, including minor surgery, during the final four-week phase spent in the casualty department of a military hospital. In medicine, also, there is another more advanced course for eligible SF personnel. This is longer and more intensive, and includes major field surgery such as amputation.

Engineering This 25-week course covers both demolition and construction techniques, including bridge building and demolition, the manufacture and use of explosives and the construction of fortified emplacements.

Weapons The use of both heavy and light weapons is taught on this course which lasts approximately 25 weeks; instruction is given on foreign weapons of all types.

Operations and Intelligence This course is designed for the Operations Sergeant and lasts for 16 weeks. Operational technique is studied and there is instruction in intelligence gathering, collation and evaluation. Although not a qualifying course, 'ops and int' is an MOS and is open to

While all SF personnel are trained in first aid many receive further instruction in preventive medicine and field surgery.

sergeants who already have one other skill qualification.

Detachment Officer All commissioned and warrant officers undergo this 19-week introductory course on joining Special Forces. On the course they learn about the techniques employed by the SF A Teams and how to handle the skilled personnel under their command.

Special Forces training always includes an SF military occupation speciality (except in the case of officers and warrant officers), common SF skills such as 'escape and evasion' and a final end-of-course field-'raining exercise. After the basic qualification course (mentioned above), the new SF soldier undergoes further operational training. Military freefall parachuting, either high-altitude/low-opening (HALO) or high-altitude/high-opening (HAHO), is an important skill that is learned by SF personnel who elect to attend this five-week course.

Special Forces also carry out missions requiring underwater divers and thus some personnel go on the five-week underwater operations course. They learn to use both open and closed breathing apparatus and dive as deep as 41 m (135 ft). There are three courses: combat diver, combat supervisor and diving medical technician.

A number of other Army courses are open to SF personnel and these include such courses as: ranger; pathfinder; jungle expert; mountain expert; jumpmaster; and

Opposite: An SF instructor about to detonate an explosive charge from behind cover.

survival, evasion, resistance and escape (SERE). In practice the list is endless.

Although Special Forces are highly trained for maximum effectiveness in wartime operations, they have proved, since their formation, that they are also valuable assets in peacetime. Apart from aiding and advising friendly powers, they have been involved in a number of civic assistance programmes. After their return from Vietnam, the Special Forces launched an intensive civic action campaign. Named 'SPARTAN' (special proficiency at rugged training and nation-building), the 5th and 7th Special Forces Groups worked with American Indian tribes in Florida, Arizona and Montana. The SF personnel constructed roads and medical facilities, and generally improved the living conditions of these tribes. Other minority groups within the United States were helped, such as the lower income groups in Hoke and Anson Counties of North Carolina, who were

given free medical treatment by SF medical personnel.

The Special Forces are now increasing in number and are more active today than at any time since the end of the Vietnam War. Units in the active Army include: the 5th and 7th SF Groups at Fort Bragg; the 10th Group at Fort Devens, Massachusetts; the 3rd Battalion/7th Group in Panama; and the 1st Battalion/10th Group and Bad Tölz in Germany. The 1st Special Forces Group has recently been reactivated at Fort Lewis, and its 1st Battalion is now based in Okinawa. There are also a number of Reserve Army units. These include the 11th and 12th Groups (US Army Reserve) and the 19th and 20th Groups (Army National Guard). The 'Green Berets', the US Army Special Forces, are professional soldiers in both peace and war. They are in the business of helping others and proudly live up to their motto, *De Oppresso Liber*, 'Free the Oppressed'.

Below: US Army Special Forces are instructed in the use of both foreign and domestic weapons. Although heavy weapons are not usually carried on missions, mortars are man-packable and provide excellent close-in fire support.

A number of US Army Special Forces' soldiers undergo training in underwater diving and some go on courses with the US Navy SEALs. Army Special Forces sometimes have to demolish bridges and other targets where underwater diving is a definite asset.

Left: Ranger skills include demolition. The main difference between Rangers and US Army Special Forces is that SF engineers are also trained in construction.

Below: Camouflage is an important aspect of fieldcraft and is taught to all SF personnel.

SPECIAL WARFARE CENTER

The US Army John F Kennedy Special Warfare Center is responsible for the training of US Special Operations Forces. Based at Fort Bragg, the Special Warfare Center (SWC) conducts a number of individual training courses for members of all the US armed forces, government departments and selected foreign personnel, in a number of fields including foreign policy, international affairs, security assistance, special forces operations and low-intensity conflict, to name but a few.

The SWC is also responsible for developing operational concepts and doctrine, and for the organization, matériel and systems for the support of all Special Operations Forces for all types of conflict.

The 1st Special Warfare Training Battalion is a part of the SWC and is responsible for conducting the various training programmes and for providing logistical support to the Center. It is also responsible for the Special Forces School which trains SF personnel on their basic qualification courses.

The Army's survival, evasion, resistance and escape (SERE) programme is also conducted by the Special Forces School which trains both recruits and instructors in codes of conduct, the Geneva Convention and SERE techniques. On these courses there is much emphasis placed on lessons learned by prisoners of war in Vietnam. One such Vietnam 'lesson' is that strict adherence to the Convention – giving only name, rank and number to your captors – is likely to result in your death.

Also within the Special Warfare Center is the School of International Studies.

Right: Providing medical
aid to friendly third-world
countries is one of
SOCOM's responsibilities.

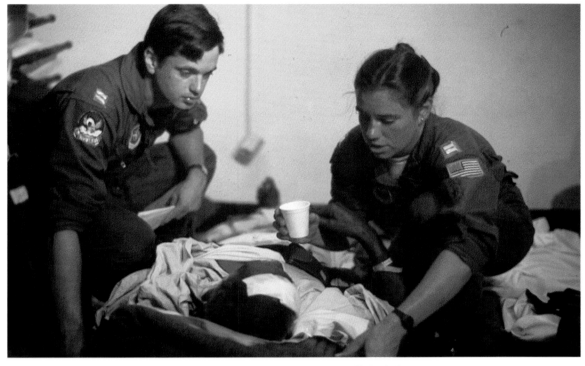

In keeping with the SWC doctrine of keeping courses in line with current affairs, a special SERE course is due to start in 1986. Due to the rapid increase in international terrorism, a 17-day course has been designed to instruct selected high-risk personnel in the advanced techniques of survival and resistance. The Individual Terrorism Awareness Course (INTAC) is aimed at both army and civilian personnel.

There are a number of other departments and programmes within the Special Warfare Center such as a Civil Affairs Department, which instructs officers and enlisted men in the use and the provision of support to civil authorities, and the Psychological Operations Department, which instructs US and Allied officers in the employment of psychological techniques. There is a Soviet PsyOp Awareness Programme (SPAP) currently being developed in conjunction with the 4th PsyOp Group; it is designed to counter the threat of Soviet disinformation and propaganda.

One of the key elements of the SWC is the Security Assistance Training Management Office (SATMO). This office is responsible for the Mobile Training Teams (MTTs), which operate outside the US assisting friendly governments. These teams comprise not only SF personnel but also specialists such as engineers, doctors and various technicians. MTTs play a vital role in American foreign policy.

The Special Warfare Center represents the focal point of Special Operations training in the US Army of today. It provides training in unconventional warfare, internal security and defence, psychological operations, civil affairs and military assistance, for the United States armed forces and its allies.

SPECIAL OPERATIONS COMMAND

The US Army 1st Special Operations Command (Airborne) (SOCOM) was activated at Fort Bragg in 1982 with the aim of consolidating all US Army Special Operations Forces under one command. SOCOM is responsible for all overt, covert or clandestine special operations conducted by the United States throughout the world. It offers direct support for national and military strategic objectives, including the targetting of foreign military and civilian resources. Employing SF teams, or other trained units, its units can mount independent operations which could not be carried out by conventional units.

The mission of 1st SOCOM is to task and support Special Operations Forces in unconventional warfare, strategic reconnaissance and intelligence, psychological operations and other related special missions, many of which are classified. To carry out its mission, SOCOM liaises closely with the Special Warfare Center, US intelligence organizations, such as the Central Intelligence Agency (CIA) and the National Security Agency (NSA), and other similar Allied SF directorates, such as Britain's Special Air Service Group.

Units assigned to 1st SOCOM include the 1st, 5th, 7th and 10th Special Forces Groups; the 4th Psychological Operations Group; the 1st, 2nd and 3rd Battalions/ 75th Infantry (Ranger); the Ranger Regiment; the 96th Civil Affairs Battalion and Task Force 160 (Army Aviation). This force, under one command, is the largest of its kind in the world.

Opposite: UH-60A Black
Hawk helicopters fly in low
to avoid detection.
Helicopters are playing an
increasingly important role
in delivering small parties
of men to the battlefield.

Today there are three Ranger Battalions (1/2/3), all of which belong to the 75th Infantry under the command of the US Army Special Operations Command.

RANGERS

The US Army has three Ranger battalions. The 1st, 2nd and 3rd Battalions of the 75th Infantry (Ranger) are under the command of the 1st Special Operations Command (Airborne) and are capable of conducting a variety of missions including tactical reconnaissance, strike and other special operations.

The Rangers take their name from a unit formed by a Major Robert Rogers to fight marauding Indians in the days before American Independence. The US Army's 1st Ranger (Infantry) Battalion was formed in 1942 at Carrickfergus, Northern Ireland, under the command of Major William Derby. The intention was to create a force similar to the British Commandos so the Rangers were trained and equipped accordingly. They underwent a variety of training including rock-climbing, amphibious landings and unarmed combat. About the same time the 2nd Ranger (Infantry) Battalion was formed in the United States. The 1st Battalion took part in the Allied invasion of North Africa, where they received a Presidential Citation for their part in the battle of El Guettar. The 3rd and 4th Battalions were raised in North Africa, but were disbanded along with the 1st Battalion after receiving heavy casualties during the Allied invasions of Sicily and Italy. The 2nd and 5th Ranger Battalions remained; they fought throughout north-west Europe, and played an important role in securing the beachheads during D-Day. In 1944, towards the end of the war, there was no longer the need for troops capable of amphibious assaults and deep-penetration raiding. The remaining Rangers together with a 6th Battalion, which had been raised and had fought in the Pacific, were deactivated.

During the Korean War (1950-53), a number of Ranger Infantry Companies were formed. Trained at the Ranger School at Fort Benning, Georgia, the Ranger Companies carried out a number of special operations, especially long-range patrols. Two Companies, the 2nd and 4th, took part in the 187th Regimental Combat Team's airborne assault during the battle of Munsan-ni.

After Korea the Rangers were again deactivated. The Ranger School at Benning remained, however, and continued to train the army in Ranger skills. During this period and throughout the Vietnam War, the Rangers remained deactivated, many of their tasks being undertaken by the Special Forces. Then, following the US withdrawal from South-East Asia and the cutbacks in Special Forces, it was decided to reactivate the Rangers. The 1st and 2nd Battalions/75th Infantry (1/75 and 2/75 Rangers) were reformed in 1975, and the 3/75 followed in 1984.

ORGANIZATION

The Ranger Regiment consists of three infantry battalions: 1st, 2nd and 3rd Battalions/75th Infantry. Each battalion is organized along the same lines as a conventional infantry battalion and is divided into three rifle companies plus a headquarters company. Each battalion has a total strength of 606 personnel and is based in a different location: 1/75 at Hunter AAF, Georgia; 2/75 at Fort Lewis, Washington; and 3/75 together with the Ranger School and Regiment, at Fort Benning, Georgia.

TRAINING

The Ranger School at Ford Benning has been operating since the Second World War, regardless of whether or not there have been active Ranger units. The Ranger course itself lasts for eight weeks and teaches basic Ranger techniques, mountaineering, survival, navigation, patrolling, weapons handling, ambushing, reconnaissance and hand-to-hand combat. It is a hard, challenging and, ultimately, confidence-building course. It is designed to bring out an individual's leadership qualities and is, for that reason, used by the US Army as an advanced leadership course for its officers and NCOs (and to a lesser extent by the Marine Corps and Air Force). Most of those who graduate from the course return to other units, but they take with them the Ranger qualification and a memorable, if not unforgettable, experience.

The Ranger battalions, as is claimed, pick up where the Ranger School leaves off. Volunteers for the Ranger battalions are, like the men of the Special Forces and 82nd Airborne, triple volunteers. They volunteer first for the Army, second for airborne training and third for the Ranger battalion. New applicants, including those who have passed through Ranger School, must go through an intensive three-week course which determines whether or not they are suitable Ranger material. This course is known, rather ominously, as the RIP (Rangers Indoctrination Program). The physical-fitness aspect of the course is highly stressed and all newcomers are given a PT (physical training) test on arrival.

The Ranger Indoctrination Program course is rigorous, and as each course has only between 10 to 30 students, the ratio between instructors and students is extremely good. The emphasis is placed on the individual and his performance, and

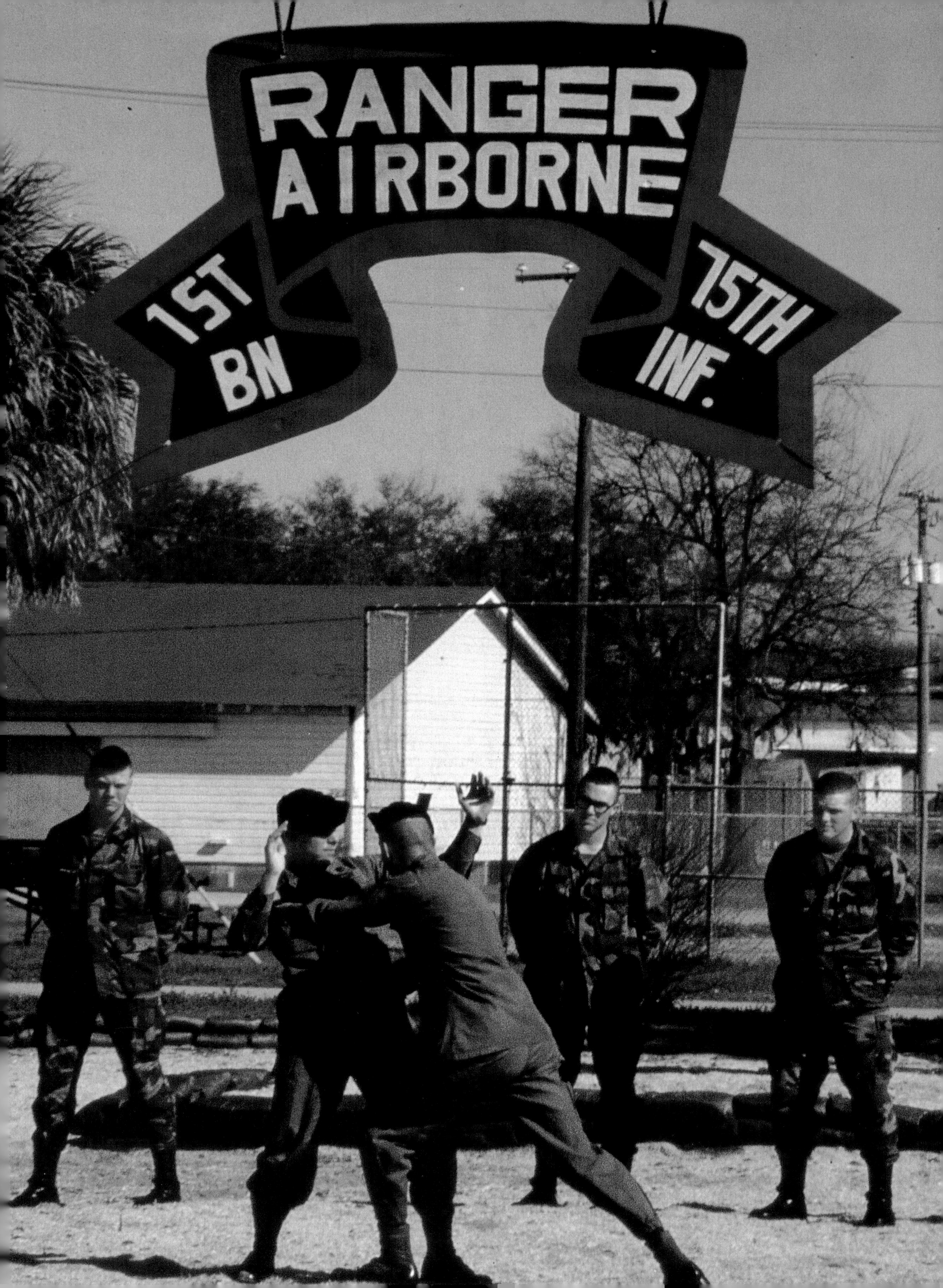
RANGER
AIRBORNE
1ST
BN
75TH
INF.

Small-scale amphibious assaults are another Ranger speciality, a skill they share with Special Forces.

each student's progress is constantly monitored and assessed. Always under stress, the students begin the course with two days of static-line parachuting (eight jumps), usually from CH-47s using MC1-B steerable parachutes. The course then goes on to test the basic infantry combat skills. Students go through an airmobile operation, then an advance to contact. They practise ambush techniques, reconnaissance, raiding patrols and abseiling.

Between 50 to 70 per cent of applicants make it through the Ranger Indoctrination Program. Those who do not are returned to other units, some to airborne units, some not. Those who pass, on the other hand, spend six months to a year with one of the Ranger battalions before being considered for the Ranger School. There are a number of young soldiers in the battalions; the average age is between 18 and 19. The average age of a qualified Ranger is about 20 to 22, so many of the young soldiers who have spent up to a year with a Ranger battalion, will then undergo a pre-Ranger School course before returning to the battalion. This will prepare them for the course itself which is, in any case, primarily designed as a leadership course.

On qualification (about 95 per cent of those who have passed the pre-Ranger course qualify), about 50 per cent of those who have served with a battalion will return to it; the others will be sent on to Fort Bragg for further training. This occurs because the Ranger battalion manning levels are restricted. Those who do pass and join the battalions wear the distinctive black beret of the Rangers and begin the full 22-month tour. (A six-month extension is possible if authorized by the battalion commander.)

All three Ranger battalions have an extremely arduous training cycle. Their year is divided into two five-and-a-half-month training periods, separated only by two two-week leaves. They train throughout the United States either as a battalion or in individual companies. They also train abroad and, as part of 1st Special Operations Command, are involved in a number of joint exercises in a variety of climates and terrains.

WEAPONS AND EQUIPMENT

Ranger battalions are the most lightly equipped infantry troops in the US Army and, apart from a two-man Air Force Forward Air Controller (FAC) team with each company, they have no outside support. Each squad has one 7.62 mm M60 machine gun, which will soon be replaced, it is to be hoped, by the new Squad

Above: Climbing is an important Ranger skill and men in the Ranger battalions regularly train in mountainous areas.

Left: The Rangers in Honduras. As in Grenada, the Rangers are often chosen to spearhead the assault.

35

Automatic Weapon (SAW). Both these weapons are belt-fed, but the SAW is 5.56 mm calibre and compatible with the M16 A1s carried by the rest of the squad. M16 A1s are now being replaced by M16 A2s. Each squad also has one 40 mm M203 grenade launcher. Each Ranger company is equipped with one M224 60 mm mortar, which has the same effective range as the 81 mm mortar but is far lighter, weighing only 20 kg (45 lb). Some officers, NCOs and personnel such as radio operators carry the 5.56 mm CAR-15, shorter-barrelled than the M16 with a telescopic butt.

Although the heaviest weapon in the Ranger battalion is the 90 mm recoilless rifle or occasionally the Dragon anti-tank missile launcher, they are both capable of massive firepower for short periods. All Rangers are, in addition, trained in the use of foreign weapons such as the Warsaw Pact's AK-47 and RPG, and NATO's MP-5 submachine gun and G-3 rifle.

Rangers carry very little non-essential equipment. Since their usual method of insertion is by air or water and then foot, they take only what they can carry. There is a Ranger saying, 'Travel light, freeze at night'.

OPERATIONS

The first operation in which the Rangers were involved since their reformation in the early 1970s was Operation Urgent Fury. On the morning of 25 October 1983 several hundred Rangers from 1/75 and 2/75 Ranger Battalions parachuted onto the Caribbean island of Grenada.

The Rangers were part of a large United States force, which included 82nd Airborne Division and the US Marine Corps, that invaded Grenada in a successful attempt to restore law and order and to secure the lives of a large number of American students on the island.

The first troops into action, the Rangers made a combat-jump onto the runway at Point Salines Airport. This airfield was of vital strategic importance to the operation and was held by a force of Cuban and Grenadan troops. Intense anti-aircraft fire prevented the first two C-130 aircraft from dropping their troops. The third aircraft succeeded and the Rangers, led by Lieutenant Colonel Wesley B Taylor, parachuted in from 150 m (500 ft). 'This way, my troops spent less time in the air, exposed to hostile fire,' said Lt Col Taylor. Once on the ground, this small force of 50 Rangers

The Rangers in Grenada. Their success during the campaign more than proved the value of their training.

or so engaged the enemy while directing suppressive fire from AC-130 'Spectre' aircraft. For 20 minutes this small group fought off attacks from a force over ten times stronger, until the main body of Rangers could be parachuted in. Under fire, the Rangers cleared the airfield of obstacles, including wire barricades and vehicles, before assaulting well-prepared enemy positions on the outskirts of the runway.

The Rangers then moved onto their secondary objective, the True Blue medical college, which they quickly secured, thus assuring the safety of the American medical students resident there.

The operation was a success. Point Salines Airport had been captured, which allowed the 82nd Airborne to land rather than jump into Grenada.

The 1st Special Operations Command's three Ranger battalions constitute its rapid strike force. Capable of forced-entry operations, the Rangers undergo intensive training in a variety of special operations including deep-penetration raids and the destruction of vital targets behind enemy lines. The Rangers have proved time and time again they are masters in their art.

82ND AIRBORNE DIVISION

The US Army's 82nd Airborne Division is the largest airborne formation outside the Soviet Union. As the mainstay of America's strategic combat forces, 82nd Airborne (known as the 'All American' Division) must be prepared to deploy anywhere in the world without notice and to go into combat immediately upon arrival. The Division has a total strength of 18,000, and nearly all its personnel are qualified to parachute, including the pilots and aircrew. All the Division's combat equipment — transport, artillery, mortars, tanks, ammunition and medical supplies — can be parachuted into the battle zone, giving the 82nd more firepower and more mobility than all seven wartime Allied airborne divisions combined.

The 82nd was originally activated as an infantry division in August 1917. The name 'All American' came from the discovery

Parachuting is still one of the airborne soldier's most important skills although today's paratrooper is more likely to be airlifted into the battlefield by helicopter.

that the division consisted of some men from each state of the United States, and the red, white and blue shoulder flash with 'AA' in the centre was adopted and is still worn today. The unit was deployed in France in 1918 and, before its deactivation in 1919, saw more consecutive days on the front-line than any other American unit.

In 1942 the 82nd was reactivated and designated as the US Army's first airborne division under the command of Major General Omar N Bradley. After training in the USA the division deployed to North Africa whence, under the command of Major General Matthew B Ridgeway, the 'All Americans' took part in the airborne assaults into Sicily and Salerno. After Salerno one element of the 82nd, the 504th Parachute Infantry Regiment, fought with distinction at Anzio. In June 1944 the 82nd parachuted and air-landed the 505th, 507th and 508th Parachute Infantry Regiments as well as the 325th Glider Infantry Regiment into France as part of the Allied invasion of Normandy. The landings were successful and the 82nd was responsible for confusing the enemy and for tying up German reinforcements that were badly needed to counterattack the Allies at the beachheads.

After a brief period of rest and retraining in England, the 'All American' Division took part in what was the largest Allied airborne operation of the war. Operation Market Garden took place in September 1944 and the 82nd had the task of capturing the bridges at Nijmegen and Grave, while the US 101st Airborne Division secured the road in between. The aim was to create a 'corridor' through which the British 2nd Army, led by the 30th Corps, could advance to Arnhem, to meet up with the British 1st Airborne Division and the Polish Independent Parachute Brigade. Although the British Division was unable to hold the bridge at Arnhem, which would have given the Allies a bridgehead over the Rhine, the 82nd achieved its objectives at Grave and Nijmegen.

During the final stages of the war the 'All American' Division took part in the 'Battle of the Bulge' in which 30 German divisions attempted a breakthrough in the Ardennes, with the object of reaching Antwerp and cornering Allied forces to the north of the Antwerp-Brussels-Bastogne line. The area in which the Germans attacked was held by only four American divisions. After some of the fiercest fighting of the war, the German advance was halted and the Allies counterattacked. The 82nd Airborne Division went on to make assault river crossings of both the Rhine and the Elbe, and eventually received the surrender of the 21st German Army at Ludwigslust. In July 1945 the 82nd was ordered to Berlin as the American contingent of the Allied Army of Occupation. It was here that it became known as 'America's Guard of Honor'.

By the end of the Second World War the 82nd Airborne Division had spent nearly two years overseas, including a total of 442 days in combat. During this time the Division had lost over 3,000 killed and over 12,600 wounded. Men of the 82nd had been awarded three Medals of Honor, 79 distinguished Service Crosses, 894 Silver Stars, 2,478 Bronze Stars and a number of Allied awards.

Since the end of the Second World War, the 82nd Airborne Division has been into combat a further three times. After the Division's return to Fort Bragg in North Carolina, the 'All Americans' underwent a number of changes in organization and training. New equipment and weaponry were introduced, and different tactics were tried and tested. Then, in 1965, the 82nd was deployed to Santo Domingo in the Dominican Republic as part of the Inter-American Peace Force. The aim of the operation – codename 'Power Pack' – was to rescue US nationals trapped in Santo Domingo, the island's capital, during the revolution. The mission was a success and the 1st Brigade spent over a year on the island carrying out peacekeeping duties before returning to Fort Bragg in mid-1966.

At the start of 1968 the 'All Americans' were again called into action, this time in Vietnam. During the New Year, the North Vietnamese and the Viet Cong (VC) launched the Tet offensive. In January and early February the VC attacked 36 of the 44 South Vietnamese provincial capitals and five of the six autonomous cities. They

Above: 82nd Airborne Division's parachute training is conducted at Fort Benning, Georgia. Here a trainee learns the basic skills of static-line parachuting.

Left: Physical fitness is an important part of the 82nd Airborne Division's daily programme which includes calisthenics and a 6-km (4-mile) run.

Training is realistic and each year the 82nd Airborne conducts a number of combined-arms, live-fire exercises or CALFAX, during which large quantities of live ammunition are fired.

also assaulted 64 district capitals and 50 hamlets. Fighting was protracted in Saigon and Hue and, in the case of the latter city, only the Citadel area housing the Allied 3rd Division HQ remained unoccupied. The decision was taken to deploy the American strategic reserves so the 3rd Brigade, 82nd Airborne, flew to South Vietnam to reinforce 1 Corps. Here the Division took part in a number of counteroffensive combat operations against the North Vietnamese in the Hue/Phu Bai area. After the situation was brought under control, the 'All Americans' moved down to the South where they were involved in the repacification programme in the area surrounding Saigon. The Brigade eventually returned to Fort Bragg at the end of 1969 after serving nearly 22 months in Vietnam.

Most recently the 82nd Airborne Division took a major part in the operation to safeguard the lives of American nationals on the Caribbean island of Grenada. [The part played by the Rangers was mentioned earlier.] Two brigade-sized infantry units of 82nd Division were deployed, supported by an army aviation task force and a large contingent from the Divisional Support Command (DISCOM). On 25 October 1983 the Division was alerted for combat operations. Within 18 hours of being notified the force had not only left Fort Bragg but was also in combat with enemy forces on the island of Grenada, where they defeated a hostile Cuban and revolutionary force. After the fighting they helped to restore civilian democratic control to the island.

The 'All American' Division has proved that it is able to deploy anywhere, without any notice and to fight and win. This high state of combat readiness, together with the ability to deploy at 'no notice' and the intense training, has made the 82nd Airborne Division the US Army's primary reaction force and the mainstay of the US Central Command Rapid Deployment Force.

TRAINING

The US Army trains its paratroopers at the United States Army Infantry Center, Fort Benning, Georgia. The training is carried out by the 4th Airborne Training Battalion and is designed to produce, among other qualities, the correct attitude of mind in the airborne soldier. There is a belief that the paratrooper is just an infantryman who drops from the sky by parachute. This is not the case. From the beginning students at the airborne school are expected to have the 'airborne spirit'. Training is hard and aggressive, and students are expected to perform their tasks quickly and

correctly, regardless of whether they are cooks, clerks or pilots.

All the men and women who 'go airborne' are 'two-time' volunteers. They volunteer to join the army and they volunteer to parachute. There are a number of women in the US airborne forces, and although they are not expected to fight in combat they are airborne-qualified and serve in the support areas, thus releasing the men for combat duties.

The 4th Airborne Training Battalion consists of four training companies, to one of which all basic airborne students are assigned. They are administered by a headquarters company and receive instruction from a training cadre. The instructors — known as 'Black Hats' — are also responsible for pathfinder and jumpmaster students.

The Basic Airborne Course (BAC) is designed to train both officers and soldiers of the US and Allied armed forces in the art of military static-line parachuting. The three-week course is divided into three phases: Ground Week, Tower Week and Jump Week. Before starting the course students must be passed as medically and physically fit. Regardless of age they must pass the Army Physical Readiness Test (APRT) in the grade established for the 17–25 year age group. Having qualified for the course they begin the first phase of the course which is designed to develop their confidence. During the next two weeks the students start with one hour of physical training which includes a number of stretching exercises and calisthenics and finishes with a 5-km (3-mile) run. At the end of the first week this is increased to 6 km (4 miles). Each trainee must learn the basic skills of static-line parachuting which includes aircraft drills, exiting procedure, parachute control and the parachute landing fall (PLF). Students are monitored while practising these techniques and only those who are judged satisfactory are allowed to advance to the second week.

During Tower Week the trainees progress from the 10-m (34-ft) mock tower to the 76-m (250-ft) free tower. They start to practise mass exits. The 'mass exit' technique is used in airborne operations and involves paratroopers leaving the aircraft in quick succession, usually about one man per second from each of the side doors. This allows the troopers to land closer together and therefore less vital time is spent regrouping on the ground. The trainees also practise steering their parachutes from suspended harnesses and have the angle of their landing approach varied on the swing-landing trainer. By the end of the week all students must demonstrate their ability to perform all the skills that they have been taught including how to deal with malfunctions, before they progress into Jump Week.

Men of the 82nd emplaning before a parachute jump during Exercise Bright Star in Egypt. The Division spends much time training overseas and constitutes the major part of the US Rapid Deployment Force.

Paratroopers jumping from a C-130 aircraft during a training mission. The 82nd Airborne also uses C-141 Galaxy and C-5A Starlifter aircraft.

Jump Week, the final phase, is the culmination of the previous two weeks' training. During this week the students make five static-line parachute descents from both C-130 Hercules and C-141 Starlifter aircraft. The first jump is made from 380 m (1,250 ft) using a type T-10 parachute. The second jump is from 460 m (1,500 ft) with a T-10, but in this case the jump is made carrying combat equipment. This consists of a full rucksack suspended under the reserve parachute which is lowered on a strap after the parachute has deployed. The third jump is also from 460 m (1,500 ft), but this time the parachute used is a MC1-1B. This type of parachute is more advanced than the T-10 and has an excellent safety record. The next jump, the fourth, is from 380 m (1,250 ft) with a T-10 plus combat equipment, but this time the jump is done at night. The fifth and final jump is a day jump from 610 m (2,000 ft) using a MC1-1B parachute and is considered to be the easiest of the course.

After the fifth parachute jump the students qualify for their wings and are badged 'airborne'. Over 21,000 personnel attend the 4th Airborne Training Battalion's courses each year and qualify. Almost 95 per cent of those who pass are from the Army, the remainder coming from the Navy, Marines, Air Force and Allied nations. Those who pass wear their wings on their left breast, and some of them move on to join 82nd Airborne Division at Fort Bragg.

FORT BRAGG, NORTH CAROLINA

Fort Bragg is the 'home of the Airborne'. It is one of the largest military bases in the world and the home of XVIII Airborne Corps, 82nd Airborne Division, 1st Special Operations Command (1st SOCOM) and the Army's largest support command. It is to Fort Bragg that the soldiers of 82nd are posted when they have successfully completed their basic airborne training at Fort Benning.

Each trooper in the Division has what is known as a primary Military Operation Specialty or MOS. This is the trade in which he has specialized before joining the Airborne and will remain his primary task while he is with the 82nd. The trooper may be an infantryman, in which case he will join one of the airborne infantry battalions, or he may be a gunner or a cavalryman, a clerk or a driver. Whatever his speciality he will find a use for it within the Division.

Climate and terrain are two major factors affecting 82nd Airborne's ability to be deployed immediately, anywhere in the world. Although the training at Fort Bragg allows the paratrooper the opportunity to practise his own basic skills and to learn how to operate within his particular sub-unit and formation, the extremes of climate

and terrain he is likely to find on active-duty deployment are not available at Fort Bragg. Thus, in order to carry out the rapid-deployment role, the Division must train in a variety of different regional areas both within the United States and overseas.

Therefore, the 'All American' Division conducts an extensive off-post training programme. Throughout the year various battalions will be training in the Panamanian jungle, the Alaskan tundra, the Mojave Desert and any number of military installations and training areas within the US. The off-post training programme provides both the troopers and their officers with a number of benefits. They experience varied climatic conditions, learn how to fight in arctic conditions, to move on snowshoes, to climb mountains and to survive in the desert and jungle. Another benefit is the experience gained by Army and Air Force planners, who co-ordinate and execute these training exercises with the realism of an actual contingency mission.

Local training continues all year round at Fort Bragg, which remains the most reliable and immediate training area available for the Division. The Division's yearly training statistics are impressive: its actual training days (per year) average 230; it runs more than ten million man-miles (16 million km) during physical training; it

Above: A group of men and women from the 82nd Airborne during desert-warfare training. The women in the Division train alongside their male colleagues and, although they serve in non-combative posts, many are airborne-qualified, including a number as helicopter pilots.

Opposite: Patrolling along the shoreline during Exercise Bright Star. As the US Army's primary reaction force, the 82nd Airborne Division regularly deploys overseas and trains in a variety of terrains.

Above: Paratroopers seated in a C-130 before a training jump. The men and women of the 82nd Airborne Division get plenty of opportunity to practise their jumping skills.

parachutes more than 100,000 personnel; it conducts between 100–125 mass tactical parachute assaults; it fires more than three million rounds of machine-gun ammunition; and it uses over 130,000 rounds of mortar and artillery ammunition during the course of each training year.

Each year there are a number of combined arms, live-fire exercises (CALFAX) held at Fort Bragg. These are battalion-sized exercises organized by the Division with the aim of training its infantry and supporting arms to operate as a team. During a CALFAX, the paratroopers fight across several miles of simulated battle field, in the most realistic conditions. They use live ammunition on a variety of different targets, while artillery rounds and aerial bombs land in close proximity. This is the most realistic and dangerous training available to the men of the 82nd Airborne Division, and also the most physically gruelling. The troopers mount one assault after another, under direct artillery-fire support, with 50 per cent of rounds landing within the minimum safe zone.

Above: An 82nd Airborne trooper firing a Soviet-manufactured rifle during training.

Left: A paratrooper throws a fragmentation grenade during a platoon live-fire exercise (LFX) at Fort Bragg.

49

ORGANIZATION

The 82nd Airborne Division is the key element of the United States Armed Forces Rapid Deployment Force. As such it has a unique organizational structure which enables it to carry out its immediate 'no notice' deployment. The Division has a full manned strength of 18,000 personnel, nearly all of whom are qualified to jump, and it is this ability to deploy from the air that makes the Division elite.

In order to fulfil its primary task there are elements of the 'All American' Division constantly 'on call', 24 hours a day, every day of the year. These units vary in size, depending on their task and state of readiness. The key unit is the Initial Ready Company (IRC) which comprises one infantry company with specialist supporting elements (an artillery forward observer team, an engineer squad and an anti-aircraft team). When 'on call', the IRC assembles all its personnel, weapons and equipment; packs all its equipment and supplies; loads its vehicles and containers

Men of 82nd Airborne move forward from Point Salines Airport during Operation Urgent Fury, Grenada 1983.

A USAF C-130 transport aircraft delivers heavy supplies by low-level parachute extraction. All the 82nd's heavy equipment, with the exception of helicopters, can be delivered by this method.

ready for parachute drop; and stands by, ready for immediate deployment. Should there be an alert, it is the IRC who will be the first in. It is its task to parachute in and secure the area for the larger, more powerful infantry battalion.

After the Initial Ready Company has deployed, it is followed by the Divisional Ready Force (DRF). This Force is designed to accommodate larger threats, after the IRC has carried out its 'show of force' mission and secured a landing zone. In each infantry battalion there are three infantry companies, a combat support company and a headquarters company. When a battalion is 'on call' it is referred to as DRF-1, and can have extra support added to it as required. Support includes an artillery battery, an engineer platoon, water-point and bulldozer teams, a military police squad and a helicopter crew. With these extra elements the DRF-1 is able to clear a landing zone for the Brigade which may follow and to reinforce the Initial Ready Company that has already secured the area.

The final force that is placed on routine rotating 'on call' status is the Brigade. When 'on call' the Brigade is referred to as the Division Ready Brigade (DRB), and is composed of three infantry battalions and an anti-tank company (referred to as 'Echo Company'). The DRB is augmented with an engineer company, an artillery battalion, an air cavalry platoon, a military intelligence detachment and elements from medical, supply and maintenance services. Also attached to the DRB are United States Air Force forward-air-control personnel.

The Division also has several 'packages' at its disposal which it can add to either the Divisional Ready Force or the Divisional Ready Brigade. These packages include Vulcan anti-aircraft weapon systems; airfield construction units; civil affairs units; attack, transport and observation helicopters; and an armoured unit. All these packages are capable of being air-dropped by parachute, with the exception of the helicopters which would be air-landed by transport aircraft. With these additional packages the Division can put together a force designed to meet the requirements of any specific mission.

The structure of 82nd Airborne Division itself is rigid, and the Division is composed of three infantry brigades, one Divisional artillery, one Divisional support command, and seven separate battalions (aviation, cavalry, signals, engineer, armour, air defence and military intelligence). The 82nd Airborne Division is organized as follows:

A child receives medical attention during Operation Urgent Fury.

1st Brigade
1st Battalion (Airborne), 504th Infantry
2nd Battalion (Airborne), 504th Infantry
2nd Battalion (Airborne), 508th Infantry
E Company, 504th Infantry
2nd Brigade
1st Battalion (Airborne), 325th Infantry
2nd Battalion (Airborne), 325th Infantry
3rd Battalion (Airborne), 325th Infantry
E Company, 325th Infantry
3rd Brigade
1st Battalion (Airborne), 505th Infantry
2nd Battalion (Airborne), 505th Infantry
1st Battalion (Airborne), 508th Infantry
E Company, 505th Infantry
Divisional Artillery
1st Battalion (Airborne), 319th Artillery
1st Battalion (Airborne), 320th Artillery
2nd Battalion (Airborne), 321st Artillery
Support Command
307th Medical Battalion
782nd Maintenance Battalion
407th Supply and Service Battalion
82nd Adjutant General Company
82nd Finance Company
182nd Material and Management
    Center
Separate Units
307th Engineer Battalion
82nd Signal Battalion
3rd Battalion, 4th Air Defense Artillery
82nd Combat Aviation Battalion
3rd Battalion, 73rd Armor
1st Squadron, 17th Cavalry (Air)
14th Chemical Detachment
Headquarters and Headquarters
    Company Division
82nd Military Police Company
313th Military Intelligence Battalion
    (Combat Electronic Warfare
        Intelligence)

WEAPONS AND EQUIPMENT

The 82nd Airborne Division is the most strategically mobile division in the free world. Because of the American policies of realistic deterrence and rapid deployment, the 82nd Airborne must be capable of carrying out a variety of different missions. The Division's weaponry and equipment are among the most advanced in the world.

Armour has always posed a great threat to the airborne soldier, but with the significant improvements in anti-armour weapons over the past few years, the paratrooper is now able to combat this threat. Each infantryman carries an M72 A2 light anti-tank weapon (LAW) as part of his basic combat load. The LAW is a lightweight, self-contained system, capable of firing a single 66 mm high-explosive rocket. With a maximum effective range of 200 m (220 yd), the LAW is a weapon the infantryman can employ against enemy armour, soft-skinned vehicles and fortified emplacements. Also available to the paratrooper is the tube-launched, optically-tracked, wire-guided (TOW) anti-tank missile. The TOW is the most widely used anti-tank missile in the world and one of the most effective. Its 2.4-kg (5.3-lb) high-explosive warhead is capable of knocking out a tank at a range of up to 3,750 m (4,100 yd) during either the day or night.

Aircraft provide another threat to the paratrooper, a threat to which he is now less vulnerable with the introduction of the Stinger anti-aircraft missile. This man-portable, shoulder-fired guided-missile system is effective against low-level ground-attack aircraft and helicopters up to a range of 5,000 m (5,500 yd). The 3rd Battalion, 4th Air Defense Artillery has 72 organic Stinger teams. Five teams are normally deployed with each infantry battalion, and three teams with each artillery battalion. Other elements of the Division also receive Stinger assets, the particular allocation depending on the air threat and the mission.

The most important element of the Division's air-defence capability is the Vulcan M167 air-defence system. This is a six-barrelled 20 mm cannon with a rate of fire between 1,000 and 3,000 rounds per minute. This weapon is extremely accurate and has a built-in radar system which calculates the correct lead angle and elevation of the target aircraft and automatically sets the gun. The system, which can also be used against ground targets, is towed by the M561 Gamma Goat and can be deployed by helicopter (Black Hawk), aircraft or parachute.

The Divisional artillery's main asset is the 105 mm M102 howitzer which provides direct fire support for the Division with a range of 11,500 m (12,580 yd) and a sustained rate of fire of three rounds per minute. The Division artillery has 54

Capable of flying at a speed of 60 knots with an underslung load, the UH-1 Huey 'Slicks' are a vital part of the 82nd's aviation asset.

Known as the Gamma Goat, this vehicle is the 82nd Airborne Division's prime mover once it is deployed on the ground.

105 mm howitzers, 18 of which are normally deployed in support of each infantry battalion. Together with its prime mover, the Gamma Goat, the complete system can be air-dropped.

The M-551 Sheridan with its 152 mm gun/missile launcher provides the 82nd Airborne Division with the ability to defend itself against enemy armour and also acts as the Division's armoured reconnaissance vehicle. The 'All American' has 54 of these light tanks which can be delivered either by parachute or by the low-level wedge delivery system. The Sheridan is armed with a 152 mm gun/missile launcher, that is capable of firing a Shillelagh guided missile or a variety of conventional ammunition up to a range of 3,000 m (3,280 yd), and also has a 7.62 mm co-axial machine gun and a 0.5 in anti-aircraft machine gun. Although the M-551 is no longer in service outside the Division, it provides the 82nd with a valuable asset for its anti-armour defence.

The infantry personal and support weapons of the 82nd are the same as those used by the rest of the United States Army. The 0.45 in M1911A1 semi-automatic pistol is still used but will soon be replaced by the 9 mm Beretta 92SB. The M16A2 rifle is the standard-issue personal weapon. This is an improved version of the 5.56 mm M16 and is used with the 30-round magazine. The M203 dual-purpose weapon is also used by the 82nd and consists of an M16A2 rifle beneath which is attached an M203 40 mm grenade launcher. The M203 launcher is capable of firing a variety of ammunition and is an excellent weapon for suppressing and neutralizing targets, even in dead ground. The largest infantry support weapon used by the 82nd is the 81 mm mortar. This provides close, high-angle, indirect fire support for the combat infantryman up to a range of 4,950 m (5,415 yd). Each rifle company in the Division has one organic mortar platoon (three mortars per company) and there are a total of 81 in the Division. The M151 jeep with trailer is the prime mover for the mortar, but it can, if necessary, be man-packed.

ARMY AVIATION

One of the most important elements of the 82nd Airborne Division is its 'heliborne' capability which is the task of the 82nd Combat Aviation Battalion (CAB) and the 1st Squadron (Air), 17th Cavalry (Air Cav).

The mission of the 82nd Division's integral army aviation support is twofold:
● To provide the 82nd Airborne Division with tactical air movement, airborne command and control, aerial anti-armour capability and intermediate aviation maintenance.
● To extend by aerial means the Division's reconnaissance, security and 'economy of force' potential.

The Division also has a 'Quick Fix' platoon which is part of the 313th Military Intelligence Battalion, Combat Electronic Warfare Intelligence (CEWI). The 'Quick Fix' platoon's primary role is:
● To provide general aerial support in the area of electronic warfare.

The 82nd Combat Aviation Battalion (CAB) is responsible for flying the Division's aerial anti-tank missions, and flies in the infantry for heliborne (helicopter-based) assaults. The Battalion is equipped with Black Hawk troop carriers (UH-60As), Kiowa scouts (OH-58A/Cs), Huey utilities (UH-1Hs) and Cobra anti-tank helicopters (AH-1Ss). In total the Combat Aviation Battalion has 98 helicopters which it can deploy in a variety of roles to support the Division.

The 1st Squadron (Air), 17th Air Cavalry — the 'Air Cav' — provides the 82nd with its tactical reconnaissance. One of Air Cav's

The M203 dual-purpose weapon combines the M16 rifle and the 40 mm grenade launcher, and provides infantry sections with the ability to engage targets in dead-ground as well as being effective against fortified positions.

main roles is to locate the enemy and report its position, giving the Division information on which it can base its plans. The Air Cav will then maintain contact with the enemy and is capable of either calling down artillery fire or engaging the target itself with its Cobra-mounted TOW missiles at a range of 3,750 m (4,100 yd). The Air Cav also has an aero-rifle platoon (ARP) which is capable of reconnaissance and long-range observation. Its personnel can either air-land or rappel from hovering helicopters to carry out reconnaissance on foot or motorcycle. The 1st Squadron, 17th Cavalry have a total of 82 helicopters, comprising Black Hawks, Kiowas and Cobras.

The smallest element of the Division's aviation contingent is the 'Quick Fix' CEWI platoon. It is responsible for the Division's aerial electronic warfare and is capable of radio direction finding, communication monitoring and jamming and electronic target acquisition. 'Quick Fix' has three EH-1H helicopters specially fitted out for its operations.

Aviation is the Division's combat-manoeuvre asset. The 82nd's helicopters are capable of being air-transported by United States Air Force C-141 Galaxy and C-5A Starlifter aircraft. The OH-58 Kiowas and the aero-rifle platoon are capable of carrying out reconnaissance missions and supplying in-depth intelligence on enemy movements. The UH-60 Black Hawks provide the means of landing air-assault teams and can also be used for airlifting 105 mm howitzers and other equipment across the battlefield. UH-1H Hueys offer 'command and control' facilities to the force leaders while Cobra AH-IS attack helicopters can engage enemy armour.

The 82nd Air Cavalry acts as the Division's 'eyes and ears' while the Combat Aviation Battalion provides the 'teeth' for its anti-armour capability.

Right: The pilot of a scout helicopter demonstrates the finer points of low-level flying.

Below: The 82nd Combat Aviation Battalion and the 1st Squadron (Air) 17th Cavalry have a total of 48 AH-1S Cobras. These attack helicopters provide the Division's main aerial anti-armour capability.

UNITED STATES MARINE CORPS

The United States Marine Corps (USMC) is the largest force of its kind in the world. Formed in 1775 and permanently established by Act of Congress in 1798, the US Marine Corps is the oldest service in the United States armed forces. The Marines fought with distinction throughout both World Wars, especially in the Pacific theatre during the Second World War. They fought a number of successful battles in Korea between 1950 and 1953, and also won a legislative struggle in Congress at the same time — for years the future of the Marine Corps had been uncertain, but in 1951 a bill was passed in Congress giving the USMC equal status with the other armed services.

The US Marine Corps was extensively involved in the Vietnam War. From 1950 onwards the Marines supplied a training team to the South Vietnamese Marine Corps, and in 1965 they started to supply helicopter support. As the war escalated, so the support to the South Vietnamese increased. The Marines' amphibious capability, and the fact that they were able to support themselves via a beachhead, made them an invaluable part of the overall US strategy. Chiefly deployed in the northern provinces of South Vietnam, the Marines were involved in some of the heaviest fighting of the war, especially in the De-Militarized Zone (DMZ) between North and South Vietnam. In total the Marines lost 12,936 dead and 88,594 wounded during their eight years of conflict in South-East Asia; this was a high price to pay and brought a lot of adverse reaction from the American public.

Since the US withdrawal from Vietnam and the end of the war in South-East Asia, the Marine Corps has undergone a number of major changes. Its selection and training procedures have been revised, and recruiting standards are higher now than ever before. There is a greater emphasis on the Marines' primary role, that of conducting amphibious operations, and a marked increase in their commitment to the defence of NATO's Northern Flank.

The present active strength of the US Marine Corps is about 194,000. This considerable force is divided into three Marine Divisions and three Marine Air Wings. Each Marine Division has a strength of some 18,000 personnel who are divided into three infantry regiments, an artillery regiment, a tank battalion, an armoured amphibian battalion and a light armoured assault battalion. Each Division also has a small number of logistical support units. The Marine Air Wings each have a total of between 286 to 315 aircraft, both fixed-wing and rotary, which provide the Marine Divisions with an invaluable air capability.

MARINE RECONNAISSANCE UNITS

Before any amphibious landing, much detailed intelligence information must first be gathered on the proposed landing area. These strategic reconnaissance operations are carried out by Marine Reconnaissance Units.

Marine Reconnaissance Units, known as 'Recons', are the US Marine Corps' own special forces and are, therefore, distinct from the US Army's Special Forces and US Navy's SEALs (Sea, Air, Land Teams, discussed later in the chapter). Recon units are divided into two types: the Force Reconnaissance Company (Force Recon) and Battalion Reconnaissance Company (Battalion Recon). The role of both Force and Battalion Recons is to reconnoitre the landing area for both landing craft and helicopter assault, but their missions and training programmes differ.

The Force Recon teams operate clandestinely, in a way similar to the US Army SF teams and the British Special Boat Squadron (SBS). They do, in fact, have more in common with the latter. Both the SBS, which is part of the Royal Marine Commandos, and the USMC Force Recons have the same basic sub-unit structure — the four-man patrol. These small teams provide the ideal number of men for a clandestine mission. Each man has his own speciality and is cross-trained in a second (for instance, demolitions/signalling or medic/demolitions). A four-man team is also easier to control and easier to conceal, both vital to the success of a clandestine operation.

The training of a Force Recon operator is long and intensive. He must have passed through the USMC 11-week 'boot camp' at either San Diego or Parris Island, and then have served for a period with a Marine battalion. He must be proficient in all the basic infantry skills before he can volunteer for Force Recon. Many have served with the Battalion Recon before volunteering. He must be airborne-qualified, or willing to become so. The Marines

The UH-1H Huey is still used by the United States Marine Corps for the insertion and extraction of Recon teams before heliborne or seaborne assaults.

send a number of their personnel to the Army's Airborne and Ranger Schools to acquire further skills.

All the men in Force Recon are trained paratroopers. They must be good swimmers and are trained divers, using both open and closed breathing apparatus. They are also skilled in the handling of small boats, such as inflatable and rigid raiding craft. Other training includes forward aircraft controlling (FAC), artillery observing, long-range reconnaissance patrolling and a variety of other skills. Taken into account, the training that the Force Recon personnel receive makes them among the most highly trained troops in the world.

The Battalion Recon is a much larger force, and each Marine division has one such battalion, usually with a strength of around 500 men. Operating as platoons or companies, Battalion Recon gathers intelligence information on the landing area, which it then relays to its own par-

ticular battalion or task force. Battalion Recon can be used in conjunction with Force Recon, in which case it is introduced into the operational area after Force Recon. If the amphibious assault is battalion-sized, it is possible for the Battalion Recon alone to be used.

Apart from being fully trained Marines, the personnel of Battalion Recon platoons are experienced surface swimmers and inflatable-boat handlers. Some also receive SCUBA (self-contained underwater breathing apparatus) training.

The main difference between Force Recon and Battalion Recon occurs in the selection of their missions. Although both units gather intelligence, the Battalion Recon's role is primarily tactical while Force Recon is a strategic unit under the direct command of the Landing Force commander. Furthermore, Battalion Recon relies heavily upon helicopters and light vehicles for mobility whereas Force Recon, like the Ranger Battalions, relies on its feet.

UNITED STATES NAVY

UNDERWATER DEMOLITION TEAMS

The United States Navy also has its own special forces which consist of the Underwater Demolition Teams (UDT) and the SEAL (Sea, Air, Land) Teams. The primary mission of the UDTs is the reconnaissance and clearance of the proposed amphibious landing area, from the 6½-fathom curve (6.4 m/21 ft in depth) to the high-water mark. All obstacles that may prevent or hinder the free movement of landing and supply craft are cleared by the use of explosives, laid by the UDTs. They also mark out channels, guide in the first assault wave and gather intelligence for the Amphibious Task Force commander. Their secondary missions include mine clearance, agent and guerrilla infiltration/extraction and ship/harbour installation sabotage.

Underwater Demolition Teams are also trained in a number of delivery and retrieval techniques using such means as high-speed surface craft (HSSC), low-flying helicopters, submarines, parachutes and,

A small raiding party bringing its rubber boat ashore. This method of inserting patrols is still widely used by most of the world's special forces.

lastly, on foot. Although they are not normally required to do so, UDTs are capable of short-range operations inland.

The first US Navy Combat Demolition Unit was formed at Fort Pierce, Florida, in mid-1943. Volunteers came from Navy Construction Battalions and USN/USMC Scout and Raider units. They underwent intensive physical training and were divided into six-man teams before being sent to England in time for the Allied invasion of Normandy. During D-Day the teams carried out their assigned tasks, but casualties were extremely high, with some teams being wiped out altogether. The Combat Demolition Unit losses averaged 41 per cent during the assault.

The survivors of the Normandy invasion brought back the lessons learned and these were put into effect during an additional six-week advanced-training course in Hawaii. The structure of the units changed to two/three-man groups, several of which formed a squadron, and these became UDTs. Most UDT activity occurred in the Pacific theatre, where UDT personnel were involved in combat operations on Borneo, Peleliu, Saipan, Guam, Iwo Jima and Okinawa, among others. During these campaigns the casualty rate fell to one per cent.

By the end of the Second World War there were 34 UDTs active, employing a total of about 3,500 men. By 1946 most of the men had been demobilized leaving only five standard Teams, two in the Atlantic and three in the Pacific. In 1950 the UDTs were again in combat, this time in Korea. They took part in the amphibious landing at Inchon, and conducted a number of night sabotage raids against enemy targets, such as bridges and railway lines. The Teams continued to carry out beach-reconnaissance and channel-clearing operations in Korea until the end of the war in 1953.

The US involvement in the Vietnam War gave the UDTs yet another chance to demonstrate their expertise. One complete Team was deployed in the Philippines whence it sent out various detachments on operations. Detachment Alpha provided support and training from the headquarters at Subic Bay, Republic of the Philippines. Detachment Bravo provided Beach Reconnaissance Groups in support of Far

A US Navy SEAL with members of a South Vietnamese Special Forces unit aboard a riverine craft during operations in South-East Asia.

East operations. Detachment Charlie conducted combat recon missions from two fleet-type submarines, USS *Perch* and USS *Tunney*. Two methods of entry were practised: swimmers either would ascend from a submarine resting 11 m (35 ft) down on the sea bed before swimming ashore or would paddle ashore from the deck of a diving submarine. Detachment Delta carried out sabotage missions from its base in Danang. Detachments Echo and Foxtrot carried out reconnaissance and demolition operations for the Amphibious Ready Group, and Detachments Golf and Hotel operated with the river patrol boats of the Riverine Groups. These small craft, known as PBRs (Patrol Boat, River), are crewed by the Navy's Special Boat Squadrons which fought many battles up to 160 km (100 miles) from the sea on the Mekong Delta River systems.

SEAL TEAMS

The US Navy SEAL Teams resulted from a study carried out by the Navy in 1960. This study analyzed the Navy's ability to conduct counter-insurgency operations, including unconventional and clandestine warfare. The Commander of Navy Operations recognized the need for the US Navy to have its own special forces unit and on 1 January 1962 President John F Kennedy commissioned SEAL Team 1 and SEAL Team 2.

The SEAL (Sea, Air, Land) Teams are part of the Naval Special Warfare Groups, as are the UDTs and the Special Boat Squadrons. The SEAL Teams are part of the Fleet's tactical units and are organized, trained and equipped to conduct counter-guerrilla and clandestine warfare in maritime and riverine environments. They have the same training and role as the UDTs and carry out sabotage, infiltration and reconnaissance missions. In addition, however, they have the task of conducting limited counter-insurgency civic action missions as part of counter-guerrilla operations. These include medical aid, civil engineering, boat operation and maintenance and basic education for the local indigenous population. They are also able to provide foreign and Allied countries with training teams, to organize and train their own forces.

With the increasing US involvement in Vietnam the SEALs deployed two platoons in the Rung Sat area where they disrupted Viet Cong and North Vietnamese Army sapper activity. Their results were so successful that four more platoons were deployed to carry out listening-post and ambush operations against the Viet Cong, well back from the main rivers.

As the Vietnam War escalated, both SEAL Teams 1 and 2 deployed platoons throughout the riverine areas. These platoons were usually inserted and exfiltrated by small, armed and armoured river-craft.

A group of US Navy SEALs during operations in Vietnam. The SEALs were the exclusive users of the Stoner 5.56 mm machine gun, pictured here.

A US Navy SEAL in training. It is often difficult to determine where the water ends and the land begins.

As operations increased a specially designed and equipped SEAL support boat was developed. This craft was quieter, faster and more manoeuvrable, with increased firepower and range. Its use substantially reduced casualties from Viet Cong ambush.

By late 1966 the SEALs received further support. A SEAL 'package' was introduced. This contained Seawolf helicopter support, a Boat Support Unit and a Mobile Support Team, all providing the SEAL platoons with rapid, effective assistance.

SEALs continued to operate throughout the war, carrying out a wide variety of highly successful combat missions. With the gradual withdrawal of US forces from Vietnam the number of SEAL missions began to decrease, but in late 1970 the SEALs conducted a highly successful attack on a Viet Cong prisoner of war (POW) camp. A team of 15 SEALs and 19 Vietnamese militiamen attacked the camp and rescued 19 South Vietnamese POWs, some of whom had been captive for four years. In total, SEAL units released 48 POWs from Viet Cong captivity in a series of operations conducted in 1970.

Throughout the Vietnam War the SEAL Teams continually demonstrated their courage and professionalism. SEAL Team 1 received two Presidential Unit Citations plus one Navy and one Meritorious Unit Commendation. Personal awards included one Medal of Honor, two Navy Crosses, 42 Silver Stars, 402 Bronze Stars,

two Legion of Merits, 352 Navy Commendation Medals and 51 Navy Achievement Medals.

During the war SEAL Teams accounted for more than 800 Viet Cong killed in action; even more were detained and captured.

Training All volunteers for UDTs and SEAL Teams must undergo a series of training courses before joining their assigned units. These courses, which last up to two years, begin with Basic UDT/SEAL training at Coronado, California. The BUD/S course lasts for 23 weeks and is divided into three phases: Phase 1, indoctrination and conditioning; Phase 2, diving; and Phase 3, practical field exercises including reconnaissance, demolitions and tactics.

Physical training is intensive; students run every day and swim every second day. Continuous physical stress is gradually increased and the students must complete a 21-obstacle endurance course in under 15 minutes. Only about half of the 80 to 100 'tadpoles' (as the students are known) will go on to graduate, and most drop out during the first phase. During Phase 2 the students practise small-boat handling and learn basic diving techniques for open and closed SCUBA systems. Phase 3 is taken up by land-warfare tactics, hydrographic reconnaissance, weapons' handling, demolitions and communications.

Those who graduate from the BUD/S training go on to Fort Benning, Georgia, where they undergo their three-week basic airborne course. Under Army instruction the students learn the skills of basic static-line parachuting.

After Fort Benning the students return to the Naval Amphibious School at Coronado. Here they spend ten weeks learning how to operate and navigate swimmer delivery vehicles (SDVs). These small, battery-powered, open submersibles are used in a variety of UDT/SEAL missions. After ten weeks' training with SDVs the students progress to the basic EOD course.

Explosive ordnance disposal (EOD) plays an important part in both UDT and SEAL operations. Students are taught how to use plastic explosives and TNT, and practise the neutralization of both foreign and domestic ordnance. They also learn about chemical and biological munitions. This is the final part of their training, lasts 33 weeks and takes place at Huntsville, Alabama or Indian Head, Maryland.

On graduation, the newly qualified combat swimmers go on to their assigned UDT or SEAL Teams where they receive further on-the-job training as part of an operational platoon. SEALs receive further training in unconventional warfare, including unarmed combat, jungle warfare, combat medicine, escape and evasion, fire support and freefall parachuting.

Weapons and Equipment UDTs and SEAL Teams use a wide variety of specialized equipment. These include small boats, especially the seven-man inflatable, a number of different open and closed SCUBA systems, hand-held sonar and underwater communication devices and various types of parachutes for land and water jumps. Swimmer delivery vehicles for between one and four swimmers are also used and can be launched from either surface craft or submarines.

Both standard and non-standard personal weapons are used. The CAR-15 assault rifle is popular, as is the Stoner M63A1 light machine gun. The latter weapon, although not officially adopted by US forces, uses the same ammunition as the M-16 and CAR-15. It is also relatively light and with its 150-round drum magazine gives extra firepower to a small team.

The US Navy UDTs and SEALs provide the United States with a unique force, capable of the following: collecting information about enemy military installations in coastal areas; carrying out the reconnaissance and demolition of natural and manmade obstacles before an amphibious landing; conducting sabotage raids against military targets ashore; limpet-mining enemy shipping; operating as small patrols on reconnaissance or ambush missions; and, in the case of the SEALs, carrying out counter-insurgency operations, aiding the civil population with medical, engineering and other assistance, and providing training teams for other military and para-military forces.

UDT/SEAL Teams operate throughout the world, in the Arctic and Antarctic, in the jungles, on sea and land, and are a vital strategic and tactical force for the United States and its Allies.

All US special operations' forces are instructed in unarmed combat, mostly a mixture of various oriental martial arts.

SPECIAL AIR SERVICE

In May 1980 a Counter-Revolutionary Warfare team from 22nd Special Air Service Regiment stormed the Iranian Embassy in London. Inside the building a group of Arab terrorists was holding 22 hostages, including a number of Iranian diplomatic staff, a BBC employee and a uniformed police officer. The SAS troop, after days of careful preparation and rehearsals, assaulted the Embassy and released the hostages. All but one of the terrorists were killed, their captives were rescued unscathed and the CRW team suffered no serious casualties.

This dramatic assault and rescue operation was filmed by television crews, one of which had managed to slip past the tight cordon of police controlling the area. The entire operation was broadcast live on television and, for the first time, brought the Special Air Service Regiment to the attention of the public.

Up until that time few people, either inside or outside the British armed forces, knew what the Special Air Service was or did. The siege at the Iranian Embassy changed that: a number of books have been written on the Regiment; there have been films of fictional, heroic deeds carried out by its members; and the letters 'SAS' have been used to describe black Balaclava helmets and West German-manufactured submachine guns — often to the great amusement of the Regiment itself.

The Special Air Service is a military formation. It constitutes a major part of Britain's special forces, and its main role is one of strategic reconnaissance and attack, a role that has changed little since the Regiment was formed.

FORMATION

The origins of the Special Air Service lie in the Western Desert during the Second World War. At the time of its formation the Germans controlled most of western Europe and had recently captured Yugo-slavia, Greece and Crete. General Rommel's Afrika Korps had won a number of successful battles in North Africa and together with the Italians posed a grave threat to British forces.

In Egypt at this time was a Scots Guards Lieutenant by the name of David Stirling. Stirling was not a professional soldier. He was a Cambridge graduate and an experienced mountain climber who had joined the Scots Guards at the beginning of the war and went on to join Laycock's No 8 Commando in the Middle East. This formation, known as 'Layforce', was one of the early Army Commando units, and by 1941 was in the process of being disbanded. During this period of inactivity, Stirling came up with the basic idea of the Special Air Service, a concept of operations now employed by almost all special forces throughout the world.

The theory was that small parties, consisting of four to five highly trained commandos, could carry out strategic raids on vulnerable enemy lines of communication and targets such as airfields, vehicle parks and fuel dumps. These small groups could be inserted behind enemy lines by parachute or, in coastal areas, by small boats launched from submarines. These teams, because of their size, would be less easy to detect, for example, than a commando troop of 50 men. They could then approach their target unnoticed and attach time-delay explosive devices before leaving the area, without attracting enemy attention. Such small teams could exploit the maximum possibilities of surprise and, if properly equipped, cause as much damage as a much larger force.

Once the plan had been conceived, Stirling was presented with the problem of delivering it to the right authority. Since a unit of the type Stirling envisaged would have to be responsible for its own training and operational planning, Stirling felt that it should come under the direct command of the C-in-C. Only a young Lieutenant at

the time, Stirling thought it unlikely that his plan would ever reach the man at the top by normal channels, so he decided on the 'direct approach'. What followed has become Regimental history within the Special Air Service, and it is fitting that such a Regiment should have an imaginative and daring beginning.

In order to see the Commander-in-Chief Middle East, General Sir Claude Auckinleck, Stirling first had to get into the GHQ Cairo. Despite being incapacitated by an injury he had received two months previously in a parachuting accident, Stirling managed to climb over a high security fence before staggering into the headquarters' building. Unable to find Auckin-

leck, Stirling was able to give his plan to Lieutenant General Neil Ritchie before being caught and ejected. Luckily the plan was passed on to Auckinleck who was impressed with both the concept and its method of delivery. Auckinleck realized that a unit of this kind, if successful, could be of great strategic value and could also provide him with a most useful intelligence asset. Subsequently a meeting between the two men was held, and Stirling was authorized to establish 'L' Detachment, Special Air Service Brigade, the name 'brigade' being a ruse to confuse enemy intelligence.

'L' Detachment established its headquarters and training camp at Kabrit in the

Members of the SAS team cross the balconies just before their assault on the Iranian Embassy. After placing a framed charge against one of the armoured windows, they moved into the building where they rescued the hostages.

The American-manufactured jeep, originally acquired by the SAS in 1942 and similar to the type still used by the Belgian Para-Commandos. This jeep is armed with one .5 in Browning machine gun and three .303 in Vickers K machine guns (one twin-mounted). In addition it carries 409 litres (90 gal) of fuel, a large quantity of explosives and ammunition and rations for up to 60 days.

Canal zone. Stirling was promoted to Captain and given command of this new unit for which he was authorized to recruit 66 officers and men. It was from these inauspicious beginnings that the Special Air Service grew. Stirling was very selective about the men he chose, and those he recruited were to have a lasting influence on the character of the Regiment. Among the first to join was Jock Lewis, an Oxford graduate. It was he who shortly afterwards designed the well-known explosive/incendiary device, aptly named the Lewis bomb, which was to be used to great effect in the Desert War. Another recruit was Paddy Mayne, an Irish rugby international and an excellent boxer. An exceptional leader of men, he too was to have a great effect on the Regiment, and was later to command the 1st SAS when Stirling was captured by the Germans. Other officers who joined included Fitzroy Maclean and Anders Lassen, and Stirling was able to recruit four invaluable NCOs: Bennet, Cooper, Lilley and Riley. Both Bennet and Lilley rejoined the postwar Regiment when it was re-formed in Malaya.

Above all it was a combination of leadership, ingenuity and toughness that Stirling was looking for and it is because of these high standards of selection and training that the SAS has survived.

'L' Detachment's first operation, however, was a disaster. Due to adverse weather, aircraft became lost, and many of the men who parachuted in were swept away. From then on ground vehicles were mostly used as the method of transport. Initially 'L' Detachment hitched rides to its targets in the trucks of the Long Range Desert Group. These raids were more successful, and within a few weeks they had destroyed over 100 enemy aircraft. By the latter part of 1942 'L' Detachment had grown to become the 1st Special Air Service Regiment and had within its ranks a number of French paratroops. They also had their own transport. A number of jeeps were acquired and specially equipped with extra water and fuel tanks. Usually armed with either three machine guns or twin Vickers K and a .30 Browning, these two-man vehicles were used throughout the war.

The 1st SAS Regiment was a great success. By the end of the campaign they had destroyed almost 400 German aircraft on the ground plus a number of supply depots and countless enemy vehicles. By 1943 the 1st SAS Regiment was commanded by Paddy Maine (Stirling having been captured by the Germans); David's brother, Bill Stirling, was in command of the recently formed 2nd SAS Regiment, which was conducting raids in Sicily and along the Italian coastline.

After operations on the Italian mainland the two Regiments returned to England in 1944. Here they formed the 1st Special Air Service Brigade together with a Belgian Independent Parachute Squadron (later 1st Belgian SAS) and the 3rd and 4th Free French Parachute Battalions. Attached to the Brigade was F Squadron GHQ Reconnaissance Regiment (Phantom) which acted as the Brigade's signal squadron.

The Brigade was commanded by Brigadier Roderick McLeod and came under the direction of HQ Airborne. A number of roles were considered for the new Brigade, but it was eventually decided to deploy them both strategically and, to a lesser extent, tactically. Their initial task was to support the Allied invasion of Normandy but in the longer term they were to fight right across north-west Europe, in central and southern France and again in Italy.

A number of strategic operations were carried out behind enemy lines after D-Day, with reconnaissance parties operating within 80 km (50 miles) of the advancing Allied armies. These groups varied in size, but their main mission was to co-ordinate attacks on enemy lines of communication with local agents and guerrilla movements. In this action they were ably supported by the RAF, mostly 38 Group, and liaised closely with the Special Operations Executive, who had 'Jedburgh' teams operating with many of the resistance units.

In the four months following D-Day a total of 43 operations were conducted by the 1st SAS Brigade. Ammunition, weapons, vehicles and other supplies were flown in to the groups. The results achieved by these operations were out of all proportion to the manpower involved. Trains were derailed, vital supplies destroyed, enemy captured and important targets indicated for RAF bombing raids. The well-armed jeeps were used to devastating effect, shooting-up enemy transports and occasionally engaging light armour. As the Germans fell back, SAS support to the various Belgian and Dutch resistance groups was increased and attacks on the retreating Germans were stepped-up.

During the winter of 1944–45 the Allied offensive in north-west Europe drew to a standstill and there was little suitable employment on hand for the SAS. In Italy, however, Field Marshall Kesselring's army was putting up stiff resistance, and this was to provide the Brigade with their next task.

In Italy the Allies had air superiority but because of appalling weather during the winter their aircraft were almost always

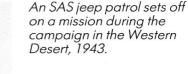

An SAS jeep patrol sets off on a mission during the campaign in the Western Desert, 1943.

69

grounded. The road and railway networks in and out of Italy were vitally important not only to Italy herself but to her German defenders as well. Furthermore, there were a large number of partisan units operating in the north of the country and in December 1944, 3 Squadron of 2nd SAS, led by Major Roy Farran, was sent in to coordinate their attacks. One troop, led by Major Walker-Brown, was so successful that a force of 6,000 Germans was tied-up just searching for them. Walker-Brown is renowned for pioneering the use of heavier weapons in these attacks. Apart from successfully employing 3 in mortars and medium machine guns, they also used a 75 mm howitzer which had been parachuted in at his request.

While operations in Italy were severely hampering the German withdrawal, most of the 1st SAS Brigade were being employed in their jeep reconnaissance role in north-west Europe, and towards the end of the war were responsible for rounding-up and disarming many German troops.

By the end of the Second World War the Special Air Service was recognized as being a strategic force of vital importance. During the campaign in Europe it had been responsible for killing or seriously wounding over 7,500 German soldiers, and capturing nearly 5,000. Out of the 2,000 men in the Brigade, there were only 330 casualties. They had destroyed scores of trains and hundreds of vehicles, and provided the RAF with innumerable bombing targets. In addition to this they had trained, armed and led resistance movements and had a great effect on the morale of Allied civilians in German-occupied territory.

At the end of the Second World War the Belgian and French Regiments were officially handed over to their respective armies, both of which kept them going. This, however, was not the case with the British 1st and 2nd SAS Regiments, and in October 1945 they were disbanded. In 1946 the War Office in London carried out an analysis on the employment of Special Air Service troops and concluded that in the event of a war there would be a definite role for such a unit. So it was that their role went to a recently disbanded Territorial Army regiment, the Artists Rifles. The 'Artists' as it was known, had been created in 1859, had served with distinction throughout the First World War and had achieved a total of eight Victoria Crosses. During the Second World War, however, it had been made into an Officer Cadet Training Unit, and had not taken part in the fighting.

The 'Artists' was something of an elite itself and it was therefore rather fitting that

it should take on the SAS role and become 21st Special Air Service Regiment (Artists).

MALAYA

The next conflict in which the Special Air Service was to become involved was known as the 'Malayan Emergency'. In 1948 Malaya, a British colony, was becoming increasingly vulnerable to Communist subversion and terrorism. This was a new and different enemy for the British. During the Second World War large groups of Chinese guerrillas had been supported by the Allies in their fight against the occupying Japanese Army. After the defeat of Japan, these guerrillas, who were nearly all Chinese Communists, were inactive for a period, and many left their jungle hideouts and returned to their homes. However, they were soon to return, in an attempt to replace British control of Malaya with their particular form of Communism.

Malaya was, at this time, an important trade and strategic asset to Britain. It produced one-third of the world's rubber and over half of its tin. Besides possessing such great mineral wealth, Malaya was geographically linked to the British army and naval base at Singapore, which controlled the Strait of Malacca and access to the South China Sea. Malaya was also an ideal country in which to mount a guerrilla-type revolutionary war. Over three-quarters of the country was covered in thick jungle, much of it unmapped. The majority of the rubber plantations were bordered by jungle, and most of the tin mines were in remote areas.

The political situation worsened, and by 1948 there were over 5,000 disaffected Chinese 'guerrillas' in the jungle. These groups of 'Communist Terrorists', or CTs as they became known, were led by Chin Peng, a Chinese who had fought for the British against the Japanese. He and his 'hard-core' CTs knew both the jungle and the British, and had vast supplies of weapons and ammunition left over from the war. The campaign started with attacks on mines and plantations and soon escalated to the ambushing of convoys and the assassination of both British and Chinese civilians. Initially they operated with impunity. Living in camps deep in the jungle they coerced the local native aborigines into aiding them by providing food and, more important, information about British movements. Employing these tactics they were quickly able to build up a formidable intelligence network, which even extended into the towns. By early 1950 the CTs had killed a total of 836 civilians, 323 police officers and 154 soldiers and, although they had suffered heavy casualties them-

Opposite: This jungle 'basha' provides the trooper with temporary accommodation while in the field. Constructed by using a poncho and local materials, this simple shelter gives the man a place to cook, eat and sleep and takes only a few minutes to erect.

selves, the opposing British infantry battalions from Singapore were making little headway.

A new strategy against the terrorists was conceived by the Director of Operations, General Sir Harold Briggs. Known as the Briggs plan, it called first for the isolation of the terrorists by the building of 410 fortified villages in which to house the local population. This would deny the CTs their main source of food and, more important perhaps, their information on security forces' activities. The second part of the plan involved the deployment in the jungle of specially trained troops. These special forces troops would be able to operate in the difficult jungle environment for long periods, and would be used to cultivate the local aborigines. The man chosen to establish and train this unit was Major Mike Calvert, who was, at the time, a Staff officer at Headquarters Far East, and had commanded the 1st SAS Brigade at the end of the Second World War. He formed the Malayan Scouts and recruited them throughout the Far East.

As the recruits started to come in they were put through an exhausting training programme, much of which was planned by Major John Woodhouse who was later to organize the SAS selection and continuation course in Britain. The standard of these early recruits varied. Some had previous experience in the SAS or SOE, but there were a small number of men who were to prove to be below standard. The Regiment started to take shape, and Calvert travelled thousands of miles to recruit. The new force was now called the Malayan Scouts (SAS) and was based at Johore. It started to take shape as a three-squadron regiment, which was soon to become 22nd SAS. 'A' Squadron was composed of Calvert's volunteers, 'B' Squadron were Reservists from 21st SAS in England, and 'C' Squadron came from Rhodesia.

Thus 22nd Special Air Service Regiment was formed in Malaya, and a number of commanding officers left their mark on the Regiment. Mike Calvert was invalided out in 1951 and was replaced by John Sloane, an orthodox soldier who brought traditional military discipline to the Regiment. In 1953 Oliver Brooke took over and did much to further the 'hearts and minds' campaign with the aborigines. Brooke was seriously injured while parachuting into the jungle and was replaced for a short time by Mike Osborne who, in turn, was replaced by George Lea. Lea, who later became a Lieutenant General, had much to do with shaping the Regiment and was responsible for building a strong cadre of officers. A number of squadron commanders also left their imprint on the Regiment. Among them were Harry Thompson, John Edwardes, Dare Newell (who later became the Regimental Adjutant) and John Woodhouse and Peter de la Billiere (now Lieutenant General), both of whom later came to command the Regiment.

Over the nine years of the Malayan campaign the Regiment perfected its jungle operations, and its experiences were to prepare it for the campaigns that followed. The hot, humid and mostly hilly jungle posed great navigational problems, and the Regiment perfected its use of the prismatic compass. Living conditions were primitive, and the troopers became masters of the art of survival. They learned how to build 'bashas', jungle shelters made from issue ponchos and local materials; they learned preventative medicine and how to deal with various tropical diseases; they learned tracking from the Iban Dyaks, natives from Borneo who were brought to Malaya in the early stages of the emergency because of their tracking abilities; and they pioneered the technique of tree-jumping, a very important method of infiltration. Tree-jumping involved parachuting into the jungle canopy which was often up to 60 m (200 ft) above the ground. Once the parachute was firmly lodged in the trees, the man would then lower himself to the jungle floor by abseiling down a rope. By tree-jumping into the jungle, the patrols could increase their range of operations, and could deploy quickly deep into the jungle without alerting the enemy. Food was also a limiting factor for the duration of patrols, and a special 7–14 day SAS patrol ration was introduced.

Throughout the campaign the SAS were ably supported from the air. Because of the extended nature of their patrols, the Regiment relied heavily on air support for resupply as well as for casualty extraction. Initially they were supported by helicopters flown first by the Royal Navy and later by the RAF. Various types of fixed-wing aircraft were used for parachute operations and resupply; these included Hastings, Valettas and, towards the end of the campaign, Beverleys. The 55th Company Royal Army Service Corps were responsible for the air-delivery of supplies, and during the conflict lost over 100 men in aircraft crashes.

The organization of the Regiment changed during its time in Malaya. In 1956 C Squadron returned to Rhodesia and was replaced by a New Zealand Squadron. The latter was commanded by Major Frank Rennie and a third of the men were Maoris. One squadron of men from the Parachute Regiment, commanded by Major Dudley Coventry, also joined the Regiment as did a number of Fijians. This brought the total number of squadrons to five. The Fijians made excellent soldiers

and many stayed with the Regiment throughout their service with the British Army.

The Special Air Service left Malaya at the end of the emergency with three major achievements. First, they had proved themselves capable of providing valuable intelligence on the enemy, an achievement more important than the 108 confirmed CT kills they had made in their nine years in the jungle. They had proved that specially trained troops could operate for long periods in a hostile environment. Patrols had stayed out in the jungle for months at a time whereas before their formation the maximum duration for an infantry patrol was considered seven days. Second, they had proved the value of 'hearts and minds' in modern counter-insurgency operations. They had lived for long periods with aboriginal tribes, had won over the natives to their cause and gained valuable allies. They had provided medical aid in the form of treatment for malaria and tuberculosis, both of which were prevalent among the tribespeople. These lessons were put to good use by the Regiment in future cam-

paigns in Borneo and Oman, and by the US Special Forces in South-East Asia. Third, they had won the battle for their right to exist as a regiment. Whitehall had finally agreed to their permanent establishment, and they became part of the British Order of Battle in 1958.

BORNEO

After its return from Malaya, the Regiment found itself reduced to two squadrons, A and D. B Squadron had been incorporated into the other two squadrons, C Squadron had returned home in 1956 and was part of the Rhodesian Army and the 'Kiwi' Squadron had returned to New Zealand. Apart from four months' active service in Oman between 1958–59 both squadrons were actively involved in reorganization and training in the UK and the United States.

In December 1962 there was an internal rebellion in the British protectorate of Brunei, which together with Sarawak and North Borneo formed the top one-third of an island to the west of Malaya. The

Above: A four-man patrol during operations in Malaya. As the 'hearts and minds' campaign got underway increasing use was made of the local native population, seen here acting as porters.

remaining two-thirds of the island formed the independent country of Indonesia. The 'Brunei Revolt', as it was known, was short-lived. Small groups of armed guerrillas carried out simultaneous attacks on a number of strategic targets in Brunei, including police stations, government buildings and a power station. The British response was to bring in troops from Singapore. Gurkhas, Royal Marines Commandos and Queen's Own Highlanders played a part in suppressing the revolt. Within eight days it was over and the rebels, who at this time numbered about 1,000 men, took to the jungle.

Although the revolt was over, it seemed likely that the general situation would worsen. The rebellion had been organized by a young Brunei sheikh named Azahari whose aim was to unite the three British dependencies. The Indonesian Communists were ready to exploit the situation for their own gain and had a trained army poised along the 1,120-km (700-mile) border. It was into this scenario that A Squadron 22nd SAS was propelled in January 1963.

The Director of Operations in Brunei was Major-General Walter Walker. He had, under his command, five battalions with which to secure the border, a seemingly impossible task. The terrain was varied: primary and secondary jungle, mountains and swamps, wide fast-flowing rivers along which small tribes lived in long houses. Walter realized that the SAS with its experience in conducting long-range reconnaissance patrols and living in the jungle, would be a vital asset in the coming struggle. He was right.

Soon after their arrival, A Squadron had a total of 21 three-man patrols spread out along the border with Indonesia. After deploying his patrols, Major John Edwardes visited them on foot. Edwardes had served as a squadron commander in Malaya, was well-liked and respected by his men and a typical example of an SAS officer. The border itself was difficult to define, but A Squadron were aided by two factors: first, because of the terrain there were only a limited number of crossing-points; and second, the local tribes provided the patrols with intelligence. The latter was most important. During its time in Malaya the Regiment had come close to perfecting the 'hearts and minds' technique. After keeping a village under observation for a period and establishing whether it had allegiance to the Indonesians or the guerrillas, patrols would visit the village and speak with its headman. Depending on their reception they would either sit around and talk or, if lucky, eat and drink with the natives. They would then move back to their jungle hideout, and return a day or a week later, to pick up where they had left off.

Visits were never hurried, and the business of establishing relations with the Ibans was never forced. It did not take long for mutual respect to develop, however, and before too long a number of patrols were operating from long houses in these remote villages. The tribespeople provided food, accommodation, transport, if on a river, and trackers, and the patrols provided payment for their work, as well as gifts, medical treatment and, in some cases, construction work. For example, the soldier Gipsy Smith constructed an improvised hydro-electric generator. He is also reputed to have used the frame of a Bergen rucksack in the construction of an alcohol still (the details of this remain a closely guarded secret, presumably until some agreement on the patent has been agreed).

The local natives proved to be invaluable and provided the patrols with information which was subsequently collated and sent back to the brigade HQ. The first raid took place in April 1963, just before A Squadron's withdrawal. A police station at Tebedu, which was close to the Sarawak-Indonesian border, was attacked by a group of 30 Indonesians. It was a quick guerrilla attack — only one policeman was killed and two wounded — but it was significant because General Walker was given reinforcements on account of it.

Advanced survival skills are taught to all members of the Special Air Service Regiment during their continuation training.

74

D Squadron replaced A Squadron at the end of April and spent much of its tour training locally raised scouts with the aid of the Gurkha Independent Parachute Company. These border scouts proved themselves both efficient and useful, and were later to take part in cross-border operations with the SAS. In the meantime surveillance of the border and long-range patrols were stepped up.

During 1963 there was a great deal of behind-the-scenes political activity. A United Nations team visited Borneo in the summer and ascertained that the majority of the local population would prefer to be part of the Malaysian Federation rather than Indonesia. In late summer the Federation was formed and included Sarawak. The Sultanate of Brunei and Northern Borneo remained a British protectorate. Indonesian activity along the border continued and in August, just before D Squadron's tour ended, the Indonesians launched their first large-scale offensive.

As the Borneo confrontation escalated it was decided to raise a new B Squadron, and by the time D Squadron returned for its second tour in December 1963, the training of the new squadron was already underway. By October 1964 B Squadron was ready and, supported by experienced NCOs from the other two squadrons, it deployed in Brunei. The two SAS squadrons were now augmented by the Guards Independent Parachute Company, which was later to become G Squadron 22nd SAS.

By the end of 1964 there were 18 British battalions involved in the confrontation. This total included eight Gurkha battalions, but there were, in addition to these, three Malaysian Army battalions, a grand total of 14,000 troops including supporting arms. Most of these men were deployed in the jungle and were maintained largely by aerial resupply. As the year drew to a close, permission was received from London to carry out cross-border operations. These clandestine operations were kept hidden from the rest of the world by both the British and the Indonesians, as adverse public reaction could effect either side.

These operations, codenamed 'Claret', were conducted by the SAS patrols which penetrated Indonesian territory up to a distance of 10 km (6 miles). Reconnaissance missions were carried out by the

Members of a patrol are briefed before going into the jungle. In-depth briefings such as this one have always played an important part in SAS operations, with members of the patrol not only asking questions, but also putting forward suggestions.

Helicopters proved invaluable during the counter-insurgency operations in Malaya and Borneo.

four-man patrols and a great deal of intelligence regarding the enemy's forward bases was collected. Ambush patrols were then sent out to cover the trails and rivers used by the Indonesians, and these often met with great success. Enemy bases were also attacked, and the SAS often acted as guides for larger forces on these missions.

In the summer of 1965 the battalions in Borneo were reinforced by the arrival of Australian and New Zealand forces from the 28th Commonwealth Brigade in Malaysia. These included a New Zealand and an Australian SAS squadron. There was much activity along the border and patrols often found themselves up against large groups of Indonesian regulars, often paratroopers or marines. Throughout this period the SAS was constantly involved in the conflict, with the squadrons rotating back to the UK for leave on the completion of their four-five-month tours.

In August 1965 Singapore opted out of the Malaysian Federation. This was followed two months later by a coup in Indonesia, resulting in months of political confusion as the various factions fought to gain control. This ended in the President, a man named Sukarno (known as 'The Mad Doctor' by British troops), being replaced by General Suharto. A peace agreement ending the conflict was signed in August 1966.

At the height of the three-and-a-half-year confrontation there had been as many as 17,000 soldiers on active service in Borneo of whom 114 had been killed by the time the peace agreement had been signed. Many of those killed were Gurkhas and it was they who had borne the brunt of much of the fighting. An estimated 590 Indonesians had been killed, and the SAS had lost three men dead and two wounded. The squadrons had done nine four-five-month tours, in what was one of Britain's most difficult but least-publicized campaigns since the end of the Second World War. It was also one of her most successful, a victory in which the Special Air Service had played an important part.

OMAN

Oman is the largest state in the Persian Gulf, and because it dominates the Hormuz Strait leading from the Gulf to the open Arabian Sea, a major oil route, it is important strategically. In the early 1960s it had a population of about 500,000, many living in the remote areas of a country about the same size as England and Scotland.

Members of D Squadron working with the local population, seen here in the Radfan, building a well. While they were in Aden, the Special Air Service did much to improve the lot of the local inhabitants.

The Sultanate of Muscat and Oman had long been friendly with the United Kingdom, and the British had been supplying officers for the Muscat and Oman Field Force. In 1952 the Saudis occupied Buraimi Oasis, thus initiating what would become a long and bloody struggle for the control of Oman. In 1956 Saudi-trained guerrillas, who had become increasingly successful in their attacks on the Sultan's Field Force, were driven back into the mountains by a British force. A company of the Cameronians plus the Trucial Oman Scouts and aircraft of the Royal Air Force drove the rebels into the Jebel Akhdar, the highest point of which reaches 2,400 m (8,000 ft). There were a number of small villages on the fertile plains 600 m (2,000 ft) below and they kept the rebels in the mountains supplied with food and information. This area was the centre of operations conducted by both A and D Squadrons 22nd SAS against the rebels between November 1958 and the end of January 1959. After some fierce fighting the rebels were eventually defeated and Oman remained reasonably quiet for the next decade.

Between 1970 and 1976 trouble flared again in Oman, this time in Dhofar, the southern part of the country. Here the Dhofar Liberation Front, a rebel force which was backed by the People's Democratic Republic of the Yemen (PDRY), were fighting to gain control of Oman. The Dhofar Liberation Front had been formed in 1962 with the aim of overthrowing the Sultan and abolishing the archaic feudal system of government. In 1970, Qaboos, the 29-year-old son of the Sultan, deposed his father and began a programme of modernization and development in an attempt to bring Oman into the twentieth century. He also offered an amnesty to the rebels, some of whom took it. This was not, however, good enough for the PDRY and they stepped up their support of the hardcore rebels in an effort to overthrow the Qaboos government.

It soon became apparent that the Sultan's armed forces were not equipped to handle the mounting number of rebel attacks. The rebels held the Jebel and could not be shifted. Qaboos turned to Britain for help and it was decided to send in an SAS squadron which, apart from being trained in counter-insurgency and guerrilla warfare, would also be able to offer medical assistance to the Dhofaris.

The first squadron arrived in February 1971, and until September 1976 there would always be at least one SAS squadron in Oman on a four-month tour. The squadrons were known as BATTs (British Army Training Teams) and they were deployed in the Dhofar with the aim of

training tribesmen to fight the rebels. Two Civil Action Teams established clinics in the towns of Taqa and Mirbat to the east of Salalah. These four-man teams were extremely useful; containing a medic, a vet and at least one Arabic speaker, they did much to win over the Dhofaris.

The most important task of the SAS in Oman was, however, the raising and training of the 'Firqats'. These were groups of local tribesmen, including many former rebels, who were enlisted in the government cause to fight the rebels themselves. Both sides were extremely skilled in the art of war; they knew the areas in which they fought, were intensely tribal and, above all, enjoyed fighting. At the start the rebels,

Men of the SAS-trained Firqat emplaned aboard a transport aircraft in Oman. The success the Regiment had with these irregulars was a vital element in the final victory over the insurgents.

with Soviet AK-47s, were better equipped than the Firqats were with Lee-Enfield .303 rifles and the rebels also had a number of heavy weapons such as rocket-launchers, mortars and heavy machine guns. The situation changed as the war progressed and weapons were captured from the enemy and used by the Firqats. Also the rebels who came across and joined the Firqats were allowed to keep their personal weapons.

Apart from training the Firqats and going on patrol with them, the BATTs also conducted their own operations, mostly four-man reconnaissance patrols. They were also involved in operations with the Sultan's armed forces, and throughout the

campaign were ably supported by the Sultan of Oman's Air Force. The best account of the Oman campaign can be read in Major-General Tony Jeapes's book *SAS: Operation Oman*; Jeapes was a squadron commander with the SAS in Oman.

It was the success of the Firqats that led to the eventual defeat of the rebels. By 1974 the Sultan had 15,000 troops fighting the rebels, and by 1975 they were supported by 1,600 men from 21 separate Firqats, all trained and administered by the SAS. By the end of 1975 the Sultan announced that the war had ended, brought about by lack of support, both inside and outside Oman, for the rebel cause. By the

Good communications are vital to the Special Air Service Regiment, and today all recruits must achieve regimental signaller's standard before joining their squadron.

A trooper equipped for high-altitude low-opening (HALO) parachuting. In military freefall parachuting the Bergen is worn suspended beneath the main parachute.

time the last SAS squadron left Dhofar in September 1976, Oman had at last become part of the twentieth century.

POST OMAN

There was no major campaign for the SAS between their return from Dhofar in 1976 and the Falklands Campaign in 1982. However, the SAS has been involved in Northern Ireland since D Squadron was deployed there in 1969, and men from the four squadrons rotate through Northern Ireland for short periods as part of their tour with the Regiment. Although the internal security operations do not lend themselves to the SAS role, they have been particularily useful in the border area of Crossmaglen. There, in 'bandit country' as it is known, their skills in extended surveillance operations have been put to use, together with their ability to live in concealed hides for two weeks or more, supporting the local infantry battalions.

Contrary to popular opinion, the Regiment's role in Northern Ireland is a purely military one. Like other soldiers in the Province, the SAS trooper has a difficult and often distasteful assignment. The Army is an aid to the civil power, and the SAS is *not* an undercover 'hit squad' that quietly eliminates known terrorists and their sympathizers.

THE FALKLANDS

When the Falklands Islands were invaded by Argentina on 2 April 1982 it shocked the British public and presented the government with a major diplomatic problem. The United Kingdom did not have the equivalent of the US Rapid Deployment Force and was not set up to fight a campaign over 12,800 km (8,000 miles) away across the Atlantic. As the government discussed its options and reviewed its military assets, 22nd SAS Regiment prepared for possible deployment.

A parachute assault of the Falklands was not an option open to the British as the distances involved and the limited airlift capability made this type of operation impossible. This left the government with one main course of action open to it, that of mounting an amphibious operation followed by a landing. While the government entered into political negotiations with Argentina, it started to prepare and organize the troops and ships for an invasion force.

On 5 April D Squadron, which was on standby in Hereford, plus its supporting elements flew to Ascension Island, which was to be the main staging area for operations in the South Atlantic. It was followed, one day later, by G Squadron

The Special Air Service Regiment was among the first British troops to specialize in arctic warfare.

and the Regimental HQ. After much planning and preparation it was decided to recapture the island of South Georgia, which lies 1,280 km (800 miles) to the east of the Falkland Islands. D Squadron, together with a Royal Marines company and SB detachment from the SBS, embarked with the fleet at Ascension.

On 21 April D Squadron Mountain Troop landed by helicopter on the Fortuna Glacier. The weather was appalling. With winds gusting up to 160 km/h (100 mph) and crevasses 30 m (100 ft) deep, it was impossible to survive let alone carry out the reconnaissance of Leith, Stromness and Husvick as planned. After spending the night on the Glacier the Troop was evacuated by helicopter. The weather was so bad that two helicopters crashed on the ice before the Troop, together with the crews of the two downed aircraft, were lifted to safety by a third helicopter.

Furthermore D Squadron Boat Troop's attempted reconnaissance also failed because of the weather, and they were unable to land their Gemini inflatables on the coast. Luckily there were no lives lost in either attempt, and on 25 April a combined Royal Marines and SAS force landed by helicopter and made a direct assault on Grytviken. By the evening, the 75-man force had captured the town with virtually no fighting and South Georgia was back in British hands.

By early May it seemed certain that there would be British landings on East and West Falkland, and between the 1–3 May eight reconnaissance patrols from D Squadron were flown onto the islands. These night-time landings were unopposed and the patrols moved off to establish their various observation posts. These patrols passed back the first real intelligence on the enemy while the Royal Marines SBS carried out detailed beach reconnaissance before the amphibious landings.

On 14 May D Squadron carried out a three-troop attack on the airfield at Pebble Island. The actual assault was conducted by Mountain Troop, led by Captain Hamilton; Boat Troop covered the approaches to the settlement; and the third troop stood by in reserve. Supported by naval bombardment which was supervised by an attached team of artillery observers from 148 Battery, 29 Commando RA, Mountain Troop attacked the airfield and destroyed all 11 aircraft. Despite being under fire from Argentinian positions during both the assault and the withdrawal phases only two men were wounded, and the operation was a complete success.

Five days after the Pebble Island attack, however, D Squadron suffered a tragic loss. A Sea King helicopter, carrying men

Men of the 22nd SAS Regiment practise freefall parachuting, unencumbered by heavy Bergen rucksacks.

to HMS *Intrepid* for a briefing, crashed into the sea from a height of 90 m (300 ft). Nineteen men from D Squadron plus two attached specialists were drowned. Most of the men lost were from Mountain Troop, and the crash was the worst single cause of casualties to the Regiment since the Second World War.

As 3 Commando Brigade's 2,500-strong force began its amphibious landing at San Carlos, 40 men from D Squadron made a 20-hour forced march to Darwin. That night they attacked the 600-man strong Argentine garrison with mortars, machine guns and anti-tank missiles. The enormous amount of firepower directed at the enemy positions led the Argentinians to believe they were being attacked by a larger force, and the SAS were able to withdraw without being counterattacked or receiving any casualties.

Once the beachhead at San Carlos was secure and the 2nd Battalion the Parachute Regiment had captured Goose Green, the SAS squadrons carried out continuous night reconnaissance patrols ahead of the advancing Paras and Royal Marines. D Squadron captured Mount Kent after a night assault and held it until relieved by 42 Commando Royal Marines. This 460-m (1,500-ft) peak was vital as it overlooked the approaches to Port Stanley, the final objective.

By 1 June both Mount Kent and the neighbouring Mount Challenger were in

British hands. D and G Squadrons had four-man patrols on both West and East Falkland, establishing observation posts (OPs) and probing the enemy's defensive positions. Then on 10 June, the inevitable happened. A four-man patrol, led by Captain Hamilton, came into contact with a much larger enemy force in the Port Howard area. Two men managed to escape but Hamilton and his signaller were surrounded. Hamilton, though badly wounded, put down covering fire in an attempt to allow his signaller to escape. In the ensuing fire-fight, Hamilton was killed and the signaller captured.

The final operation in which the SAS were involved was a combined SAS/SBS amphibious assault on Wireless Ridge, just to the north of Port Stanley. On 13/14 June three troops from D and G Squadrons

Camouflage and concealment, the 'business end' of a hide.

Nearly all of the movement by British troops during the Falklands campaign was done on foot.

took part in the 60-man seaborne assault, but the 'rigid raider' craft in which they were travelling came under intense enemy fire and they were forced to withdraw. Luckily only four men were slightly wounded.

One operation that was planned but not carried out involved the use of SAS soldiers disguised as Argentinians who, together with a Spanish-speaking Royal Marines Captain, Rod Bell, were going to attempt to capture the Argentine commander, General Menendez. Bell and the commanding officer of 22nd SAS had for some time been striving to negotiate an early surrender with the Argentinians. At the same time, Bell had spent a lot of time talking to

Argentinian prisoners-of-war and had, in the process of picking up valuable information on the enemy, been brushing-up on his colloquial Spanish as well. In the event there was no need to use this option, and on 14 June Captain Bell flew into Port Stanley and began the negotiations that led to the Argentinian surrender that evening.

The campaign was over, and the SAS had been successful in spite of D Squadron's tragic loss. They had provided strategic and tactical reconnaissance for their Government in Whitehall and the Task Force, and their raids had done much to lower the morale of the Argentinian opposition.

The SAS Regiment's Boat Troops receive training in a number of skills similar to those of the Royal Marines Special Boat Squadron. Here a combat swimmer comes ashore to carry out a beach reconnaissance while his partner covers him from the sea.

SELECTION AND TRAINING

One of the major reasons behind the Special Air Service's successes is its method of selection. The Regiment is made up of volunteers from all corps and regiments in the British Army. Unlike many of the world's special forces, it is impossible to enter the SAS directly, and all volunteers must pass through stringent selection procedures before being put forward for training.

The Regiment looks for a particular type of recruit. Obviously all volunteers must be physically and mentally fit, but the main emphasis is on the 'self'. They need men who are self-confident and believe that they will make it no matter what the odds. They need men with self-discipline and self-determination, men who have the will to keep on going in spite of physical pain. And they need men who will put the challenge above all else, and to many the Special Air Service offers the most challenging career in the army.

Today's selection course is based on the one designed by John Woodhouse on his return from Malaya in 1952. The course, like everything else in the Regiment, is constantly under revision, but the SAS still needs the same kind of soldier. Selection courses are held twice a year, last for approximately four weeks, and are designed to test a man's personal qualities rather than his skills. As the Regiment says 'techniques can be taught; qualities are inborn'.

Selection takes place in the Brecon Beacons and Black Mountains of South Wales. The area is mountainous and rugged; there are few tracks and what roads there are, are out-of-bounds. The only way to get from point-to-point is on foot, using a map and compass. The weather varies; in summer it can get extremely hot, and all the recruit wants to do is get out of the sun and drink water; in winter the weather varies between rain, sleet and snow, and all the recruit wants to do is get under cover and drink something warm. However, those who stop for a rest are not those who will pass. The only way to get through is to keep going from one rendezvous to the next, never knowing which is the last. The course is designed to test physical and mental stamina under controlled conditions – and it does just that.

Map reading in both theory and practice is stressed at the beginning of the course. Visibility in the mountains can drop to

below 10 m (30 ft), so the ability to navigate and walk on a compass bearing are most important. Initially the recruits go off into the mountains in small groups of five or six. As the course continues the groups get smaller until the recruit is on his own. As he struggles along between two rendezvous points with his 25-kg (55-lb) Bergen rucksack he is competing against himself and the clock, testing not only his map-reading and fitness but also his will-power. If he is lucky enough to make it to the fourth week of selection, he is faced with his hardest test to date. Known as 'long drag', the final selection test is a 60-km (38-mile) march, carrying his 25-kg (55-lb) Bergen plus rifle and belt-kit, over the steepest peaks in the Beacons, within 20 hours.

The two Territorial Army Regiments, 21st SAS (Artists), based in London and the south of England, and 23rd SAS, based in the Midlands and north of England/Scotland, do a similar selection course. The TA selection is spread over a six-month period at the end of which they do a final week culminating in 'long drag'.

For those who pass the selection course (often less than 10 per cent of the original number), the next challenge is continuation training. This consists of three phases, lasting a total of 14 weeks, and concentrates more on testing each man's basic soldiering skills.

The first phase is seven weeks long and consists of general training. During this time the recruit comes across SAS standard operating procedures (SOPs) for the first time. He is taught how to operate as part of a four-man patrol, and practises ambushing techniques, raiding and reconnaissance. He also learns the basics of demolition and first aid, trades in which he may specialize later.

The second phase is three weeks long and deals with all aspects of combat survival. Recruits are trained in the art of survival in the wilds and testing includes spending up to five nights out in some isolated part of the country, wearing old serge battledress (with a greatcoat in winter) and being equipped only with a knife and a box of matches. The recruits are also taught how to resist interrogation, and can spend up to 24 hours being interrogated. This assignment is carried out by professionals under strictly controlled conditions and relies on mental rather than physical pressure. Escape and evasion (E & E) is also taught during this phase, a reminder that it is better not to get captured.

The third and final phase is given over to the standard army static-line parachuting course at RAF Brize Norton. This is generally considered to be the easiest part of

continuation training, and after completing the seven qualifying jumps, the recruits are finally 'badged' SAS, and receive their beige beret and 'sabre' wings. Both 21st and 23rd SAS undergo similar continuation training but their courses are shorter and spread over a longer period, usually between 18 to 36 months, depending on their individual civilian commitments.

INDIVIDUAL SKILLS

Once the newly 'badged' SAS trooper has completed his continuation training, he spends the next nine (or so) months as a 'probationary' while learning an individual skill. Usually the first month after parachute training is spent in the Far East or Brunei learning jungle-warfare skills. This is followed by individual training in demolition, signals or medical skills, and each man must qualify in at least one of these skills. This usually takes the man to the end of his probationary period. On starting his three-year tour with the Regiment, the trooper joins one of the troops in a squadron.

The 22nd SAS Regiment consists of four 'Sabre' Squadrons, A, B, D and G, a Headquarters Squadron and various supporting elements. These are all based at Stirling Lines, Hereford, together with R Squadron, which is a reserve unit. There are also the two Territorial Army SAS Regiments, 21st and 23rd, but their organization and primary role differs from the regular Regiment.

The squadrons in 22nd SAS are divided into four troops, each with its own speciality. In Boat Troop the men are trained as combat swimmers, and learn how to handle canoes, inflatable boats and rigid raiders. Air Troop members are trained freefall parachutists. Military freefall parachuting differs from civilian parachuting in a number of respects. Exits from the aircraft are usually made from heights in excess of 6,100 m (20,000 ft) and each man carries his own oxygen supply in addition to his Bergen. There are two types of descent: high-altitude/low-opening (HALO) and high-altitude/high-opening (HAHO). Both methods allow the parachutist to land a considerable distance away from the aircraft's drop-off position. Mountain Troop concentrates on mountain and arctic climbing, including high-altitude movement techniques. Mobility Troop learns how to drive, maintain and repair all types of vehicle.

Each troop, regardless of its speciality, consists of 15 men commanded by a captain. Each troop is divided into four four-man patrols where each man will have his own speciality: demolitions, medical, linguistic or communications. During a trooper's three-year tour with the

SAS he is given further advanced training in his specialist skill. Many men attend the Army School of Languages at Beaconsfield where a variety of languages are taught, and many learn minor surgery in the UK or the United States. Communications skills are constantly being improved as equipment becomes more sophisticated. Troop skills are also improved. For example, a man in Boat Troop will usually go on to a diving course where he will learn how to use both open and closed SCUBA equipment.

In fact, training never ceases in the SAS. Men are cross-trained in each other's skills which will be tested under arctic, mountain, jungle and desert-warfare conditions. Individuals and groups train with foreign special forces such as the US 'Green Berets' and Germany's GSG-9. Counter-revolutionary warfare constitutes an increasing part of the Regiment's role. Special Project Teams, such as the team that released the hostages during the Iranian Embassy siege, are constantly training, and there are always two teams on standby in Hereford to counter any threat of this nature that may suddenly arise.

WEAPONS AND EQUIPMENT

The Special Air Service use the widest variety of small arms in the British Army. This is mainly because of their sphere of operations and their counter-revolutionary warfare role. Like all special forces they do not have much in the way of heavy weapons, and the largest weapon they normally carry is the belt-fed 7.62 mm general-purpose machine gun (GPMG).

The standard British Army personal weapon is the 7.62 mm self-loading rifle (SLR). This rifle is still used by the SAS but the American M-16/AR-15 is more common now. It is a lighter weapon and fires a 5.56 mm round; this calibre is smaller but means that more ammunition can be carried, an important consideration when weight must be kept to a minimum. The M-16, unlike the SLR, can also fire fully automatically, another consideration when immediate heavy firepower is an important factor. The only real drawback to the M-16 is that it is not general issue, and therefore marks out anyone armed with it as being 'special forces'. The M-203 40 mm grenade-launcher is also used. This useful weapon fires a 40 mm grenade and can also be fitted beneath an M-16.

The 9 mm Browning pistol is used extensively. Its 13-round magazine is useful when engaging more than one target and it is accurate and reliable. Like the SLR, the 9 mm Browning is British Army issue. So is

The SAS Regiment is often called on to play the role of 'enemy' during internal security exercises. From these trials, the SAS gains experience in evasion and, on occasion, in interrogation.

the 9 mm Stirling submachine gun (SMG), and this weapon, especially the silenced version, is used by the SAS. The latter is an excellent weapon for quietly disposing of enemy sentries.

Over the past few years Heckler and Koch submachine guns have gained favour with the SAS, and the MP5 A3 was used to great effect during the Iranian Embassy siege. Other small arms of various types are used, especially shotguns. Jungle warfare, in which the ranges can often be under 15 (50 ft), are ideal for shotgun use, and they were used extensively in Malaya and Borneo. Heavy weapons such as 81 mm mortars and .30/.50 Browning machine guns are used by the SAS in fortified bases, such as those in Oman. MILAN wire-guided anti-tank missile launchers have also been used. These are ideal for attacking enemy emplacements on short-range raids, but are too heavy for long-range patrols, where the lighter 66 mm light anti-tank weapon would be used.

Because of the wide variety of missions that the SAS undertakes there are no hard-and-fast rules as to the weapons and equipment used. The SAS role often requires a patrol to be inserted by parachute or helicopter, so there is often a limit to what each individual man can carry. Usually a man will carry most of his equipment in his Bergen rucksack. This will weigh 23–36 kg (50–80 lb) depending on the length of the operation. It is generally considered that carrying anything over 27 kg (60 lb) detracts from a man's ability and performance, so weight is kept as low as necessity will allow. Each man wears 'belt kit' in which he carries ammunition, water, rations and survival equipment. 'Belt kit' is made up to the individual's requirements and consists of a number of canvas pouches.

The largest piece of equipment normally used by the SAS is the 'Pink Panther'. This vehicle is a specially converted long-wheelbase Land-Rover, and is the modern version of the Second World War SAS jeep. It has a crew of three: driver, gunner/navigator and gunner. Usually armed with one GPMG at the front and twin-GPMGs at the rear, this vehicle is a virtual weapons

Known as the 'Pink Panthers' because of their camouflage, these modified Land-Rovers are the descendants of the jeeps used by the SAS during the Second World War.

platform. Mainly used by Mobility Troop, it is an ideal vehicle for desert warfare, although there is a similar version for the European theatre.

The list of types of equipment used by the Special Air Service is virtually endless. Many items are special-to-purpose, for instance, Special Project Teams' equipment. Much of the personal equipment, including weapons and uniforms, depends on personal preference to a large extent as well as the particular theatre and operation.

The Special Air Service is a Regiment of highly skilled professional soldiers, and has within its ranks some of the most dedicated and experienced special forces men in the world. Officers, NCOs and junior ranks form a team and have proved time and again in places such as Malaya, Borneo, Oman, the Falklands, the United Kingdom and Northern Ireland, that they can carry on the successes of their Second World War predecessors.

ROYAL MARINES COMMANDOS

The Royal Marines Commandos is one of the best-trained amphibious fighting forces in the world. The Royal Marines is an independent Corps consisting of three battalion-sized Commandos, 40, 42 and 45 Commandos Royal Marines, which come under the direct command of the Ministry of Defence Navy. The main role of the Corps is to provide military units, primarily trained in amphibious operations. The basic force is the Commando Group which consists of one of the Commandos plus supporting elements. The Commando Group is then capable of operating on either light or heavy scales, depending on its particular operational requirement.

In addition there are a number of smaller detachments such as landing craft, raiding squadrons and Special Boat (SB) sections that are capable of either providing support to the Group, or operating independently in the amphibious role. The Corps also has its own Air Squadron capable of operating from amphibious ships and maritime task forces.

The Corps has three main deployment priorities; first, deployment in support of NATO; second, other national commitments outside NATO; and third, deployment in support of the United Nations. The

Corps' primary role is the security of NATO's Northern Flank in Norway; this is the responsibility of 42 Commando RM and 45 Commando Group, which are part of 3 Commando Brigade RM. The Royal Marines have played an important part in the internal security operations in Northern Ireland since the beginning of the present 'troubles' and have done tours as 'peacekeepers' with the UN Forces in Cyprus.

HISTORY

The Royal Marines Corps has a long and proud history dating back to its formation as the 'Duke of York and Albany's Maritime Regiment of Foot'. The Corps served the Crown loyally throughout the world during the eighteenth and nineteenth centuries and won its first VC at the Battle of Inkerman in 1854. During the First World War, the 4th Battalion Royal Marines took part in the amphibious raid at Zeebrugge on 23 April 1918, and won its eighth and ninth VCs, both of which were awarded by ballot.

During the Second World War, the first Commando units were formed to conduct raids on the German-occupied coasts of Europe. The British Army formed ten Com-

mandos and in 1943 these were reorganized into brigades with Royal Marines Commando units. These newly formed Commandos RM served with distinction for the remainder of the war, and on 6 June 1944 over 18,000 Royal Marines took part in the Normandy Landings. In November 1944 one of the combined brigades, the 4th Special Service Brigade, fought the Battle of Walcheren, subsequently capturing this strategically important island which is just off the Dutch coast. Three Royal Marines Commandos, 41, 47 and 48, took part in this successful amphibious operation but, in doing so, suffered heavy casualties.

After the end of the Second World War, all the Army Commandos were disbanded and their men were returned to their original corps and regiments. Three of the Royal Marines Commandos were retained however, and 40, 42, and 45 Commandos RM went on to form 3 Commando Brigade RM.

Subsequently 3 Commando Brigade RM has been employed in internal security and counter-insurgency operations in Hong Kong, Palestine, Malaya, Kenya, Egypt, Cyprus, Borneo and Northern Ireland. During the Korean War, 41 Commando RM was reformed as an independent unit

Rock climbing and abseiling have long been specialities of the Royal Marines Commandos. Today the Mountain and Arctic Warfare Cadre RM teaches recruits ice climbing, one of the more difficult mountaineering techniques.

Men of Commanchio Company, training on a North Sea oil rig. The Company, based in Arbroath, Scotland, specializes in off-shore protection.

Overleaf: Specialists in the amphibious warfare role, the Royal Marines played a vital part in the Falklands Campaign.

The Royal Marines Commandos saw action in both the Malayan and Borneo campaigns. Many have experience in jungle warfare, which is still taught today in Brunei.

and was on active service from August 1950 until 1952 when it was disbanded. In 1961 41 Commando RM was reformed only to be disbanded again in 1968.

In November 1956 3 Commando Brigade took part in the amphibious landings at Port Said, Egypt, during the Suez Crisis, and 45 Commando RM conducted a heliborne assault. Between 1955 and 1959 both 40 and 45 Commando RM were periodically engaged in the EOKA campaign in Cyprus. Between 1960 and 1967 45 Commando RM were also actively engaged in the Radfan, and were part of the covering force during the British withdrawal from Aden. While on duty in the Middle East, 45 and 42 Commando RM undertook a defensive deployment in Kuwait in order to counter an Iraqi armoured threat.

During 1964 both 42 and 45 Commandos deployed in Africa where they were responsible for putting down mutinies in the Tanganyikan, Kenyan and Ugandan armies. In 1960 3 Commando Brigade HQ together with 42 Commando RM moved from their base in Malta to a new one in Singapore, and in 1961 40 Commando RM deployed into South Jahore in Malaya. In 1966 40 Commando RM joined the Brigade HQ and 42 Commando RM in Singapore at the Fleet Amphibious Forces base.

In December 1962 there was an internal revolt in Brunei. Brunei, Sarawak and northern Borneo were British protectorates to the north of Indonesia. 'L' Company, 42 Commando RM carried out an amphibious attack on the town of Limbang which was held by the rebel forces. The town was recaptured and a number of hostages who had been taken by the rebels were released.

From 1963 until 1966 both 40 and 42 Commandos RM were involved in counter-insurgency operations in Borneo. Operating in the border areas of Sarawak and Sabah, they were involved in numerous engagements against the Communist-backed guerrillas and Indonesian regulars who were attempting to infiltrate the country.

In November 1970 40 Commando RM took part in relief operations in Bangladesh after the area had been devastated by a tidal wave. Aided and abetted by helicopters, ships and other vessels, the Royal Marines Commandos can be a great asset to the civil powers during this type of relief operation.

Since 1969 the Corps' major involvement has been its deployment as part of the British counter-terrorist force in Northern Ireland.

TRAINING

Commando training is generally considered to be one of the most physically exhausting courses in the British armed forces. Recruits spend a total of 30 weeks, excluding leave, undergoing their 'basic' training. Initially all recruits must pass a potential recruits' course where both parties assess whether each is suitable for recruit training. After they have been assessed and selected, the recruits undergo an induction period at the Commando Training Centre Royal Marines at Lympstone, Devon.

At the CTC RM the new recruits carry out a 14-week course, known as Part I, 'Basic' Training. During this phase the recruits learn how to handle their section and troop weapons, and are taught all the individual infantry skills in preparation for the advanced course. Recruits are also taught how to operate successfully with helicopters and small boats, such as

Overleaf: Geminis and other small craft are widely used in and around Hong Kong.

Below: Royal Marines of 3 Commando Brigade RM enter Port Stanley in the Falkland Islands after the Argentinian surrender. These Marines, experienced in mountain and arctic warfare, were an invaluable asset to the British Task Force and played a vital part in its ultimate victory.

Gemini inflatables and rigid raiders.

The Part II Training, or group training as it is known, lasts for a further 12 weeks. During this phase the recruits are trained in the use of the remainder of the infantry 'support' weapons, and receive instruction in basic seamanship and amphibious operations. They are also taught the basics of internal security tactics, including such aspects as riot control and rapid deployment from vehicles. During the Commando course recruits are introduced to rock climbing and the course culminates with a final exercise on Dartmoor during which they will be tested on all they have been taught. At the end of the final exercise the recruits take the Commando 'Pass Out' tests which consist of a 9-mile speed march, an assault course and an endurance course, the 'Tarzan' course and a 30-mile march across Dartmoor.

On successful completion of the Commando 'Pass Out' tests, the recruit becomes a qualified Royal Marines Commando and is awarded his green beret and Royal Marines Commando shoulder flashes. Most Royal Marines then go on to join a Rifle Troop in one of the Commandos, although some go on for further specialist training to become cooks, clerks or drivers. Further specialist training is available for the Royal Marine who wishes to qualify for such trades as assault engineer or heavy weapons specialist, but these courses are only available after the man has spent some time with one of the Commandos.

A number of Army and Royal Navy personnel become Commando-qualified

The Royal Marines, like all other British infantry units, use the 84 mm Carl Gustav anti-tank weapon.

and wear the green beret. These two services provide the Royal Marines with their support elements, such as artillery, engineers and medical. These attached soldiers and sailors do not do the 30-week training course as do the Royal Marines themselves, but they do undergo the Commando 'Pass Out' tests as a culmination of a four-week All-Arms Commando Course, after which they receive their green berets and begin their two- to three-year attachment to the 3rd Commando Brigade.

MOUNTAIN AND ARCTIC WARFARE

The primary role of 3 Commando Brigade RM is the security of NATO's Northern Flank in Norway; 42 Commando and 45 Commando Group RM, 1 Amphibious Combat Group and Whisky Company Royal Netherlands Marine Corps, the Commando Logistics Regiment and supporting arms and services form a ski-borne force trained in mountain and arctic warfare.

For three months every year the Brigade deploys in Norway for a series of winter warfare exercises. Norway is of vital strategic importance to NATO and is located between two of the largest Soviet maritime concentrations, one to the north and the other to the south. In the event of a Warsaw Pact invasion, control of Norwegian territory would be vital for NATO's defence. Norway itself has a peacetime

The 7.62 mm general-purpose machine gun (GPMG) is one of the most versatile weapons of its class and is effective in both the suppressive and sustained-fire roles.

Another weapon that is capable of being mounted on a helicopter is the general-purpose machine gun (GPMG), which can be used to give suppressive fire during a heliborne assault.

force of 55,000, many of whom are conscripts doing their national service. In the event of mobilization, this force could be increased to 300,000, but Norway's defence relies heavily on NATO's reinforcement capability.

At present this consists of four brigades and 16 air squadrons. The brigades include the ACE Mobile Force, a US Marine Amphibious Brigade, the Canadian Air-Sea Transportable (CAST) Brigade Group, and 3 Commando Brigade Royal Marines.

Arctic and mountain warfare is the primary role of 45 Commando Group RM, a role it has been assigned since 1969. In 1977 42 Commando RM was designated as the second mountain and arctic warfare Commando and in the winter of 1978 3 Commando Brigade Headquarters deployed in Norway for the first time. The experience gained by the Brigade in operating in arctic conditions proved to be

of great value during the Falklands Campaign in 1982.

All members of the Brigade must pass the Arctic Warfare Training course before being deployed on exercise in Norway. The three-week AWT course is designed to teach all personnel how to survive and fight in arctic conditions. They are taught how to ski by MLs (mountain leaders) from the Mountain and Arctic Warfare Cadre RM and MSIs (military ski instructors) who are specially qualified Marines from within the rifle companies. Over the three-week course, the men being trained learn how to live in ten- or four-man shelters and snow holes, and spend a total of 11 days in the field, including four continuous nights. At the end of the course, the students must pass a series of practical and written tests before becoming 'ski-qualified'.

Those men in the Brigade who are 'ski-qualified' but have not deployed in

A Royal Navy Sea King disembarks Commandos during arctic-warfare exercises in Norway.

Norway for a year must go on a week's Arctic Survival Training by way of a 're-fresher'. Both the three-week AWT and one-week AST courses are carried out in the first five weeks of the Brigade's three-month deployment in Norway. During weeks six and seven the Commandos test their individual and section battle drills. Patrolling, camouflage and concealment, ambushing and anti-ambush procedures are practised, and in week eight the entire Commando conducts a tactical exercise in preparation for the final exercise which is run at Brigade level and involves the armies of various other nations. During tactical exercises at Commando level, the rifle companies ski-march up to 25 km (16 miles) each day before either lying-up for the night or carrying out assaults on 'enemy' positions.

The final exercise at the end of the Brigade's three-month deployment in Norway varies from year to year, depending on which countries are taking part. Usually the Brigade initially fights a defensive battle before counterattacking, although some elements act as the enemy. The Brigade's amphibious capability usually plays a vital role in the defensive and counter-offensive manoeuvres. Landing craft are the most efficient method of transporting men and material on the Norwegian fjords, and Geminis and rigid raiders can land raiding parties, undetected, at a number of vulnerable points.

The Brigade's mountain and arctic warfare capability, coupled with its specialized amphibious role, makes it one of the most versatile brigade-sized fighting forces in the world. A high peak of physical fitness is constantly maintained and regular exercises in Norway and elsewhere keep the Brigade in a high state of operational readiness.

An 81 mm mortar is brought into action during a tactical exercise in Norway. In arctic conditions these weapons are mounted on large bags packed with snow, without which they would sink with the recoil.

Royal Marines on a ski-march patrol in northern Norway. Under such conditions it is usual for the Commandos to carry loads of up to 45 kg (100 lb).

ORGANIZATION

The 3 Commando Brigade is a totally autonomous force. It is composed of a Brigade Headquarters and Signal Squadron RM, 539 Assault Squadron RM, Tactical Air Control Parties and an Air Defence Troop. Three battalion-sized Commandos, 40 and 42 Commando RM and 45 Commando Group, comprise the major fighting elements. These are supported by the Commando Logistic Regiment which consists of Army elements: RAOC Ordnance stores and supply, REME Workshop, RCT Transport, and a Royal Navy medical element. The 3 Commando Brigade has its own Air Squadron consisting of Lynx and Gazelle helicopters. These provide the Brigade with its aerial observation and reconnaissance asset and the Lynx can be fitted with TOW anti-tank missiles to counter the armoured threat. Artillery support is provided by 29 Commando Regiment Royal Artillery which is equipped with 105 mm light guns, and 289 Battery Royal Horse Artillery (V). The 59 Independent Commando Squadron and 131 Independent Squadron Royal Engineers provide engineering support and are, like the artillery, arctic-trained. They are capable of building complex defensive positions and bridges as well as clearing and laying minefields, a difficult task in the arctic environment.

The movement of men and equipment in Norway is extremely difficult because of the great distances involved and the adverse climatic conditions. The Brigade's amphibious capability is supplemented by the aerial support provided by two Naval Air Squadrons, 845 and 846 Squadrons, equipped with Westland Sea King helicopters. This aviation asset is supported by other Commando Helicopter Operations and Support Cell (CHOSC), a combined Naval and Royal Marines unit that provides ground reconnaisance and establishes the landing zones (LZs).

Both of the arctic-trained Commandos, 42 and 45, consist of three Rifle Companies, a Support Company and a Headquarters Company. The Support Company includes a Mortar Troop, equipped with 81 mm mortars; an Anti-Tank Troop, equipped with MILAN wire-guided missiles; and a Recce Troop, which is divided into six four-man patrols.

In addition to the Commandos and support elements, 3 Commando Brigade Headquarters can also have operational control of Whiskey Company and the 1st Amphibious Combat Group of the Royal Netherlands Marine Corps (RNLMC). Other units, such as the Naval Air Squadrons (NAS) and Special Boat detachments

(SBS), also come under the Brigade's command during its winter deployment in Norway.

MOUNTAIN AND ARCTIC WARFARE CADRE

The Royal Marines are themselves an elite Corps. The 3 Commando Brigade RM is a specialized amphibious force, trained in arctic warfare. The Royal Marines have, however, two integral special forces units, and they are the Mountain and Arctic Warfare (M&AW) Cadre and the Special Boat Squadron.

The main responsibility of the M&AW Cadre is to provide mountain leaders (ML

1s and 2s) for the Commando's arctic-warfare instruction; they also instruct the Recce Troops in mountaineering and climbing techniques. The secondary role of the M&AW Cadre is to provide 'tactical reconnaissance' for 3 Commando Brigade. In 1981 the M&AW Cadre acquired their special forces operational role in addition to their primary role of instruction, and are now capable of carrying out deep-penetration reconnaissance patrols for HQ Commando Forces RM. During the Falkland Islands Campaign, the M&AW Cadre successfully accomplished its various missions and has become established as Britain's newest special forces unit.

The selection and training of recruits wishing to join the M&AW Cadre are among the toughest in the British armed forces. The course itself lasts over eight months and all applicants must be qualified RM commandos who have passed their Junior NCOs course. M&AW training starts with a seven-day selection phase which takes place in Devon and Cornwall. During this period the recruits live in barracks but are taken out every day and are pushed to the limit while being constantly assessed by the instructors. This initial part of the course is so strenuous that it is not uncommon to loose 12 out of 20 applicants. The next two weeks are spent learning the techniques of military mountaineering at Stonehouse Barracks, and then practising these skills in the Welsh mountains. Physical fitness is steadily built up to a high peak and the recruits are worked over 12 hours a day on average.

Marines undergoing the mountain leader (ML 2) course run by the Mountain and Arctic Warfare Cadre. This is one of the toughest courses in the Royal Marines and lasts almost a year.

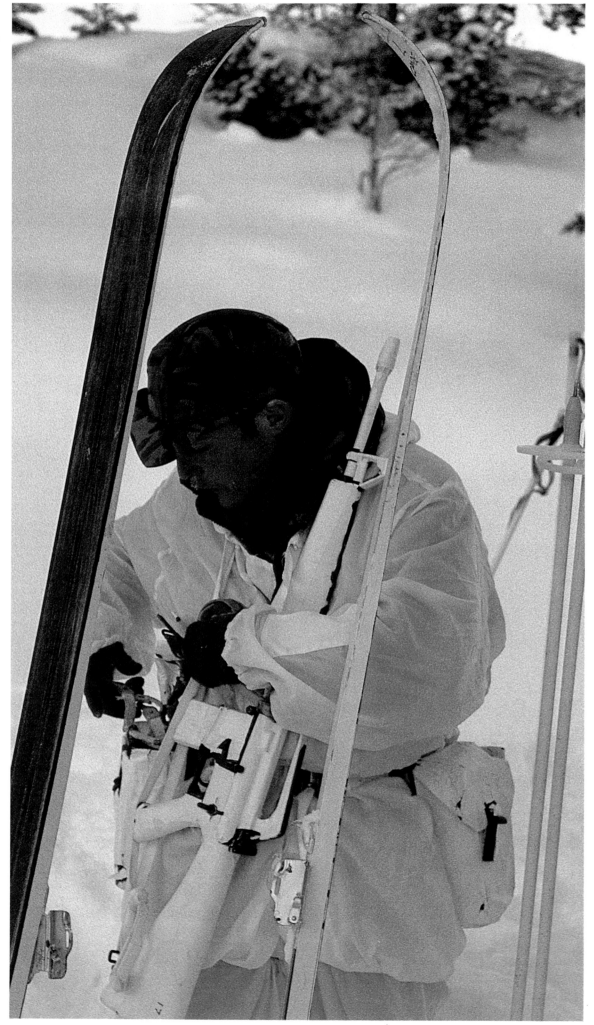

A member of the Mountain and Arctic Warfare Cadre carrying the M-16 rifle. This weapon is favoured by most of Britain's special operations units because of its light weight and its fully automatic capability.

This phase is followed by two to three weeks operational training in the Plymouth area and during this time much emphasis is placed on night operations, including free-climbing. Seaborne assaults and small raiding missions are also practised with the aim of 'fine tuning' the recruits' advanced military skills.

After Plymouth the aspirant mountain leaders move to Rjukan in Norway for their military ski instructor course. These MSI courses are normally about 80-strong and are open to all Royal Marines units. The instructors for the courses are Norwegian and they assess the ML recruits not only on their skiing ability but also on their instructional qualities.

A brief break for Christmas leave back in the United Kingdom follows the MSI course before the ML 2 recruits return to Norway for three months of intense arctic training. On average the recruits spent six days a week living and training out in the field. They learn how to survive in sub-zero temperatures without the aids of modern technology. They learn how to break trails and cross obstacles and practise route selection and navigation. Once they are proficient in all aspects of arctic warfare the ML 2 recruits spend seven days in the field practising for the final tactical exercise.

After a short break the recruits are deployed in the field for the 11-day exercise during which all the skills learned in the UK and Norway are tested. Split up into four-man reconnaissance patrols, the recruits ski-march and climb up to 40 km (25 miles) a day before lying-up for the night. They undertake a wide variety of tasks such as target reconnaissance and attacks. They report intelligence back to their headquarters and receive further orders before finally contacting a Norwegian 'agent' to arrange for exfiltration.

This tactical exercise is the major test of the recruits on the ML 2 course. Although it is still possible to fail, nearly all who reach this phase go on to pass the course. The exercise is followed by a 'relaxing' three days of parachuting for those recruits who are para-qualified, and finally one week of snow and ice climbing in the area around Lom.

After spending the winter in Norway, the ML 2 recruits return to the UK and spend about three weeks in the Ben Nevis area receiving instruction in pathfinding techniques. This is followed by the four-week parachute-training course at Brize Norton for any ML 2 recruit who is not para-qualified, and a further one week of instruction and practice in the use of 'steerable' parachutes. As in the Army's SAS selection course, this phase is considered to be the easiest part of the course.

The final three months of the ML 2 course are spent in England and Switzerland. The ML 2 recruits go on a special one-month snipers course at the Commando Training Centre at Lympstone. Here they are taught camouflage and concealment and learn to

Sniping is another important skill which must be mastered by those wishing to join the Mountain and Arctic Warfare Cadre. They are not only expert marksmen but also highly skilled in the art of camouflage and concealment.

A Lynx helicopter of 3 Commando Brigade Air Squadron lands in the Arctic. Flying in these conditions requires great skill from the pilots, nearly all of whom are Royal Marines officers or senior NCOs from the Brigade's rifle companies, serving a three-year tour with the Air Squadron.

cover ground unseen. The standards are high and an excessive degree of patience is required, as the recruits wait motionless for hours at a time or stalk a target inch by inch. The final test on the snipers course is to move within range of the target without being seen and 'kill' it with a single shot, from between 500–600 m (1,640–2,000 ft).

After qualifying on the snipers course, the ML 2 recruits move to the Lake District in England for 'instructor' training and practice in the 'Alpine Technique' for Exercise Ice Flip which takes place in Switzerland. Ice Flip is the final phase of the ML 2 course and lasts for one month. The first two-week period is spent under the supervision of the course instructors and for the second two weeks the recruit is teamed up with a qualified ML 1 or 2. During this final month of their training all the recruits' technical knowledge and practical skills

are assessed, and if they pass the final assessment, they pass the course.

In true military fashion the final judgement is reserved until the recruits have returned to the UK. After nearly a year of training and months away from their homes and families, the recruits will find out whether they have passed one of the most difficult courses in the British armed forces.

The pass rate for the ML 2 course is about 20 per cent which is a good indication of how tough the training is, especially when one considers the high standard possessed by those who merely apply. Once qualified, the ML 2s are assigned to a company within a Commando where they will be responsible for all the arctic-warfare training, as well as being able to form part of a four-man patrol to carry out their special forces role.

Two members of the Royal Marines Special Boat Squadron in a Klepper canoe. These small craft have a low silhouette and provide an excellent method of infiltration.

SPECIAL BOAT SQUADRON

The Royal Marines Special Boat Squadron is the other Royal Marines special forces organization and, like the Army's SAS, it traces its lineage back to the Second World War. The SB Sections of the SBS are, in some ways, similar to the Boat Troops of the SAS Squadrons and, although their amphibious and underwater training is more thorough, the SB Sections also have a strategic role.

The origins of the SBS lie within the Royal Marines Boom Patrol Detachment, the Combined Operations Beach and Boat Section and the Small Raids Wing. Working independently or attached to one of the Commandos, the SB Sections have been involved in the Korean War, where they carried out a number of missions including reconnaissance of the Chinese coastal defences, and in the counter-insurgency operations in Malaya and Borneo, where they carried out observation and reconnaissance patrols — in the case of Borneo often using small boats and canoes. In Aden SB Detachments conducted deep-penetration patrols, often accompanied by 45 Commandos' Recce Troop.

In recent years the SB Sections have operated in Northern Ireland both on the border in support of one of the Commandos or independently along the coastline. They also played an important part in the Falklands Campaign, where they operated in conjunction with the two SAS squadrons and provided reconnaissance patrols and OPs, and, in addition, carried

out the beach reconnaissance for the Task Force landings. Together with the SAS they may well have been involved in intelligence-gathering operations on the Argentinian mainland and, although this is speculative, it was feasible and it would have made sense to monitor aircraft movement at the military airfields.

The term 'swimmer-canoeist' is used to describe the qualified SBS Marine and is one of the Royal Marines' specialist qualifications. Applicants for the SBS must first undergo a three-day selection test which is similar to that undergone by aspirant mountain leaders. Individual qualities and skills are assessed and if the man passes the initial selection test he goes onto a further 12-month training course.

Physical fitness is stressed in SBS training and trainees must be able to swim long distances above and below the water; this requires a great deal of stamina. They are taught to use both open and closed SCUBA equipment and learn both land and underwater demolition techniques.

The operation of small craft is also learned and much time is spent becoming proficient in the use of canoes and inflatable boats. Navigation is important, especially at sea, but also on land for target assaults or demolition missions ashore.

By the end of the 12-month course, the trainees will have also learned how to parachute with both standard and steerable parachutes. They will have attended all the basic special forces courses includ-

Parachuting is another SBS skill. Here a swimmer-canoeist prepares for a 'water-jump' in the Arctic from the ramp of a C-130 Hercules.

ing combat survival, escape and evasion and resistance to interrogation. Communications play an important part in the SBS strategic reconnaissance role and all men are taught to use specialized radio equipment. Photography is another SBS asset and vital for detailed beach reconnaissance before an amphibious landing.

Only 30 per cent of the volunteers for the Special Boat Squadron pass the gruelling training course. Like the Mountain Leader 2 course of the M&AW Cadre, the SBS course places much emphasis on self-reliance, determination, stamina and intelligence.

Once qualified, the swimmer canoeist takes his place in one of the SB Sections. Training in the special forces never ceases and the SBS is no exception. Like the majority of Royal Marines Commandos, much of their role involves the defence of NATO's Northern Flank in Norway. There are a number of combined exercises with the special forces of other nations, especially the US Navy's UDT/SEAL teams and the Royal Netherlands Marine Corps SBS. Both of these countries have a commitment in Norway.

The Special Boat Squadron specializes in reconnaissance operations. Its members must be adept swimmers, canoeists, divers and parachutists. They must be experienced in navigation, demolition techniques and masters in the art of reconnaissance. They are constantly perfecting these techniques and are among the elite of the world's special forces.

ASSAULT AND RAIDING SQUADRONS

Assault squadrons and raiding squadrons are two important assets for amphibious operations. With 3 Commando Brigade's commitment to the defence of NATO's Northern Flank, the need for an independent assault squadron has been realized with the formation of 539 Assault Squadron Royal Marines. It became apparent during exercises in northern Norway over recent years that the landing platform docks (LPDs) such as HMS *Fearless* would not be able to provide the support needed for the landing craft squadrons. These squadrons had to undertake specialized operations, including breaking into pack ice and lying-up in camouflaged positions against the sides of fjords. In temperatures dropping to −70°C (−94°F) including the windchill factor, small landing craft would have to be able to operate alone without the security of their own LPD.

Numerous trials were being carried out

when the Falklands Campaign began, and although the landing craft were carried down to the Falklands in their parent ships, once there, they acted independently under the command of the Land Forces Commander. A Task Force Landing Craft Squadron was formed and took part in every sea-launched operation undertaken by 5th Brigade and 3 Commando Brigade, including the amphibious operations conducted by the SAS and SBS.

The Task Force Landing Craft Squadron was commanded by Major Ewen Southby-Tailyour who had, a year previously, been elected Britain's 'Yachtsman of the Year' for his work in charting the coastline of the Falkland Islands. This information was to prove of immense value to the Task Force and obviously played a part in the success of the overall campaign. The Squadron was eventually awarded 11 decorations for gallant and distinguished service but sadly six men were killed.

On the Task Force's return to the United Kingdom the case for an independent squadron was put forward and was accepted. The principles that had evolved from the trials in the Arctic had proved successful in operations in the South Atlantic, and in April 1984 539 Assault Squadron was formed. The Squadron's first commander was Major Southby-Tailyour, who had been awarded the OBE for his service during the Falklands Campaign, and 539 ASRM became the Corps newest unit.

During the 1970s the Raiding Squadrons began to develop new techniques for arctic operations. With temperatures dropping to −70°C (−94°F) including the

Left: One of 539 Assault Squadron's LCUs in a fjord in northern Norway. These specially modified vessels are invaluable for transporting small parties of troops and vehicles.

Below: A Rigid Raider drops its passengers onto the ramp of an LCU.

windchill factor, rigid raider coxswains were prone to suffer frostbite, hypothermia or worse. An Arctic Warfare Section of raiding craft was set up and in 1975 they covered over 250 km (160 miles) in ten hours during a tactical exercise. This impressive feat was partly due to improved designs in clothing and the high level of training among the coxswains. Today 539 ASRM has its own integral Raiding Troop of around 20 rigid raiders. Their coxswains are equipped with special immersion suits, fleece-lined 'woolly bear' underwear and face masks.

The 539 Assault Squadron is equipped with two different types of landing craft. It has two specially equipped LCUs, the 'Black Pig' and the 'Brown Sow', which are capable of carrying vehicles and equipment up to a weight of 100 tons. Both LCUs have been fitted with specially constructed

'igloos', which extend over half the cargo space and are heated to warm up their passengers. The LCUs are actually capable of ferrying a complete Commando company through the fjords in one trip.

All the men in the Squadron are fully qualified Commandos who have undergone basic seamanship training at Poole in Dorset. In addition to this training, all coxswains have undergone landing-craft courses and are qualified LC 1, 2 or 3, depending on the size of craft they operate.

As well as the LCUs and rigid raiders, the Squadron also operates four LCVP Mark 4s. These landing craft are smaller than the LCUs but specially designed for arctic use, and are capable of carrying light vehicles and troops up to a maximum cargo weight of about four tons. All the landing craft and raiding craft in the

The Volvo BV202 oversnow vehicle. Known as the 'Band Wagon', this Swedish-manufactured carrier is capable of carrying eight fully equipped troops in the rear section and towing another eight on skis behind.

Squadron are maintained by an attached Royal Navy engineering section who are capable of operating under the most adverse weather conditions.

EQUIPMENT

The 3 Commando Brigade RM has, because of its amphibious and self-supporting role in arctic conditions, one of the widest ranges of different types of equipment of any similarly sized brigade in the world.

Over the past two decades there have been great improvements in the design of cold-weather clothing and these have benefited the Royal Marines Commandos operating in northern Norway. Because of this, the men of 3 Commando Brigade were the best-equipped troops during the Falklands Campaign. All the troops are equipped with windproof smocks and trousers as well as camouflaged oversuits, in addition to their standard combat clothing. Thermal underwear and specially padded liners are also issued together with an improved ski-march boot. A variety of load-carrying equipment is in use, including SAS Bergens and large-frame arctic rucksacks.

Other special-purpose arctic equipment such as tents, snowshoes, skis and sledges are also issued. The Brigade possesses about 150 BV 202E Volvo over-snow vehi-cles. Known as 'Band Wagons', these articulated tracked vehicles are an invaluable method of transporting troops over difficult terrain. They are capable of carrying eight men in the rear section with their complete issue of arctic and combat equipment. The four tracks are driven by a powerful 2,000 cc (122 cu in) engine in the front section which holds another two men including the driver, and the BV is capable of travelling at 15 km/h (9 mph) over uncleared snow with a range of 200 km (125 miles).

Aircraft provide another essential mode of transport over the vast distances that have to be covered. The 3 Commando Brigade has its own Air Squadron equipped with Lynx and Gazelle helicopters. The Lynx is a multi-purpose, twin-engined helicopter capable of carrying a fully equipped eight-man section and has a top speed of 150 knots. It can also be fitted with TOW anti-tank missiles and is one of the Brigade's anti-armour assets. The Gazelle is a small fast lightweight helicopter used chiefly for observation and reconnaissance. It has a single turbine engine and is capable of speeds up to 165 knots.

The Brigade is also supported by 845 and 846 Naval Air Squadrons. These Squadrons are equipped with Sea King helicopters flown by Royal Navy pilots. The Sea King Mk 4s are twin-engined logistic

One of the Commando Brigade's primary anti-armour assets, the TOW-mounted Lynx. Each helicopter is capable of carrying eight TOW missiles, each of which can knock out a modern battle tank.

117

support helicopters and can carry 28 fully equipped troops at a maximum speed of 125 knots. Great skill is needed by the RM and RN pilots flying in the Arctic. Conditions can change from clear skies at −30°C (−22°F) to driving snowstorms at +5°C (40°F) in a matter of hours, and nil-visibility 'white-outs' are common.

The Royal Marines Commandos are equipped with standard-issue infantry and support weapons. These include the 7.62 mm self-loading rifle and general-purpose machine gun, and the 9 mm Sterling submachine gun and Browning Hi-Power pistol. Other personal weapons issued include the 5.56 mm M-16 Armalite rifle which is sometimes fitted with the 40 mm M-203 grenade launcher. This is used by both the M&AW Cadre and the

Timing is critical in all airborne operations. It is important for the paratroopers to land in as small an area as possible so that no time will be wasted in regrouping.

SBS and is an ideal weapon for long-range reconnaissance and deep-penetration missions. The SBS also use the Heckler and Koch MP5 submachine gun and the Ingram MAC-11. Both weapons are 9 mm in calibre and can be fitted with silencers; the MP5 is more accurate but the MAC-11 is much smaller and easier to conceal.

Among the less exotic but more practical weapons are the 81 mm mortar and the MILAN anti-tank weapon. The 81 mm provides close support up to a range of 2,740 m (3,000 yd) and the MILAN fires a wire-guided missile with an effective range of over 1,830 m (2,000 yd). Other anti-tank weapons include the 66 mm LAW and the 84 mm Carl Gustav.

Artillery support is provided by Royal Artillery units under the command of 3 Commando Brigade, and this is the same regarding engineer support which is provided by Army sappers. The 539 Assault Squadron is the Brigade's tactical amphibious asset and its Raiding Troop's rigid raiding craft can each carry five fully equipped men to landing points behind enemy lines.

The Royal Marines are the Royal Navy's own infantry and Britain's commando troops. They are a small, powerful and highly trained force, able to operate in a variety of different terrains. With their amphibious capability, they are a spearhead force, second to none.

AIRBORNE FORCES

The abbreviation 'Paras', used to describe Britain's Parachute Regiment, has long stood for acts of courage and daring. The Parachute Regiment originated during the Second World War but Britain was not the first country to use airborne forces. Some time before, both the Italians and the Soviets had carried out successful trials involving the military application of the parachute. The Germans, who had seen the far-reaching effects of airborne delivery of troops had, by the beginning of the Second World War, built up a large formation of airborne troops. These were used during the invasion of Norway, and later, with devastating effect, during the invasion of the Low Countries.

The British soon realized the potential of parachute forces and began to carry out trials soon after the beginning of the war. In 1940 men of No 2 Commando, who had been carrying out specialized commando training, formed the basis for the

Left: Before landing, the paratrooper must release his Bergen rucksack from its position beneath his reserve parachute. The Bergen then dangles beneath him, suspended by a length of strap, allowing it to be recovered on landing.

Below: A patrol of paratroopers moves through ruined buildings in the village of Oosterbeek during the airborne invasion of the Netherlands, September 1944.

119

A group of British paratroops before their embarkation for the 1st Allied Airborne Army's invasion of the Netherlands, 17 September 1944.

new airborne force. Renamed Troop 11th Special Air Service Battalion, the unit carried out its first successful operation in February 1941. A small-scale target attack in Italy was carried out by men of 11th SAS Battalion; they successfully destroyed an aqueduct.

In September 1941 the 1st Parachute Brigade was formed with three Battalions (1st, 2nd, 3rd), which were later joined by a 4th Battalion. The 1st Air-Landing Brigade Group and the newly formed Glider Pilot Regiment were added in 1941. In February 1942 an airborne sabotage raid was conducted against a German radar site near Bruneval, France. The operation was a success and involved elements of the 2nd Parachute Battalion.

After the German invasion of Crete in mid-1941 a complete airborne division was formed under the command of Major-General 'Boy' Browning. In 1942 the Airborne Forces Depot was formed, and the 1st Parachute Brigade was ready for action with a 2nd Brigade being raised.

In 1942 the 1st Parachute Brigade fought a number of actions in the Tunisian Campaign and, in 1943, took part in the invasion of Sicily together with the 1st Air-Landing Brigade. By this time the 3rd and

4th Parachute Brigades had been raised and together they took part in the landings in Italy. After much hard fighting, the Division returned to the United Kingdom with the exception of the 2nd Brigade which stayed on and was renamed the 2nd Independent Parachute Brigade. The Brigade continued to fight in Italy before taking part in the invasion of southern France; by the end of the war it had fought into Greece where they carried out an airborne assault.

Meanwhile two complete Airborne Divisions, the 1st and 6th, were preparing for the Allied invasion of Europe. The 6th Airborne Division spearheaded the invasion into Normandy while the 1st Division was held in reserve and not deployed.

Arnhem is probably the best known name in airborne history. Operation Market Garden was an attempt involving three airborne divisions to capture and hold the town of Arnhem and thus secure bridges across the Rhine, Maas and Waal rivers. This would have enabled the British 2nd Army to outflank the German defences on the Siegfried Line. Initially the plan went well and the US 101st Airborne Division dropped between Veghel and Eindhoven capturing two of the bridges over which the 2nd Army was to cross. As the 2nd Army moved up to the bridges at Nijmegen and Grave, captured by the US 82nd Airborne Division, things at Arnhem were going badly wrong.

Arnhem was the northernmost bridge at the end of the 'corridor' secured by the 101st and 82nd Airborne Divisions and leading elements of 30 Corps. It was the job of the British 1st Airborne Division to capture the Arnhem bridge and hold it until the 2nd Army relieved them. From the start things began to go wrong. Because of the lack of available aircraft, the Division could not all be dropped at one time and the drop had to be some distance from the town. There was a large concentration of German troops in the area, including the IX and X SS Panzer Divisions which were quick to counterattack and stop the Allied advance at Nijmegen. Although one British battalion and some elements of divisional troops managed to reach the bridge at Arnhem, it was quickly cut-off from the remainder of the Division which was forced back into a defensive position near Oosterbeek to the west. The 2nd Army and the 82nd Airborne Division eventually broke the German hold on the Nijmegen bridge but their advance towards Arnhem was considerably slowed by intense German resistance. Meanwhile, the Polish Independent Parachute Brigade had been dropped to the south of the British bridgehead at Arnhem but had suffered casualties, and one battalion lost due to aircraft failing to arrive, so that only a few men were able to link up with the British on the north side of the river near Oosterbek.

Four gliders near a farm in the Arnhem area. The use of such gliders was an important feature of the operation and they were used to bring in both men and supplies.

By the time the 2nd Army arrived at Oriel, the 1st Airborne Division and elements of the Dorset Regiment had held out for over a week against a far larger German force. Operations to evacuate the survivors from Arnhem began, but by the time the fighting was over, more than 1,200 airborne and air-landed troops had been killed and nearly 3,000 taken prisoner. This figure is high because of the wounded and those looking after them having to be left behind. In spite of this, Operation Market Garden was not a total failure. Bridges across the Maas and Waal had been secured and the Allies had a base from which to launch their attack on Germany.

The final and largest single airborne operation of the Second World War was undertaken in the closing stages of the war in March 1945, by the British 6th and US 17th Airborne Divisions. Operation Varsity involved a single-lift daylight drop across the Rhine. The 6th Airborne Division achieved its objective and secured the high ground overlooking the town of Wesel and then went on to capture its secondary objectives, the road and rail bridges crossing the Issel 13 km (8 miles) to the north-east of Wesel. After this assault the British Division advanced across Germany and were among the first troops to link up with the Soviets.

After the end of the Second World War, Britain's Airborne forces underwent a number of organizational changes. The 1st Airborne Division was disbanded in November 1945, and this was followed by the disbanding of the 6th Airborne Division on its return from Palestine in 1948. Only one Airborne Brigade Group was retained, and in commemoration of the 1st and 6th Airborne Divisions it was entitled 'the 16th Independent Parachute Brigade'. This new Brigade was composed of the 1st, 2nd and 3rd Battalions which were formed by a complicated process of amalgamations and reorganizations.

Between 1951 and 1954 the Brigade was deployed in Egypt where it spent much of its time guarding the Suez Canal. In 1955 a Parachute Regiment Squadron joined 22nd Special Air Service Regiment in Malaya. This newly formed Squadron, composed of volunteers from the Brigade, was led by Major Dudley Coventry and proved most successful against the Communist terrorists.

In 1956 the Brigade was deployed in Cyprus where it was involved in the counter-insurgency campaign against the EOKA terrorists. While serving in Cyprus the Brigade took part in the Anglo-French airborne assault on the Suez Canal. On 5 November 1956 the 3rd Battalion the Parachute Regiment jumped into combat and secured Port Said's El Gamil airfield, before the seaborne invasion.

Between 1958 and 1964 elements of the Brigade were deployed in Jordon and Kuwait, in both cases at the behest of each country's ruler. In 1964 the 3rd Battalion, under the command of Lieutenant Colonel Tony Farrar-Hockley, took part in a series of operations in the Radfan Mountains. It was involved in a number of successful actions against the guerrillas, who were supported by both the Yemen and Egypt, and armed with a mixture of old Lee-Enfields and modern Soviet-manufactured weapons. The Radfanis operated from mountain strongholds often as high as 1,800–2,100 m (6,000–7,000 ft) above sea level and where the temperatures during the day soared as high as 55°C (130°F).

Unable to parachute onto the rocky mountain tops, 3 PARA had to mount foot-slogging assaults up the sheer slopes leading up from the valley floors. After a number of successes the combined force of Paratroopers and Royal Marines Commandos, supported by the RAF and Royal Horse Artillery, managed to gain control of the major summits dominating the area. After the capture of Jebel Huriyah, the rebels sued for peace, but the British maintained a positive presence until their withdrawal from Aden in 1967.

This withdrawal was supported by the 1st Battalion the Parachute Regiment under the command of Lieutenant Colonel Mike Walsh. Throughout the withdrawal 1 PARA came under increasing attack from the various factions wishing to take power once the British had departed. For months the Battalion attempted to keep the peace and to prevent the various warring organizations from causing widespread disruption and was, to a great extent, successful. Constantly under pressure, not only from the internal political groups but also from elements of the press, 1 PARA succeeded in maintaining a defensive perimeter around Khormaksar airfield until their departure from Aden in late November 1967.

Almost inevitably, once the colonial 'plug' had been pulled out and the Adenis were left to their own devices, another power took over. There is now a Soviet air force base at Khormaksar and a Soviet refuelling and refitting depot at Steamer Point. Little is left to show of the hard-fought campaign in the Radfan Mountains in 1964 or the well-conducted withdrawal in 1967 — except, perhaps, the roads built by the Royal Engineers in the Rabwa and Taym wadis of the Radfan. The roads, together with the eight new schools and the anti-malarial programmes started by the British Army, may be of some lasting benefit to the people of the Radfan.

During the Borneo confrontation, the Parachute Regiment was again deployed in counter-insurgency operations. Following an internal revolt in Brunei in December 1962, British and Commonwealth troops found themselves guarding over 1,120 km (700 miles) of border between the British protectorate and Indonesia. Fighting escalated over the next two years and the 2nd Battalion the Parachute Regiment was deployed in the jungle of Borneo in early 1965. C Company underwent special training with 22nd SAS Regiment and operated in small reconnaissance patrols.

The Paras soon picked up the techniques of jungle warfare and shortly after their arrival in Borneo one company fought off an Indonesian battalion attack on its position. Unlike many of Britain's enemies since the end of the Second World War, the Indonesians were well-trained and well-equipped regular troops. The end of the confrontation came after an internal coup in Indonesia which followed Singapore's rejection of the Malaysian Federation agreement. In October 1965 the President of Indonesia, Sukarno, was ousted by General Suharto and a peace agreement was signed in August 1966.

Between the end of the Borneo campaign and the beginning of the Parachute Regiment's internal security duties in Northern Ireland, the Regiment came under increasing pressure from government defence cutbacks. Shortsightedness on the part of the socialist administration forced increasing financial limitations on the armed forces, particularly units such as the Parachute Regiment and the Royal Marines. The 16th Parachute Brigade was effectively broken up with only the Brigade HQ and the Logistics Regiment left to support two of the three battalions in their airborne role. One of the battalions was released for garrison duty overseas and the Brigade's supporting units, such as artillery engineers, signals, armour and logistics gradually had their capabilities for airborne operations removed.

In 1974 the 16th Parachute Brigade was disbanded. With it went all its supporting elements and Britain's ability to mount airborne operations. This happened at a time when armies overseas were increasing their airborne formations. The Soviet Union had long since recognized the potential of airborne shock warfare and was increasing its airborne forces to eight complete divisions, including strong armoured

Paratroopers are kept busy during the long voyage south on their way to the Falkland Islands. Their physical training instructors (PTIs) led the men in daily runs around the ship so that they remained in top physical condition for the landings.

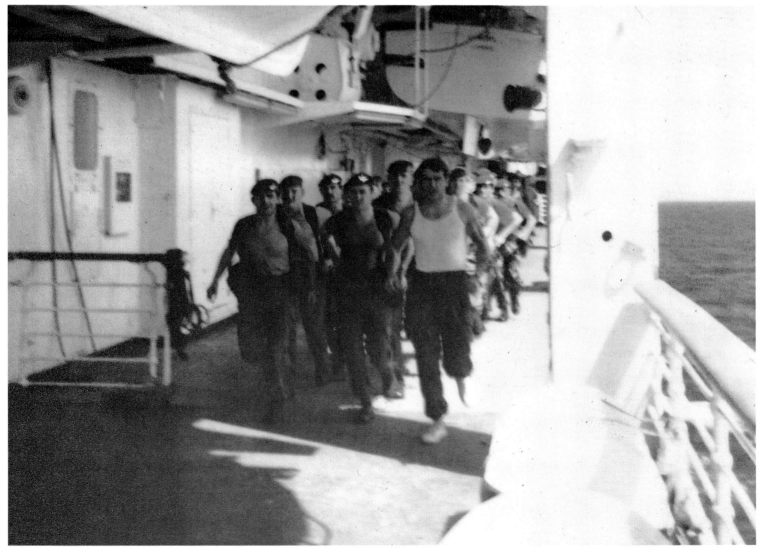

and artillery supporting elements. The United States also put faith in airborne operations and had two Divisions, the 82nd and 101st, capable of air-assault and air-landing, plus the aircraft to support them. France was moving toward the creation of her *Force D'Action Rapide* and West Germany had three *Luftlandebrigade* ready for rapid deployment.

Britain was left with one Parachute Regiment battalion in the airborne role, through which the three battalions rotated on a regular cycle between standard infantry postings. From the end of the 1960s to the present day the battalions have served two 20-month and a number of shorter tours in Northern Ireland. These tours have often been highlighted by tragic events such as 'Bloody Sunday' on 30 January 1972, or the ambush at Warrenpoint on 27 August 1979, in which 16 Paras were killed. The Parachute Regiment carries out its various duties in a thorough and professional manner and, by doing so, is bound to come under the glare of publicity, some of it adverse. The situation in Ulster is one of the most complex in which the British Army has found itself involved. Propaganda from the various factions, especially the Provisional IRA, can do some damage but has little real or lasting effect. A regiment that has fought bravely and with honour throughout its existence has little to fear from an organization that openly admits perpetrating brutal acts of terrorism. Indeed the reverse is true, and the terrorist factions on both sides are constantly aware of their vulnerability against a highly trained, disciplined force.

In January 1982 the 5th Infantry Brigade was formed under the command of Brigadier M J A Wilson and included two Parachute Regiment battalions, which were placed back in the airborne role, as the Brigade's spearhead element. They were supported by an airborne engineer squadron and an airborne gunner battery. The Brigade included the 1st Battalion, 7th Duke of Edinburgh's Own Gurkha Rifles.

Within two months of the 5th Infantry Brigade's formation, the Argentines invaded the Falkland Islands. One week later 3 PARA was on its way south with 3 Commando Brigade RM and was followed, towards the end of April, by 2 PARA, together with the airborne sappers and gunners. The Paras spent their time on board ship preparing for the forthcoming action. Weapons were zeroed and the men got some practice shooting targets dropped into the sea behind the ships and there was fitness and first aid training. Equipment was checked and rechecked, and helicopter drills were practised almost daily. By the time the Paras arrived in the Falklands they were prepared.

The main landings took place at San Carlos before first light on the morning of 21 May. Both 2 PARA and 40 Commando RM were landed by LCMs of the Task Force Landing Squadron. The landings were unopposed and shortly after dawn 3 PARA and 45 Commando RM came ashore at Ajax Bay. After consolidating the beachheads, 3 PARA moved off towards Teal Inlet while 2 PARA set off for Camilla Creek House whence they would mount an attack on Goose Green and Darwin. The Argentinian garrison at Goose Green/Darwin had previously been attacked by D Squadron 22nd SAS. This attack took place when the Argentinian garrison was around 600 men strong but shortly after the SAS attack reinforcements had been flown in by helicopter from Mount Kent. The total Argentinian strength was about 1,400 men by the time 2 PARA attacked.

The assault that followed was the most hard-fought battle of the campaign. It began at 0300 hours on 28 May and by midday had been virtually halted. The Argentinians were in very good defensive positions, well dug-in and supported by a number of light guns, mortars and heavy-calibre AA guns firing at close range in the ground role. The Paras, on the other hand, were in open ground supported by two 81 mm mortars and three 105 mm light guns.

The Battalion's commander, Lieutenant Colonel 'H' Jones, led a flanking attack on the enemy positions and, in doing so, was fatally wounded by machine-gun fire from the enemy's right flank. Undoubtedly inspired by his leadership and self-sacrifice, the Paras succeeded in taking the defensive position shortly afterwards.

Major Chris Keeble, the Battalion's Second-in-Command, then took over and, by nightfall on 28 May, the Paras had succeeded in taking Darwin and Boca House and were in position surrounding the main Argentinian entrenchments at Goose Green. During the evening Major Keeble negotiated the enemy's surrender with the help of Captain Rod Bell RM, a Spanish-speaking Commando officer. This undoubtedly saved much further bloodshed on both sides, but the surrender came as something of a surprise when, the following morning, the comparative sizes of the opposing sides became evident.

Meanwhile, the 3rd Battalion the Parachute Regiment, under the command of Lieutenant Colonel Hew Pike, had reached Teal Inlet, having walked all the way from San Carlos. From Teal 3 PARA then made its way to Estancia House, just to the north of Mount Kent, which overlooked the Task Force's final objective, the large Argentinian troop concentration in and around Stanley. Most of the troop movements in the Falklands Campaign were carried out on foot. Very few medium- and heavy-lift helicopters were available and the men had to carry their heavy loads long distances, often over very difficult ground and in appalling weather.

As 3 PARA consolidated its position and prepared to advance against the enemy holding the high ground to the west of Stanley, 2 Para was shuttled into Fitzroy by helicopter. Fitzroy had been vacated by Argentinian forces on 2 May and 2 PARA moved in the day after.

The next major action took place on the night of 11/12 June as the British moved in to secure the high ground to the west of Stanley. In this instance 3 PARA was under orders to capture Mount Longdon. As the Battalion moved forward, one of the sections from B Company walked into a minefield and soon came under heavy fire from the Argentinian defenders. The Paras fought back with grenades and light anti-tank weapons against the fortified enemy positions. In this way the Battalion moved

forward and one platoon leader, Sergeant Ian McKay, cleared three enemy machine-gun positions using grenades before being killed. By first light the entire Battalion was committed and, during the final series of assaults, bayonets were used in close-quarter combat. Enemy resistance crumbled resulting in 3 PARA capturing Mount Longdon.

The final assault was made on Wireless Ridge by 2 PARA on the night of 13/14 June. Wireless Ridge, a feature just to the north of Stanley, came under heavy artillery fire and naval gunfire support barrage during 2 PARA's assault. However, a simultaneous seaborne operation conducted by the SAS and SBS drew a lot of the enemy's fire. The attack was a success and the enemy withdrew to Stanley in disorder, closely followed by men of 2 PARA who reached the outskirts of the town before halting. The Argentinians had been defeated and the following evening, 14 June, General Menendez, the Argentinian commander,

A Para observation post to the west of Port Stanley. During the Falklands Campaign much of the fighting revolved around the taking of high ground, which was often fiercely defended by Argentinian troops.

signed the declaration of surrender thus ending a violent confrontation.

The victory had not been an easy one. Unfortunately 2 PARA had lost 15 killed and 30 wounded in their attack on Goose Green but this should be weighed against the enemy's losses in this action: 50 killed and 140 wounded. In the attack on Mount Longdon 3 PARA lost a total of 14 men dead and 35 men wounded, and the subsequent enemy shelling of the captured position cost them a further 11 killed and 12 wounded. In spite of these losses, which could easily have been far greater, the Paras had achieved their objectives. The two VCs won during the campaign had both been awarded postumously to Paras, the first to Lieutenant Colonel 'H' Jones of 2 PARA, and the second to Sergeant Ian McKay of B Company 3 PARA. Both the Battalions had proved themselves yet again, and the future of Britain's airborne forces was once more assured.

5TH AIRBORNE BRIGADE

In October 1983 the 5th Airborne Brigade was formed under the command of Brigadier Tony Jeapes, a former squadron commander and commanding officer of 22nd Special Air Service Regiment. The

During peacetime the Royal Air Force is responsible for laying out the drop zone (DZ). In wartime this role is carried out by 5th Airborne Brigade's Pathfinder Platoon.

Brigade's formation was a direct result of the lessons learned in the Falklands Campaign and the need for Britain to have its own force of paratroops, complete with airborne-trained supporting elements.

At present the 5th Airborne Brigade consists of two airborne battalions, and 2nd and 3rd Battalions, the Parachute Regiment, and one air-landing battalion, the 2nd King Edward VII's Own Gurkha Rifles. These battalions are controlled by the Brigade Headquarters which has its own Signal Squadron. The Life Guards provide the Brigade's armoured support with Fox armoured cars and Scorpion light tanks, and the 7th Field Regiment Royal Horse Artillery provide the artillery support with their 105 mm light guns. Both the armour and artillery can be delivered by air.

The Brigade's airborne-trained engineer asset is the 9th Para Field Squadron Royal Engineers. The 5th Airborne Brigade is also supported by a further three ground-based engineer squadrons, 20 and 50 Field Squadrons RE, and 61 Field Support Squadron RE. These are capable of carrying out a number of complex engineering tasks, including airfield repair.

Logistical support includes 63 Squadron Royal Corps of Transport and 23 Field Ambulance Royal Army Medical Corps; about two-thirds of their personnel are para-trained. The 10 Field Workshops

REME and 82 Ordnance Company Royal Army Ordnance Corps provide the Brigade with repair and supply facilities.

The Brigade has its own Scout and Gazelle helicopters of 658 Squadron Army Air Corps, capable of carrying out a variety of tasks including reconnaissance and casualty evacuation. Two Royal Air Force Squadrons, Nos 47 and 70, based at RAF Lyneham, are equipped with Hercules C-130 aircraft and provide the Brigade with its aviation asset. The RAF also provides the Brigade with one of its two Tactical Air Control Parties; the second one is provided by the Army. They are known as 613 and 614 TACP and one of their responsibilities in peacetime is to guide the aircraft onto the drop-zones (DZs).

The 5th Airborne Brigade also has its own 'Pathfinder' Platoon to reconnoitre, markout and secure the DZs. After the main force has arrived the Pathfinders go on to provide medium-range reconnaissance and surveillance. This unit is specially trained in HALO (high-altitude, low-opening) parachuting and the use of sophisticated radio equipment.

The Brigade is capable of carrying out a number of different missions, with many of its elements able to operate independently or as a 'package' in a special-to-purpose force, in much the same way as the larger US Rapid Deployment Force or France's

Advances in air-delivery now mean that much of the paratrooper's heavy support weaponry and equipment can be landed with him onto the battlefield.

Force D'Action Rapide. Constant and realistic training keeps the Brigade in a high state of readiness, capable of immediate deployment.

TRAINING

The high standard of training received by the British armed forces is well known throughout the world. This is especially true of Britain's airborne and commando forces. Selection and basic training of Parachute Regiment recruits takes place at the Regiment's home at Aldershot, Hampshire.

The Parachute Regiment conducts its own basic training, which is similar to that carried out by other British infantry regiments, but at regimental rather than divisional level. Since 1953 the Regiment has recruited civilians directly rather than from other regiments and corps as was previously the case. The initial seven-week phase concentrates on fitness and basic military skills, such as weapons drill and elementary fieldcraft. The physical aspect is constantly stressed and recruits must pass a number of tests, such as endurance runs, assault courses and confidence courses, before going on to the first field training exercise where they practise their newly found skills. This exercise takes place in the rugged mountainous area around Senneybridge in Wales and the recruits are constantly under pressure, both physical and mental, while being assessed on individual qualities such as team spirit and determination.

Those who pass this phase go on to the second stage of their training back at the depot in Aldershot. For the next three weeks they are instructed in the use of more sophisticated infantry weapons such as the general-purpose machine gun and the Carl Gustav anti-tank weapon. The pressure is still not relaxed at this stage and the recruits are constantly assessed on their personal skills, such as weapons' handling and marksmanship. At the end of this phase the instructors review the individual recruit's progress to decide whether he is suitable for further training. If found wanting in certain qualities, the recruit may be transferred to a line infantry regiment or, if it is the man's physical ability or military skills that are letting him down, he may find himself 'back-squaded' to a group lower down the training cycle. This is the only second chance the man is given by the Regiment.

For those who pass the assessment, further physical and 'confidence' training are in store. Now in the peak of physical condition, the recruit must undergo a variety of tests designed to assess his determination and self-confidence. These tests

A member of 5th Airborne Brigade's Pathfinder Platoon lies-up under cover, after a HALO parachute insertion.

involve crossing a series of obstacles between 9–15 m (30–50 ft) above the ground. The recruit must crawl along parallel bars, swing from one structure to another and jump between platforms, all the time overcoming a perfectly natural fear of falling. Few people actually enjoy this part of the course but refusals are uncommon at this stage. For any recruit who did refuse, it would mean the end of his selection training.

Controlled aggression has always been a part of the paratroopers' training and the old 'milling' tradition lives on. All recruits must take part in a 'boxing match' during which the man's courage and self-discipline are assessed. At the end of this stage of training, the recruit must be capable of running and marching 16 km (10 miles) in under two hours while carrying his rifle and full fighting order, running with a weighted stretcher over 11 km (7 miles) as part of an eight-man section, and completing three circuits of the assault course within a certain time. Only after passing these tests is the recruit permitted to wear the 'red beret' of the Parachute Regiment.

The next phase of the man's training is a four-week advanced field training exercise in the Senneybridge Training Area. During these four weeks, the recruit is tested as part of a section within a platoon rather than as an individual. Recruits are assessed on all their infantry skills, such as camouflage, concealment and movement, and basic tactics and on more advanced techniques such as patrolling and raiding. At the end of this phase, the training platoons carry out a live firing exercise in which they assault an 'enemy' position on one of the open ranges. This is the final phase before parachute training.

After Wales the recruits go to RAF Brize Norton in Oxfordshire where they undergo the British armed forces standard four-week parachute course. Here, together

Right: Like all infantry soldiers, paratroopers are trained in close-quarter combat. During an exercise this paratrooper can be seen checking a 'body' while being covered by his partner.

Left: A camouflaged paratrooper carrying a general-purpose machine gun (GPMG) goes to ground during an exercise on Salisbury Plain Training Area.

Overleaf: A Westland Scout helicopter of 5th Airborne Brigade takes off during an airborne exercise. These helicopters are used extensively for reconnaissance and the evacuation of casualties.

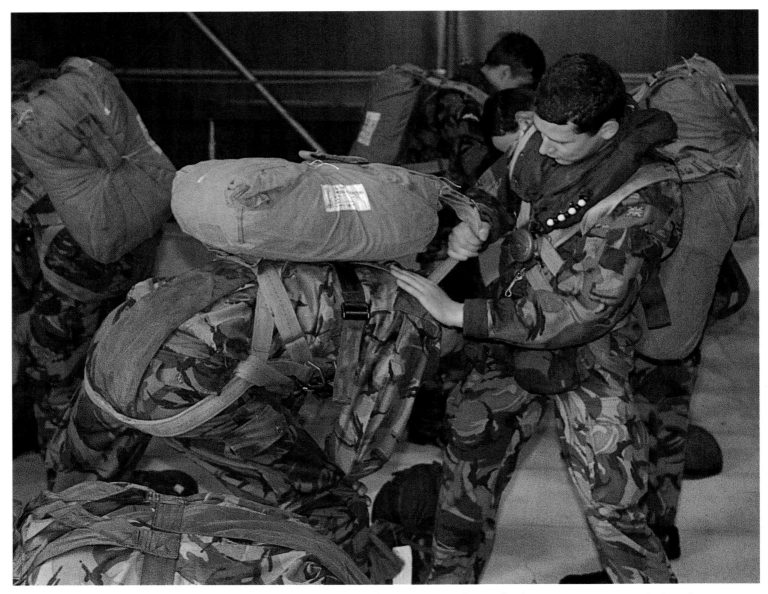

All parachutes are checked before embarking onto the aircraft to ensure a good fit. Parachuting with an ill-fitted parachute can be most uncomfortable, if not dangerous.

with men from the SAS, Royal Marines and airborne supporting arms, they receive instruction from RAF parachute jumping instructors. The men are trained how to make a parachute landing fall, how to correct the parachute's drift while in the air, and how to exit from the aircraft correctly. This 'ground training' is carried out in huge hangars and is the only part of parachute training that goes on regardless of the weather. Practice jumps are made from a 'wind machine' or fan exit trainer which controls the man's rate of descent to around 15.2 km/h (9.5 mph). For the next stage of the training programme, the men have to go outside to the 'tower' where they make longer drops and practise how to correct faults such as tangled rigging lines and oscillation.

The next facet of training is the 'balloon jump'. This is a method of training peculiar to the British and which may seem old-fashioned, but it is retained because it provides realistic training in a semi-con-

trolled environment – and also if a recruit is going to refuse to jump he is more likely to do it in a balloon than in an aircraft. It is also an excellent training aid for practising descents and very cost-effective.

Once the balloon jump has been successfully completed, the man goes to make a further six static-line descents from C-130 Hercules aircraft. Three of these are made with full equipment, contained in a Bergen, strapped up and suspended beneath the reserve parachute, and one of the jumps takes place in darkness. After he has completed this course, the man is presented with his parachute wings, which are then worn on his right arm just below the shoulder. This presentation takes place at the passing-out parade at Browning Barracks, Aldershot, which is attended by the recruits' parents, family and friends.

The newly qualified paratrooper then takes his place in one of the three Parachute Regiment battalions. Most men join

All equipment is checked and rechecked before emplaning. Every precaution is taken to prevent unneccessary accidents.

135

one of the rifle companies, and if the man has shown promise during training he may go into the battalion's 'patrol' company, where he would receive extra training in patrolling and reconnaissance operations. Each battalion also has a Reconnaissance Platoon, commanded by an experienced lieutenant or, sometimes, a captain. The men in this platoon are all experienced soldiers and when on operations, they provide the battalion with tactical intelligence. These men go on to receive further training in communications and some become part of the Brigade 'Pathfinder' Platoon.

While some men go into the rifle companies, others learn new skills in the battalion's support company. Here, they receive further in-house training in the role of their particular platoon. For example, in the Mortar Platoon they would learn how to operate the 81 mm mortar, while in the Anti-Tank Platoon they would learn how to use the MILAN anti-tank missile launcher. Others go on to become signallers or work

Each battalion has a number of qualified army parachute jumping instructors (APJIs) who are responsible for training within the battalions.

Above: Paratroopers board an RAF C-130 Hercules. The 'Herc', as it is known, is the primary transport aircraft of Britain's armed forces.

Members of a PARA battalion's Reconnaissance Platoon checking their weapons immediately after landing, while in all-round defensive positions. This is standard procedure before moving off the drop zone (DZ).

Paratroopers prepare to fire the MILAN anti-tank missile. This sophisticated weapon has greatly improved the airborne soldiers' ability to engage enemy armour effectively.

The MILAN missile immediately after firing. The empty launcher tube is ejected to the rear of the weapon allowing a fresh missile tube to be loaded.

Opposite: A soldier from the 1st Battalion the Parachute Regiment during winter warfare exercises in northern Norway. The Battalion is currently part of NATO's ACE Mobile Force and is trained in arctic warfare.

in the Battalion intelligence cell. But first and foremost, all men are paratroopers and capable of becoming part of a rifle section.

Training in the British Army never ceases and it is generally considered it takes a full three years to train a first-class paratrooper. This is also the minimum period of service for which a man can sign-up, but many extend their period of service and go on to become non-commissioned officers or, in some cases, officers. The Parachute Regiment has high standards and a higher proportion than is normal for an infantry regiment go on to become officers.

The particular nature of the airborne role means that members of the Parachute Regiment must also learn how to operate in a variety of terrains and under different climatic conditions, from the hot, humid jungles of Belize to the cold, frozen wastes of Norway. In 1984 the 1st Battalion the Parachute Regiment (which is not, at present, part of the 5th Airborne Brigade) became the British infantry battalion in the ACE Mobile Force. AMF, as it is known, is part of NATO's commitment to the security of the Northern Flank. As part of this multi-national force, 1 PARA has undergone intensive arctic warfare training in Norway.

Initially this training was carried out with the help of outside units but now the Paras have their own trained military ski instructors. The Battalion has now learned how to survive and fight in the arctic environment and is a valuable contribution to the ACE Mobile Force.

EQUIPMENT

Apart from the specialized arctic warfare equipment used by 1 PARA in Norway, the Para battalions are equipped with standard-issue weapons and equipment. Their prime mover once on the ground is, as with most airborne forces, the 'foot'. Unlike some airborne formations, such as the US 82nd Airborne Division, the Paras do not have a wide range of vehicles but rely on the ½-tonne short-wheelbase Land-Rover, ¾-tonne Land-Rover or other readily available transport. Both the ½-tonne and the stripped-down 'recce' version of the long-wheelbase Land-Rover are capable of being air-dropped on platforms, as are most items of support weaponry and

equipment, such as the 105 mm light gun of the RHA.

The standard parachutes used by Britain's airborne forces are the PX 1 Mark 4, which replaced the old X-type parachute, and the PR7, which replaced the old X-Type Reserve Mark 2. Pathfinders and special forces have tactical assault parachutes, specially designed for freefall use. By using these ram-air parachutes, Pathfinders are able to jump from over 6,100 m (20,000 ft) and by employing the high-altitude high-opening (HAHO) technique they are able to 'glide' to their DZ up to a distance of 48 km (30 miles) away.

There are a few differences between the combat uniform and equipment of the paratrooper and that of the standard infantryman. A paratroop jump smock is worn, which is based on the design of the old Second World War 'Dennison' smock. This is now in the standard British disruptive-pattern camouflage material. A new lightweight ballistic helmet was introduced in the late 1970s and early 1980s to replace the older version which, like the

Left: The commander of a battalion's reconnaissance platoon collects his men before moving off the drop zone.

Overleaf: On landing, the paratrooper's first priority is to release himself from his parachute harness and collect his equipment.

Below: A warrant officer of the Small Arms School Corps (SASC) demonstrates the new 5.56 mm Enfield weapon system which is currently replacing the ageing 7.62 mm self-loading rifle. Britain's airborne forces have been among the first to receive this new weapon.

Right: British airborne forces depend heavily on the intelligence provided by their companies' reconnaissance platoons.

Above: Due to the necessity of working unsocial hours, meals have to be taken when the opportunity arises. Here two NCOs attached to 10 PARA (v) prepare breakfast after a 20-km (12.5-mile) night march while on exercise in West Germany.

smock, dated back to the Second World War. The Bergen rucksack is the only other main difference and is carried by airborne troops and special forces instead of the infantry's 1958-pattern large pack.

British airborne forces are equipped with standard infantry weapons. The 7.62 mm self-loading rifle is being replaced with the more advanced 5.56 mm individual weapon made by Enfield. This is, at present, being introduced together with the section support version which will replace the 7.62 mm general-purpose machine gun in all but the sustained-fire role. Other support weapons include the 81 mm mortar, the 66 mm LAW, the Carl Gustav and the MILAN anti-tank missile launcher, all of which are proven weapons.

Since the Falklands Campaign there has been increased interest in Britain's airborne forces and a realization of their usefulness and capabilities in time of conflict. The formation of 5th Airborne Brigade has done much to redress the balance after the loss of the 16th Airborne Brigade and the general reduction in Britain's airborne capability.

Apart from the three regular Para battalions, Britain also has three Territorial Army battalions; 4 PARA (v) based in the Midlands; 10 PARA (v) based in London and the South-East; and 15 PARA (v) based in Scotland. These highly trained airborne battalions are, like their regular counterparts, more than capable of carrying on the tradition of Britain's airborne forces.

Left: The Carl Gustav is still employed as the section's medium anti-tank weapon. In addition to the Carl Gustav, each man in the section would also carry up to two 66 mm light anti-tank weapons (LAWs) on operations.

Below: A signaller cleans his 9 mm Sterling submachine gun during a short break. The Sterling SMG is standard issue to signallers and is an excellent close-quarter weapon.

UNION OF SOVIET SOCIALIST REPUBLICS

HISTORY

The Soviet Union was one of the first countries in the world to recognize the potential of airborne shock warfare and, indeed, the Red Army made history when, during an exercise held as long ago as 2 August 1930, a platoon executed a successful parachute attack against a corps headquarters. The next decade saw a steady expansion in this field, so much so that, at the outbreak of 'the Great Patriotic War' (the Second World War), the Soviet Union was able to field 12 first-line airborne brigades. During the war airborne forces fought a number of actions, including, in 1942, the dropping, behind enemy lines, of a corps of 10,000 men which operated independently for six months.

In the postwar period the Soviets made vigorous efforts to improve the potential of shock troops of all kinds. It was realized that any future war would roll westwards rather than eastwards and that not only would it be necessary to train elite fighting troops to operate behind enemy lines but also methods of getting them there would have to be improved. Although scant regard was paid to them by Stalin after the war, the important role played by irregular 'partisans' in the disruption of Nazi lines of communication was recognized, and methods of operating and supplying fifth-column partisans in the West were evolved.

SPESNAZ

The Soviet special forces of today, known as Spesnaz, have evolved as a direct result of the lessons learned during and immediately after the Great Patriotic War. Subordinated to Soviet Military Intelligence (GRU) and not, as is often erroneously stated, to the Committee for State Security (KGB), Spesnaz is an integral and structured part of the Red Army. Because of the delicacy of much of Spesnaz training and the total government control of the domestic press, its existence is shrouded in secrecy and it is unlikely that the majority of Soviet citizens even know of its existence.

Structure Great precautions are taken within the Soviet Union to disguise the strength, organization and deployment of Spesnaz troops. All potential recruits undergo particularly stringent examination to ensure political reliability and are left under no illusion that any breach of security, however accidental, will be regarded as espionage and thus carry the death penalty.

The 'Independent Company', one of which is attached to each Army, consists of a headquarters and three parachute platoons plus logistics-communications support. Although the exact size will vary according to manning availability and the nature of any specialist task allotted to it, company strength is always in the region of nine officers, 11 warrant officers and 95 men. Although capable of operating as a single unit, each company will normally divide into smaller groups, to a maximum of 15. The structure of each sub-unit is not rigid and may even change during the course of an exercise. Communications with each group can be maintained over a distance of 1,000 km (625 miles), although radioactivity and the effect of disruptive radio emissions after a nuclear explosion would inevitably reduce this potential distance considerably.

A Spesnaz regiment would be under the command of each theatre leader. Consisting of six or seven companies, a regiment would comprise between 700 and 800 men. Three regiments, one of which is believed to be based in the west European theatre, would be available at the outbreak of war.

The Special Operations Brigade (*Brigada Osobovo Naznacheniya*) (of which 16 exist) is the basic Spesnaz unit. Allotted one per 'Group of Forces' or 'Military

Above: A student at the Ryazan High School of Expeditional Forces parachutes from an AN-2 during a winter warfare exercise. For nearly 70 years the Ryazan School has been teaching tactics, parachuting and unarmed combat and driving.

Left: The Soviet Army has long been experienced in deep-penetration missions. Apart from airborne insertion, other methods of infiltration, such as the use of over-snow vehicles, have been developed.

District', each brigade comprises a headquarters element, a headquarters company, three or four parachute battalions and supporting units. One of the four battalions, although part of the peacetime organization, would be detached in time of war, presumably either to supplement a unit in an area of greater activity or to undertake secret, specialist duties. Each brigade has between 1,000 and 1,300 fighting soldiers and is trained to operate either as a single unit or in a number of sub-units, to a maximum of 135. The entire brigade would, in theory, come under the command of the Army of Front Commands in time of war.

The headquarters company consists entirely of regular soldiers, is highly trained in specialist assassination and subversion roles, liaises directly with Spesnaz field agents and, therefore, is likely to come under direct GRU operational control. Whether or not this leads to friction within the Front headquarters is not known but it is likely that the high-ranking KGB elements found at this level would use all their influence to ensure that tasks allotted to headquarters companies did not conflict with their own intentions.

Role In war, Spesnaz has several diverse roles. Of prime importance is the destruction of enemy command and control. This may take the form of the hunting down and assassination of political and military leaders (possibly in conjunction with KGB operatives), the destruction of centres of command and control and the cutting of telephone and power cables. Airfields, naval bases and air-defence installations would also be prime targets, particularly in support of an early airborne or heliborne landing, requiring localized, short-term air superiority. The disruption of the enemy power stations, oil and gas storage centres, pipelines and power lines would also be considered important. Prime targets would, however, be nuclear facilities, which would either be attacked directly or pin-pointed for subsequent aircraft or missile attack.

Although partisan operations are considered to be important, Spesnaz units, as such, are not meant to engage in guerrilla warfare, which is regarded as too wasteful in manpower and resources for such highly trained specialists.

Spesnaz troops are subordinated to a key element of the GRU central apparatus, known as the 2nd Chief Directorate of the General Staff, elements of which are found at all army levels and higher. The 2nd Directorate has responsibility for reconnaissance, intelligence gathering, information processing and radio interception, as well as Spesnaz operations. It appears that each responsibility is handled by an independent department, and that Spesnaz troops will not, therefore, assume intelligence or reconnaissance roles unless specifically meant to do so.

Operating Procedures Spesnaz soldiers must rely on speed and mobility and, in consequence, do not carry heavy weapons. Training is given, however, in the use of enemy equipments of all kinds, including tanks and armoured personnel carriers (APCs), and these would be seized and used wherever practicable. With the possible exception of experts undertaking specialist assassination duties, an operational soldier will be equipped with an AK-74 assault rifle, a silenced 9 mm PM pistol, a knife, up to six grenades (or possibly a disposable RPG-18 grenade launcher) and emergency food and medical supplies. Each group, however small, will carry, in addition, an R350M radio with encryption and burst transmission potential, an SA-7 (or possibly an SA-14) anti-aircraft missile, explosives and directional mines.

Although Spesnaz units have extreme freedom of action, operations tend to take place simultaneously in conjunction with more conventional Soviet units. Assistance may be given to long-range reconnaissance companies of a divisional 'recce' battalion, operating up to 100 km (62.5 miles) ahead of its own lines. Front air-assault brigades, landed by parachute or helicopter, may be guided to their landing zones by Spesnaz patrols, while Airborne Divisions, once landed and established in the enemy's rear areas, might well be used as Spesnaz forward bases. Independent companies or their sub-units may operate as much as 200 km (125 miles) behind enemy lines, while larger elements, derived from Front brigades, may deploy as deeply as 500 km (300 miles).

More than 50 km (33 miles) behind enemy lines, troops are deployed by aircraft rather than helicopters, which are considered vulnerable. Although conventional aircraft, such as the AN-12 *Cub*, AN-22 *Cock* and IL-76 *Candid* will be used, their crews will have been specially selected and trained in the art of low-altitude flight and navigation. It is likely that they will have undertaken several exercises with their Spesnaz passengers beforehand.

Unless an operation is so large that surprise is impossible, a dropping zone (DZ) will be chosen 15 to 20 km (9 to 13 miles) from the ultimate target. Parachutes are buried immediately and a rendezvous chosen some distance away in case of compromise. If enemy transport can be captured, the unit will move immediately to its objective. Should this not be possible, a secure base, guarded by mines and trip

flares and observed from a distance by a small stay-behind patrol, will be set up, and superfluous heavy equipment left. Once a unit has carried out its command task it will recover its heavy supplies from the secure base, abandon equipment no longer required and either undertake its secondary task or attempt to return to its own base.

Although the enemy will obviously be alerted after an attack, the Soviets will be mounting a large number of raids simultaneously and will feel that their operatives have a realistic chance of escaping in the ensuing confusion. Spesnaz units will have rehearsed their escape routes and will try to keep to these as far as possible but, if they can do so without compromising their position, will attempt to wreak as much havoc as possible upon enemy communications during their withdrawal.

Security Spesnaz forces, which include women, are rarely photographed and their selection and training are shrouded in secrecy. Although connected neither with airborne forces nor with air assault troops they share a common uniform, making accurate recognition from a distance very difficult. Airborne units were, however, awarded Guards Division status for conspicuous gallantry shown in the Great Patriotic War and now wear Guards badges on their distinctive blue-epauletted uniforms. Thus any soldier wearing airborne uniform without the Guards badge will be either air assault or Spesnaz. As Spesnaz troops always parachute and air assault troops never do, the proximity of a parachute (or helicopter) unit will be an aid to identification. Spesnaz who are stationed in Warsaw Pact countries adopt the uniforms and insignia of the nearest

The Soviet armed forces place much emphasis on the capability of conducting operations in a nuclear, biological and chemical (NBC) environment.

communications troops, making their identification almost impossible.

Units are normally co-located with airborne or air assault troops but if this is not possible they adopt the 'walking-out' uniform of the predominant unit. Co-location is not allowed to lead to fraternization and Spesnaz units shun all contact with their neighbours who live and work in the same enclosed compound. In order to accentuate security these troops are referred to by various titles which depend on the area in which they serve. Thus special forces serving in the German Soviet Forces Group (GSFG) are known as '*Reydoviki*' (Raiders), and those in the Siberian Military District as '*Okhotriki*' (Huntsmen). Only senior officers when speaking in absolute privacy refer to themselves collectively as Spesnaz, and ordinary soldiers from the various districts, meeting by chance, would not even realize that they were part of the same organization.

Officers are trained at the Reconnaissance Faculty of Kiev Higher Command Arms School and the Special Faculty of the Ryazan Higher Airborne School, where they integrate as far as possible with conventional officer cadets.

In time of peace, anonymity is further enhanced by the removal of the independent Spesnaz companies from Army Command. Instead, they are grouped to form the 4th Battalion of the Spesnaz Brigade under direct Army or Military District control. The professional Headquarters Companies are themselves removed from Brigade command and from Military District Athletics Teams belonging to the Central Army Sporting Club.

Membership The vast majority of Spesnaz soldiers are conscripts for whom the recruiting process begins many years before the start of their formal military service. Recruits must have an impeccable political background. Most will have parents in the Communist Party, and most will have attended — and excelled at — the Voluntary Society of Co-operation with the Army, Air Force and Navy ('DOSAFF'), which they will have joined at the age of 14. They will be strong, hardy and nimble-minded.

Before conscription all recruits are categorized and the best reserved for the KGB Kremlin Guard, for KGB government communications, for frontier troops or for Spesnaz. Spesnaz, therefore, has a choice of the elite, even in preference to airborne

Left: Paratroopers demonstrate freefall parachuting during the 1982 Air Force Day celebrations at Tushino.

Below: Special operations personnel are briefed at an airfield in the Baltic Frontier District, before a surveillance mission.

forces and strategic rocket troops. Basic training differs from that given to the conventional Red Army conscript. It starts with a short but highly physical and intensive course during which born leaders are picked out and sent to training battalions to become sergeants. Although only the best young men are sent on these courses, standards are so high that many are returned to their units. Most of those who get through the sergeants' course return to their companies to serve as private soldiers, thus ensuring that any existing sergeant who fails to maintain the very high standards set for him can be replaced immediately by a fully qualified reserve. The large numbers of reserves also ensure that, even with the heavy losses expected in war, standards of command would be maintained. The reserve of officers and warrant officers is also high, and whereas a conventional motor-rifle company is staffed by five officers and one warrant officer, its Spesnaz equivalent has nine officers and 11 warrant officers.

All Brigade headquarter's companies and the three independent regiments are manned exclusively by professional soldiers whose existence is shrouded in even greater secrecy. The link between these troops, many of whom are female, and major sports is denied officially but occasionally leaked inadvertently by the press, eager for details of current Soviet sporting successes. Due to an unusual recent lapse of security a photograph appeared in the Soviet press depicting four famous female all-round athletes, proudly wearing the uniform of the airborne officer, including the Guards insignia badge. As there are no females serving in airborne units the connection between those girls and Spesnaz was obvious.

Spesnaz agents belong to the Central Army Sports Club (ZSKA), where they mix and train with other military athletes from all arms of the service. Unlike their conscript equivalents, these regular soldiers are trusted to liaise directly with foreign agents, from whom they must inevitably glean a great deal of information about potential targets during their frequent 'sporting' visits abroad. Interestingly, the KGB also uses this method of sending its

A three-man patrol during a border-surveillance operation in 1985. Frontier troops receive additional training in the Soviet Army.

agents abroad but, in its case, grants them membership of the Dynamo Sporting Club. Rivalry between ZSKA and Dynamo is renowned and frequently reported in the sporting press.

Traditionally, highly successful Soviet athletes are rewarded with cars and better living accommodation and food, an excellent way of repaying a particular Spesnaz soldier for exceptional services without attracting undue attention.

Agents The description of 'agent' within the Soviet Union is restricted to a foreigner recruited by the intelligence services, and specifically excludes Soviet citizens executing spying missions abroad. Agents suit-

able for assisting with behind-the-lines Spesnaz operations are initially recruited from visitors to the Soviet Union who, it is hoped, will return home and recruit others. Ideally, an agent will be mature, involved in restricted or classified work and be able to move around freely. On no account will Spesnaz members themselves attempt a peacetime infiltration of restricted areas but instead will rely on the 2nd Directorate of the GRU to supply its agents with enough funds to move to areas in the proximity of key targets such as bridges, power stations and nuclear sites. Thereafter, they are required to report information, either via dead-letter boxes or direct

Colonel-General D Sukhorukov, Commander Airborne Troops, presents paratroopers with wristwatches after Exercise West-81.

Officer cadets train at the Higher Border-Guards Command School at Alma Ata. Over the last 50 years many Soviet special forces officers have undergone courses here.

to visiting Soviet 'athletes'. Much of this information will be piecemeal and large parts of it irrelevant but, nevertheless, painstaking analysis of thousands of facts will, when the day comes, enable Spesnaz units to execute accurate and speedy attacks on enemy key points with only a minimum of prior reconnaissance.

Spesnaz operates a small, highly specialist team of internally trained secret agents for assassination work. Little is known of these men, even within Spesnaz, although it must be assumed that they travel extensively if only to gain intimate knowledge of their potential victims. Unlike the regular army sportsmen they do not use the 2nd Directorate's pool of agents to supply them with field information but instead, and unusually for Spesnaz, liaise closely with the KGB.

Other agents, recruited to carry out acts of sabotage against supply lines and rear installations in time of war, are also supplied by Spesnaz. Small Spesnaz units (*Vysotniki*), trained in HALO parachuting and SCUBA diving, would be landed behind enemy lines, either immediately after the start of hostilities, or, if possible, before, to take charge of these agents.

Training To enhance secrecy, the combat units, foreign agents and the professional athletes of Spesnaz are kept apart in peacetime.

Secret agents train individually in small, specialist centres. Although little is known of these most are thought to be on Soviet soil. One is known to be in Odessa. The training of agents concentrates on security, communications and collaboration with professional groups. Where relevant, the theory and practice of using demolition explosives and light firearms are taught.

Although professional athletes are all members of the ZSKA, training itself takes place in small groups in various parts of the Soviet Union to enable Spesnaz operatives to merge more easily with genuine athletes. All sportsmen are trained to their highest potential, in several cases to Olympic standard, and will study at least one other language to colloquial level. They will become intimately aware of the terrain where they are likely to operate and, whenever possible, will compete in sporting events in that area. As well as normal military skills, communications and demolition are taught.

The training of combat units, although based on that of conventional airborne forces, is far more stringent. It is considered so harsh that officers and warrant officers receive not only 50 per cent more pay and an allowance for every parachute jump, but also 18 months' accountable service for every year actually served. Pay for all regular soldiers is appreciably higher than civilian rates for the same sort of trade, and pensions are far more generous. Increments to both pay and pensions make Spesnaz service very desirable.

Spesnaz soldiers spend over half of each year on field exercises, simulating combat conditions. Units usually live off the land and sleeping bags, always considered a luxury in the Soviet Army, are

154

A soldier undergoes anti-tank warfare training in the Trans-Baikal Military District.

rarely provided, however inclement the weather.

In the course of training, attacks are often made against genuine vulnerable targets deep in the Siberian wastes. These targets, such as power stations, are guarded by armed KGB or Internal Security (MVD) troops, who receive no prior warning of an impending assault. Parachute drops are often made hundreds of miles away from the objective, leaving the infiltrators vast distances of inhospitable and heavily patrolled territory to cover in limited time.

A competition involving the best Spesnaz units throughout the Soviet Union is held each year in the principal training centre near Kirovograd. Lasting three months, it covers all aspects of potential warfare. Interestingly, this area also contains the Zheltyye Vody uranium mines, which are served by one of the most horrific concentration camps in existence within the Soviet Union. Whether or not Spesnaz forces train in proximity to the camp is not known but obviously they know of its existence.

The role of the enemy in exercises is played by MVD home forces, KGB communications troops or local KGB units, and by the militia. Each has to guard vulnerable points and maintain internal security and is as keen as Spesnaz itself to see if the latter can breach its defences. The outcome is studied seriously by the leadership of the GRU, KGB and MVD to see what lessons, if any, can be learned. There is evidence that defensive tactics change drastically as a result of successful Spesnaz attacks.

No cost is spared in the simulation of 'enemy' targets and terrain. Units exercise in Yavarov, which is very like the French Alps, and along the Baltic coast, which is similar to the north German plain. Enemy uniforms are worn and their tactics and interrogation techniques are studied. Models of their dispositions are made into which, to enhance realism, are inserted inflatable models of their weaponry.

In Spesnaz the Soviet Union has a dedicated force of approximately 30,000 men and women, all highly trained and motivated. They would play a significant part in any future Soviet conflict.

NAVAL SPESNAZ

There is a naval counterpart of the Army's Spesnaz, one brigade of which is allocated to each of the Pacific, Northern, Baltic and Black Sea Fleets. Each brigade consists of a regular-staffed anti-VIP headquarters company, a midget submarine group, three combat-swimmer battalions, a parachute battalion, a signals company and

support units. Because this force is nominally part of the Soviet Navy, its conscripts serve for three years. Spesnaz forces wear the same uniform as conventional naval infantry and are, therefore, very difficult to identify. They are stationed in closely guarded barracks within the harbour area and mix as little as possible with conventional forces.

They support amphibious operations with beach clearance, reconnaissance and the neutralization of sentries and such units occasionally undertake independent

direct action against harbour facilities. Elements may even be landed by helicopter to ambush and, therefore, delay enemy reinforcements attempting to destroy a bridgehead.

Scandinavia is regularly visited by Naval Spesnaz forces and it is more than likely that the vast majority of territorial incursions complained of so publicly by the Swedes during the 1980s, especially those in the region of the big naval base at Karlskrona, have been carried out by Spesnaz forces, possibly operating from their base at Kronstadt near Leningrad. From information released by Sweden, it would appear that two types of mini-submarine have been used and there is evidence of a rendezvous between one of these and its mother ship. It is likely that small parties of frogmen are trained to operate from old diesel submarines which can use their small size and sound imprint to approach a hostile coastline. Thereafter the Spesnaz swimmer will go ashore independently, returning to his submarine at a pre-arranged time.

Naval Infantry perform a marchpast during the May Day parade in Moscow. The Soviet Union is proud of its amphibious forces and they are often seen at the forefront of major military parades.

Such actions are shrouded in total secrecy and all steps possible are taken to ensure that no intimations of such activities are leaked to the outside world. It is of interest to note that when an old 'Whisky-II' class submarine ran aground in Sweden in 1982, that submarine had not been based, as might have been expected, with the Baltic Fleet but with the Northern Fleet and had sailed from the Kola Inlet into an area never usually entered by ships of that Fleet. It cannot be coincidence that the submarine carried a senior political officer and was thus clearly involved in unusual activity. 'Whisky-II' class boats have only the most primitive electronics and it is more than likely that it was acting in close co-operation with Naval Spesnaz swimmers.

AIRBORNE FORCES

Whereas in recent years Western nations have questioned the whole concept of airborne operations in conventional warfare, the Soviet Union has no doubt as to their value in any future conflict and has steadily increased the size of its airborne forces. Today, the Soviets have some 50,000 men, deployed in seven combat-ready airborne divisions, who practise both parachute and helicopter landings on a large scale during all major exercises.

Organization and Equipment Recent modernization has transformed Soviet airborne forces into effective mechanized infantry units capable of seizing defended objectives and attacking well-armed forces deep in the enemy rear. The Soviets perceive enemy tanks and aircraft to be the two major threats to airborne units after landing and have, accordingly, equipped their units with numerous anti-tank and air-defence weapons. It should be remembered that not all the equipment allocated to airborne units is new and, indeed, some units may still be issued with the venerable ASU-57 assault gun, while the SD-44 anti-tank field gun and RPU-14 140 mm multi-barrel rocket launcher are still to be found throughout the airborne order of battle.

Possibly the most revolutionary piece of equipment to enter service recently has been the BMD amphibious infantry combat vehicle. This heavily armed fighting vehicle is equipped with a 73 mm main armament which has an effective range of 800 m (2,625 ft) and sustained rate of fire of two to three rounds per minute. It also has a co-axially mounted 7.62 mm machine gun and two bow-mounted independent machine guns, supplemented with a rail-mounted AT-3 *Sagger* anti-tank guided missile with single reload. Subsequent models, designated BMD-2, are being equipped with a 30 mm

Marines of the Naval Infantry practise their section battle drills during a recent training exercise.

The Soviet Airborne Forces have an impressive heavy-drop capability, as seen here during Exercise West-81.

gun and the more powerful AT-5 *Spandrel*. The BMD is both air-droppable and amphibious. When the BMD was under development, the possibility of dropping it with its crew and full complement of six paratroopers inside was mooted, but was soon found to be impracticable! The crew would, however, drop within seconds of the vehicle and would be operational within a very short time after reaching the ground.

Whereas most basic combat equipment is air-droppable, some support weapons, such as the D-30 122 mm howitzer, are merely air-portable and it is, therefore, more than likely that a unit will drop initially on a light scale with its BMDs, mortars and anti-tank weapons and will then secure a landing zone to enable reinforcements and air-portable equipment to be landed.

The principal manoeuvre element of each division consists of its three regiments, each comprising three BMD-equipped airborne battalions, a battery of six towed 120 mm mortars plus anti-tank and air-defence batteries. Integral support is provided by engineer, signal and transport companies and medical, supply and chemical defence platoons. Divisional fire support is provided by the D-30 howitzer, with a maximum range of 15,300m (6,700 yd), and by the RPU-14 MBRL, with a range of 9,800 m (10,700 yd). Each division has one assault-gun battalion comprising 31 ASU-85 self-propelled guns, an anti-tank guided-weapons battalion equipped with 12 BRDM AT-5 *Spandrel* (with a useful maximum range of 4,000 m/4,400 yd) and an anti-tank battalion of 18 towed ZU-23 twin-barrelled guns with a cyclic rate of 800 rounds per minute. No target acquisition

or fire-control radar is, however, available, thus degrading considerably the effectiveness of the artillery deployed.

Neither the D-30 howitzer nor the Gaz 63 truck, used to tow the ZU-23, is airdroppable and, although instances have been recorded of the ASU-85 assault gun dropping with the aid of retro-rockets, this weapon is also usually delivered by airlanding.

Training Airborne troops are among the best-trained soldiers in the Soviet armed forces. Their training is physically rigorous and mentally demanding and is conducted under conditions which simulate actual combat, including extensive nuclear, biological and chemical (NBC) training. Airborne training integrates special airborne techniques with basic motorized rifle tactics. The personnel assigned to such units enhance the quality of training and all recruits are carefully selected. Most of them are two-year conscripts who are put through a rigorous screening process which demands a high level of physical condition, education, training and political reliability.

All enlisted conscripts will have done at least 140 hours of training sponsored by DOSAFF and most will have done premilitary para-training, thus reducing the need for basic para-training. Recruits receive an initial four weeks of basic training after which they get additional instruction in the use of weapons and military equipment, parachuting techniques, equipment rigging for air drops, equipment de-rigging after air drops, aircraft loading techniques and so on. Soviet parachuting techniques differ from those of Western forces in that small drogue parachutes are employed to stabilize the faller after the main parachute has deployed at a preset height. This results in faster and more concentrated dropping, although safety is much compromised.

Many non-commissioned officers are selected for NCO training by the District Military Registration Office at the time of induction and complete a specialized

BMD amphibious combat vehicles of the Soviet Airborne Forces during the May Day celebrations in Moscow's Red Square in 1985.

training course before promotion and posting. The majority of commissioned officers attend the Ryazan Higher Airborne School near Moscow. During their four years of training, the cadets study not only military techniques but also engineering, in which they receive a diploma before leaving. Approximately 60 per cent of the cadet's time is taken up with the study of such subjects as military history, organization, weapons training, equipment operation and maintenance; a further 30 per cent is occupied with the study of such academic disciplines as mathematics, physics, psychology, foreign languages (English, German and French) and technical courses; the residual 10 per cent is devoted to political training.

Deployment Airborne operations are divided into four categories: strategic, operational, tactical and special. The depth of the objective and the size of the attacking force vary considerably with each type of mission.

Strategic missions are established in wartime by the Soviet Supreme High Command and controlled by the General Staff. The outcome of a strategic mission is expected to have a very significant impact on a war or campaign, even though targeted against areas far beyond the influence of current ground-force operations. Missions can be directed up to 500 km (300 miles) behind the enemy front-line — and could encompass the Rhine and Ruhr. The use of troops in a foreign intervention role might also be considered. No immediate link-up with advancing troops is envisaged. Because of the scope and depth of a strategic mission, substantial air-transport and air-combat support is needed and resultant in-flight vulnerability suggests that drops would be made in relatively poorly defended areas. Objectives of strategic missions might be national capitals or other administrative political centres, industrial or economic centres, ports, airfields or possibly maritime straits. They might also be used to exploit nuclear strikes, to establish a new theatre of operations or to neutralize a member of an enemy coalition.

Missions will be carried out by at least one airborne division, possibly consisting of the airborne regiments supported by divisional artillery units, signals, engineering, transport and support battalions, a chemical-defence company and a maintenance battalion.

The drop itself will involve between four and six dropping zones, each about 4 km (2.5 miles) long.

Operational missions are controlled by Fronts and Armies and are carried out at regimental level in conjunction with ground-based operations. Attacks are unlikely to be launched until local air superiority has been established and, accordingly, will be very rare during the first two to three days of hostilities. Drops may be made up to 300 km (190 miles) behind the enemy front-line. One or two DZs will be used. Operational missions may be undertaken to neutralize a headquarters or strategic position, to block enemy reserves or to frustrate a withdrawing enemy. Such missions would be expected to operate alone for up to three days until relieved by conventional land forces.

Tactical and Special missions are executed on a far smaller scale and may be used to capture key terrain such as high ground and bridges, or as small-scale deception or sabotage operations.

Wherever possible the Soviets will airlift rather than air-drop troops, thus keeping the vulnerable period between landing and becoming operational to a minimum. Subterfuge, including the use of Spesnaz agents, may be used to gain initial control of the landing strip.

In the August 1968 invasion of Czechoslovakia, the 103rd Guards Air Assault Division was air-landed at Prague airport, which had first been seized by a Spesnaz team. Late on the evening of 20 August an unscheduled Aeroflot light aircraft sought, and was granted, permission to land at Ruzyme Airport on the outskirts of the city. Once landed, the aircraft taxied to a secluded area. Later that night a second Aeroflot plane landed and disembarked a number of Soviet civilians. After a brief discussion with nervous Czech security officials, these civilians disappeared, only to return, now armed, to take over the control tower after the leading troops of the invading force had crossed the border. Two transport aircraft, guarded by MiG-21 fighters, then landed at the airport and disgorged two airborne companies, who immediately wrested control of the entire airport complex from the Czechs. The first Aeroflot plane, which had stayed at the edge of the airfield throughout, now assumed its command role, directing the landing of the rest of the Division, with its heavy equipment, throughout the night. Once established, the Division linked up with armoured units of the 35th Motor Rifle Division which was spearheading the overland invasion. Moving quickly into Prague, they then secured all communication centres and key points before the local population had time to react.

Airborne troops were again much in evidence during the invasion of Afghanistan in December 1979. Immediately before the invasion one regiment each of the 103rd and 104th Guards Air Assault Divisions were posted to the Kabul region, ostensibly in support of the existing

government. Simultaneously Soviet 'advisors' withdrew as many Afghan Army vehicles as possible for maintenance and convinced President Amin to move into his palace on the outskirts of the city, thus isolating him from his most loyal supporters. Early on the night of 24 December Soviet airborne troops, conveniently based in the area, seized control of Kabul Airport and secured it for the landing of the entire 105th Guards Air Assault Division during the hours of darkness. Two companies of Spesnaz troops then stormed the Darularnon Palace and killed President Amin, his immediate supporters and his whole family.

Air Delivery Capabilities Soldiers are transported by the 600 medium- and long-range cargo transporters of the Soviet Forces' Military Transport Aviation (VTA). Although, in order to facilitate flexibility, the VTA is subordinated directly to the General Staff, its responsibilities are so diverse that it is unlikely that sufficient planes would be found to transport two fully equipped divisions simultaneously.

The fleet includes approximately 370 AN-12 *Cubs* (similar to the C-130 Hercules), more than 170 IL-76 *Candids* (similar to the C-141 Starlifter), and over 50 AN-22 *Cocks* (which are akin to the C-5A Galaxy). The older medium-range AN-12

Soldiers of one of the Soviet Union's airborne divisions man a twin-barrelled ZU-23 light anti-aircraft gun.

Soviet airborne troops constitute one of the most important elements of the Red Army. Considerable resources are being devoted to the improvement of weapon systems and the means of transporting them and it is likely that they will play an increasingly important role in Soviet military thinking in the years to come.

NAVAL INFANTRY

Although the smallest of the Soviet Union's elite forces, Naval Infantry is the oldest, tracing is roots back to the maritime might of Peter the Great. During the Great Patriotic War it reached a zenith in numbers:

Soviet paratroopers board a transport aircraft. The Soviet armed forces have the largest airborne transport fleet in the world.

is the mainstay of the VTA. This four-engined turboprop can airlift 90 troops or 60 paratroopers, who drop from side exits. Up to 20,000 kg (44,000 lb) of cargo can be lifted, including two BMDs or one ASU-85 assault gun. However, larger engineering equipment cannot be fitted into the cargo area. Capable of operating from unimproved runways, the AN-12 has a range, with maximum payload, of 1,400 km (875 miles). It requires 115 *Cubs* to lift a complete airborne regiment.

AN-12s are now being replaced by IL-76 *Candid* long-range, four-engined jet transports. Not only can the IL-76 lift 120 fully laden troops, but it can also disgorge them very quickly through four doors. Up to 40 tonnes (39 tons) of equipment, including three BMDs or the biggest of engineering equipment, can be transported to a maximum range of 5,300 km (3,300 miles). Sixty *IL-75s* can lift a complete airborne regiment.

The AN-22 *Cock* is a long-range turboprop plane which is capable of transporting either 175 troops or 80,000 kg, (176,000 lb) weight, including four BMDs, up to a range of 4,200 km (2,600 miles). Although it can be used for parachuting, it is better suited to strategic operations and, in time of war, would most likely be utilized in large-scale airborne operations to provide follow-up deliveries of reinforcements and equipment.

During times of emergency, aircraft of the Soviet civil airline Aeroflot will be used to augment VTA capabilities. The civil fleet has some 1,100 medium- and long-range transports, approximately 200 AN-12s and several thousand short-range aircraft.

350,000 personnel in 40 brigades and six independent regiments. However, the Soviet Fleet was relatively inactive and although five of the naval brigades were awarded Guards distinctions, only four landings of divisional strength were made, the majority of the 114 recorded amphibious assaults being of company strength or less. The majority of the troops fought as conventional infantry at the front but at the end of hostilities were not given the opportunity to regain their identity. The whole force was disbanded in 1947.

When it was reformed in 1961, the Naval Infantry was then accorded a distinctive role. Admiral Gorshkov, the father of the modern Soviet fleet, appreciated that his huge new naval bases would need the protection of dedicated infantry, and that in any future war amphibious landings would inevitably be made as far afield, perhaps, as southern Turkey or northern Norway. It was essential, therefore, for him to have not only a group of specialist amphibious ships but also highly trained and motivated naval-orientated soldiers, capable of exploiting this resource to the full.

The Naval Infantry is divided between the four Fleets. One regiment each is stationed with the Northern Fleet at Pechenga, with the Baltic Fleet at Baltysk

Naval Marines of the Baltic Fleet practise amphibious assaults during one of the many large-scale exercises conducted in this area.

and with the Black Sea Fleet at Sevastopol, while a smaller division is now with the Pacific Fleet at Vladivostok.

Each Regiment consists of three line battalions — each of approximately 400 men — a tank battalion (with a mix of T-55 or T-72 main battle tanks), a battery of BM-21 multi-barrel rocket launchers, an air-defence battery of four ZSU-23-4 SP guns and four SA-13 missiles, plus an anti-tank battery of six BMDs mounting either AT-3 *Sagger* or the vastly better AT-5 *Spandrel*. Each battalion has its own dedicated support units and, clearly, an amphibious landing in such force, especially if supported by Naval Spesnaz dropping in the rear, could bring massive disruption to the enemy's communications and logistics. Unlike its American and British Marine equivalents, however, Soviet Naval Infantry suffers from the defect that it does not yet spend enough time aboard commando carriers operating far afield from the home base. It is perhaps for this reason that it took no part in the 1986 conflict in South Yemen and the speedy evacuation of Soviet citizens from Aden.

Training The Naval Infantry do three years conscripted service instead of the usual two years. Training is harsh but unusually flexible by Soviet standards, incorporating not only all facets of infantry tactics but also beach assaults and cliff-scaling. Selection for conscription is done through the usual Military Commissariat system run by the Military Districts. There is no evidence to suggest that Naval Infantrymen are specially chosen, although the

Naval Infantry, carried ashore by PT-76 light reconnaissance tanks during manoeuvres in the Black Sea. The PT-76 is armed with a 76 mm gun and is used extensively by both marine and airborne forces.

high proportion of Slavs within the ranks has been noted.

Many recruits are sent on parachuting courses, the most successful attending further courses to qualify for the Fleet Commando Platoon. This small elite force receives specialized training in reconnaissance and sabotage and will work closely with Naval Spesnaz. Some of the better recruits qualify as frogmen and join the Regimental Engineer Company or the Reconnaissance Company where they are taught beach-obstacle clearance and the choice of suitable landing sites.

Although outdated, BTR-60 PB APCs and the even older PT-76 light tanks are retained because they have good amphibious capability. The remainder of Naval Infantry equipment is among the latest and best in service and in-depth training is given to ensure that its potential is fully exploited.

Tactics Naval Infantry would be used as the first echelon of an amphibious assault, supported subsequently by a much larger second echelon of conventional motor-rifle troops. Certain divisions in the Red Army are trained in the support of amphibious operations and are usually located near Naval Infantry units. There are, for instance, two motor-rifle divisions stationed between Murmansk and the Norwegian border, ready to support the 63rd Guards Naval Infantry Regiment — attached to the Northern Fleet — should it ever have to execute landings against the Northern Flank of NATO. A defended beach would first be bombarded from the sea while paratroops (perhaps Naval Spesnaz) would drop behind enemy lines in order to deny the passage of reinforcements. Assault engineers/frogmen would then be landed by fast launch or helicopter to dismantle beach obstacles, after which the main assault would follow.

Amphibious assault exercises, especially in the Baltic, are often carried out with the support of Warsaw Pact Marines, of which the best known are the East German 'Ernst Moritz' Arndt Regiment and the Polish 7th Sea Assault Division. The great degree of progress made by Soviet Naval Infantry since its postwar inception may be judged by a study of particular exercises.

Exercise West-81 was preceded by the gathering of an 80-ship task force. Although this was slightly unrealistic in that the force included the *Kiev*, whose war station would be in the Atlantic, and the *Leningrad*, which would be protecting the Black Sea Fleet, it nevertheless indicated the seriousness with which the Soviets took the Exercise. The 36th Guards Naval Infantry Regiment formed the first wave and captured the beachhead speedily, using 24 hovercraft and 14 'Polnocny' class

landing ships. Nine 'Polnocny' and 16 'Alligator' class landing ships were used to carry the second wave.

The existence of these new classes of landing ships has given the Soviets versatility they never had before and makes large-scale landings feasible. Furthermore, their ability to carry helicopters has given Naval Infantry a new dimension, making it easier to carry out small-scale commando raids to destroy communications before a major landing.

A marine battalion commander gives instructions to a platoon commander and his section leaders. In spite of being Naval Infantry, some of these men are wearing airborne qualification badges.

Once the Cinderella of Soviet tactical thinking, the Naval Infantry is now playing an increasingly important role, and is demanding — and receiving — the best personnel and equipment. There can be no doubt that its future is secure and that it will continue to form an elite part of the Soviet armed forces.

KGB

The *Komitet Gosudarstvennoi Bezopastnosti*, the Committee of State Security, came into being on 13 March 1954 and today regards itself as the guardian of the nation, the last bastion, the Praetorian Guard, of the Soviet Communist system. Under Andropov's leadership in the 1970s, it began to dismantle much of the secrecy which had surrounded it and has even published books for domestic consumption which explain its role to Soviet citizens. Though not under military control, the KGB nevertheless operates its own uniformed and fully equipped military force, with integral armoured and artillery support.

Young men conscripted into the overt military part of the KGB serve for two years, having been chosen from the political and physical cream of the bi-annual intake. They are not conscripted in the usual way and their service is in lieu of, rather than a part of, normal military service.

The most photographed of all KGB soldiers are those who mount ceremonial guard, day and night and in all weathers, over Lenin's tomb. (Sometimes winter duty is so onerous that the guard has to be changed every five minutes to prevent exposure.) While on such duty, these men wear immaculate officers' uniforms with distinctive blue shoulder flashes. When not on public duties, they form part of the KGB Kremlin Guard which is permanently stationed in Moscow to protect the Politburo.

The largest KGB formation is the Border Guard, which has 175,000 soldiers. Responsible for the protection of the whole of the Soviet Union's borders and not just, as is often thought, the East/West border, it is recruited on the basis of competitive examination but is mostly manned by Russians, Byelorussians or Ukrainians. In time of peace it deals with internal security and the suppression of ethnic dissent (especially among the Moslems in the south). The Border Guards man immigration checkpoints, crossings and airport passport-control points. (Soviet citizens must carry internal passports and require permission to move from one state to another within the USSR.) In time of war the Border Guards would form special security units to maintain discipline in the Red Army.

The Guards are organized into nine districts, quite distinct from army districts, each of which has its own restricted zones within which there are individual detachments which are responsible for a length of frontier varying between 100 km (62.5 miles) and 600 km (375 miles). Each detachment is roughly of battalion strength (500 men) and is subdivided into a headquarters, a reserve platoon and five platoons of outpost troops. Helicopter patrols, equipped with the M1-24 *Hind* attack helicopter, are used as quick-reaction teams with mechanized armour and artillery in reserve.

POLAND

The Polish People's Army, *Ludowe Wojsko Polskie*, is the biggest of the Warsaw Pact's armies (after the Soviet) and is the only one to have divisional-sized elite forces.

The 6th Pomeranian Air Assault Division, although only formed in 1957, can trace its history back to 1938 when the first Polish parachute centre was established. During the Second World War, members of the Communist Polish People's Army dropped behind enemy lines to aid partisans and the 1st Polish Independent Parachute Brigade dropped at Arnhem as part of the British Operation Market Garden.

Many recruits have learned to parachute with one of the numerous parachute sky-diving clubs before enlistment. They must do 15 combat jumps per year. Mountain and simulated arctic warfare is practised in the Carpathian Mountains to the south of the unit's base at Krakow. The division has no extreme range capability or

The Soviet Armed Forces Border Guard is the largest single formation within the KGB, and it is responsible for the security along all the Soviet Union's borders.

role and it is likely that more emphasis will, in future, be placed on heliborne operations. An independent special operations battalion exists, trained in rear-area security and sabotage.

The 7th Lujycka Naval Assault Division, based at Gdansk, is a regular army unit and is usually not under naval command. Comprising 5,500 troops, the Division is organized into three assault regiments, each with five companies of marines mounted in OT-62 armoured personnel carriers (APCs) and a company of 13 PT-76 light tanks. *Frog-7* rockets, anti-aircraft guns, BM-21 multi-barrel launchers, tanks and reconnaisance elements are available in support. The Naval Assault Division trains extensively with the Soviet 36th Guards Naval Infantry Regiment in Baltic exercises and would almost certainly be used in any future invasion of Denmark or southern Norway.

GERMANY, DEMOCRATIC REPUBLIC

The National People's Army, *Nationale Volksarmee*, can deploy one airborne battalion, a naval landing regiment and a number of specialized diversionary units. The 40th (Willi Saenger) Parachute Battalion was formed in 1973 and is now stationed on the Baltic island of Rugen. This lightly equipped unit, which has seen service in Angola and has had some training in Syria, is under the direct authority of the GDR Ministry of Defence and would form a high-command reserve in

The Polish People's Army is the second largest in the Warsaw Pact and has a proud airborne tradition dating back to the Second World War. The paratroopers seen here belong to the 6th Pomeranian Air Assault Division.

Among the GDR's elite forces are the 'diversionary units', which are equipped with the same vehicles as the West German Army, such as this M113 armoured personnel carrier (APC). These units would be expected to cause much confusion and damage in the event of a conflict between the two countries.

wartime. Consisting exclusively of short-service men who have previously done a Civilian Sports and Technology Association course, the Battalion boasts one of the highest standards of physical training of the whole Warsaw Pact. All its members are politically secure and occasionally exercise with the Soviet Border Guards along the inner German border. They will sometimes even go 'west of the wire' to reconnoitre NATO movements from small camouflaged observation posts.

Whereas the majority of the GDR's army would be likely to engage the Dutch in a European conflict (that nation's Corps being deployed opposite them in war), small numbers of elite troops are trained to infiltrate behind the lines in West Germany to create as much confusion and disruption as possible. Known as diversionary units, they are thoroughly trained in the tactics and mannerisms of the West German forces, are equipped with M113 APCs and M48 tanks — captured in Vietnam — and would wear West German uniforms.

Although on the face of it a conventional Motor Rifle unit, the 29th (Ernst Moritz) Armoured Regiment (also based on Rugen), trains with the 36th Guards Naval Infantry Regiment and would take a leading part in any maritime landing made in war by East German troops.

The East German Army is totally controlled by the Soviet Union and provides the Warsaw Pact with some of its finest troops. Its elite units are very professional and highly motivated politically, and could be expected to play a major role in any future conflict.

OTHER WARSAW PACT COUNTRIES

Bulgaria At least one mountain warfare unit as well as a single airborne regiment comprise Bulgaria's special armed forces.
Czechoslovakia The 22nd is Czechoslovakia's only active airborne regiment and is aided by reserve, training and support elements. Over recent years Czechoslovakia's airborne forces have undergone a series of organizational changes and reductions, as have the Hungarian airborne forces, which now comprise a single battalion.
Romania The Romanian armed forces have one airborne regiment, one naval battalion and two mountain infantry brigades, the latter consisting of two mountain infantry regiments each.

Y-841 915

BELGIUM

BELGIAN PARA-COMMANDOS

In 1942 a parachute unit and a commando were formed from the Free Belgian Forces in the United Kingdom. The first para company was created on 7 May and went to Ringway in England to be trained. By 1944 they had expanded and a Belgian Squadron, developed from the Para Battalion, was attached to the SAS for operations. In July three teams were parachuted into Normandy, to the east of the Falaise gap where elements of the 7th German Army Panzer Group were being encircled by the Allied advance. They successfully carried out their mission of reconnaissance and harrassment in pursuance of the Allied advance towards the Seine. In August other teams were dropped at Beauvais and in the Ardennes, while two more operated behind the lines in occupied the Netherlands and others in Belgium.

In December of the same year the Squadron was regrouped and mounted on armoured jeeps which carried a .30 calibre machine gun. During the German offensive in the Ardennes the Squadron was attached to the 6th Airmobile Division. At the beginning of April 1945, increased in size by recruits from liberated Belgium, three reconnaissance squadrons of the Parachute Battalion were turned into the Belgian SAS Regiment, which then fought in the Netherlands and northern Germany until the end of the war. Postwar, it was dispersed and used for counter-intelligence duties in Germany and Denmark.

Three months after the paras had first been created, a Belgian commando troop was formed, in August 1942. Seven officers and a hundred other ranks were trained at the Commando Training Centre at Achnacarry in Scotland and then at Abersoch in Wales. On completion of their training they became part of a multi-national commando and, in September 1943, Number 4 Troop of 10 Interallied Commando was sent to Algeria. By October the unit had been committed to the Sangro front in Italy as part of the British 8th Army and after a series of hard-fought actions was transferred to the Vth Army where it took part in the battles for the capture of Garigliano, Monturno and Monte Ornito. From there they were sent across the Adriatic to fight alongside Yugoslav partisans and British Commando units.

By November 1944 the Belgian commandos were part of the British 4th Commando Brigade which had landed on the water-logged island of Walcheran off the Dutch coast. After a hard fight, the island was captured, thus helping to protect the left flank of the Allied advance. Once

A Para-Commando brings an 'injured' colleague down a cliff-face during a casualty-evacuation exercise.

Belgian Para-Commandos during a cliff-assault. Climbing is an important skill for the special forces' soldier and the Belgian Para-Commandos are trained in mountaineering techniques.

Belgium had been liberated, the ranks of the commandos were swelled with volunteers, as had happened with the paras; the Troop then became an Independent Commando Unit and part of the British 1st Commando Brigade which was fighting in North Germany. At the end of the war they were on the Baltic coast.

After the war the paras and the commandos were stationed in Belgium, the former based at Schaffen and the latter at Marche-les-Dames. Elements of both units took part in the Korean War. In 1952 the two units were joined to become *Le Regiment Para-Commando*. Since then, all the men who volunteer to be part of this unit have received the same training in both parachuting and marine operations. It takes the form of basic induction at the Commando Centre followed by four weeks intensive commando training. If he completes that successfully, the recruit then goes to Schaffen for parachute training, after which there is in-unit instruction on ATGW, demolitions and other specializations.

In September 1955 the 3rd Battalion Para-Commando was formed at Kamina in the Congo, to be augmented during the troubles in that nation by four other para battalions and five independent companies. They took part in a great variety of peacekeeping and counter-insurgency tasks and saved many lives during the turbulent months before the final withdrawal in September 1960. By this time all Belgian forces had returned to Europe except for two of the para battalions which remained in Africa — one in Burundi and one in Ruanda — as peacekeeping forces until the independence of those nations in August 1962. Two years later the 1st Battalion of Parachutists was recalled to the Congo to fight against 'Simba' rebels, who had taken Stanleyville, the second largest city in the nation.

Five hundred and fifty troops of the Battalion were flown in American C-130s and C-124s to Ascension Island and then on to Kamina. After regrouping, 320 of them were parachuted at dawn on the morning of 24 November 1964 onto the airfield at Stanleyville. They quickly overcame resistance from the rebels and secured the airfield in order that the remaining troops and their heavier equipment could be flown in. While the main body of the unit remained at the airport, a small force was parachuted under rebel fire onto the airfield at Paulis. Here again they held the airfield until reinforcements had been landed and, in the town, freed 370 hostages for the loss of one dead and four wounded. In the earlier action at Stanleyville they had lost two killed and had five wounded, but more than 1,200 people had been freed.

In May 1978 the Para-Commandos returned to Zaire in support of units of the French Foreign Legion, parachuting onto the airfield at Kolwezi in an assault landing. Their task was to hold the airport while the Legionnaires recaptured the town, after which they were able to release more than 2,000 hostages.

Belgium contributes troops to the Allied Command Europe Mobile Force, in this

Below: Para-Commandos demonstrate unarmed combat. All three battalions provide instructors for other Belgian Army units.

Above: Amphibious operations are another speciality of the Para-Commandos, all of whom are trained in small-boat handling.

Left: Para-Commandos at the end of their training. They wear both the para and commando insignia – the former is worn on the right breast, the latter on the right arm.

The Belgian-manufactured FN AS 24 cross-country vehicle is capable of carrying four men plus their equipment. This is one of the many purpose-built vehicles developed since the end of the Second World War to give airborne troops greater mobility.

case for the protection of the Southern Flank of the NATO alliance. In order to do this, the Para-Commandos have been modified and reorganized over the years. First, an anti-tank company was formed, equipped with ENTAC missiles (which were, in due course, replaced with MILAN) and then, some years later, a battery of artillery, equipped with 105 mm towed guns, was created to support them. In 1975 a recce squadron was added when the old-style armoured jeeps were replaced by CVRTs (combat vehicle, reconnaissance, tracked).

The Para-Commandos are now well-trained both in their task of being part of the ACE Mobile Force and in taking on any Kolwezi-type actions that may arise in the future.

CANADA

CANADIAN SPECIAL FORCES

The Canadian Armed Forces have a brigade-sized Special Service Force based at Petawawa in Ontario, on the Ottawa River about 150 km (95 miles) north of the capital. Adjoining the barracks there is a large training area of about 350 sq km (133 sq miles).

Established in 1972, the Special Service Force is a light, highly mobile airborne/air-portable brigade, equipped, organized and trained to deploy rapidly to, and

conduct operations in, any environment. It now consists of the Canadian Airborne Regiment (para-trained), the First Battalion Royal Canadian Regiment, the 8th Canadian Hussars (Princess Louise's), 'E' Battery of the 2nd RCHA, an engineer squadron and organic medical, service and provost companies. The Force uses transport and fighter aircraft based throughout Canada but has integral helicopter support in the shape of 427 Tactical Helicopter Squadron. The Special Service Force is the successor to units which were formed during the Second World War.

The 1st Canadian Parachute Battalion, Canada's first airborne unit, was raised in July 1942. A group of 25 officers and 60 other ranks, who had trained at Ringway in England, returned to Canada to join the newly raised Battalion, which then went to Fort Benning, Georgia (in the United States) and Shilo, Manitoba, for continuation training. On 7 April 1943 it was incorporated into the 6th (British) Airborne Division, becoming part of the 3rd Parachute Brigade and arriving in England on 28 July 1943, just over a year after it was created.

The Regiment's first combat operation occurred during D-Day when it parachuted into France to capture enemy-held positions. The Battalion achieved all its objectives in spite of the fact that during the drop its troops had been dispersed over an area ten times greater than the planned dropping zone.

After four months of heavy fighting in France, the Battalion returned to England but was hastily summoned back to the continent to help hold the German assault in the Ardennes, where it was the only Battalion of Canadian troops to engage the enemy. Their final airborne operation was in March 1945 when they were involved in the major landing across the Rhine. Again they achieved their objectives and won their first VC, which was awarded

A machine gunner mans a .30 inch Browning from behind a sledge. Various types of sled are used by the Special Service Force to transport its support weapons and equipment.

A combination of green and white combat clothing has proved to be the most effective form of camouflage when operating near the tree-line.

Right: A Grizzly APC of the 1st Battalion Royal Canadian Regiment supports dismounted infantry during a winter-warfare exercise in Canada.

178

to Corporal F J Topham. The Battalion then took part in the advance to the Baltic, which was reached at Wismar on the same day as the Red Army. After a short time in England, the Battalion returned to Canada, where it was disbanded at the end of September 1945 having won four battle honours.

In 1942 a highly specialized joint Canadian-United States force was created to undertake special operations in Europe. In order that 500 'all ranks' could be recruited without undue publicity being directed towards their future role, the 2nd Canadian Parachute Battalion was raised at the same time as the 1st, coming into the order of battle on 10 July 1942. On 25 May 1943 it became the 1st Canadian Special Force Battalion, with its officers and men distributed with Americans throughout the multi-national unit. The Special Service Force was trained in Helena, Montana, before being deployed in the Aleutian Islands in 1943, where it had valuable training experience.

By November it had gone into action in Italy, where it distinguished itself in the successful assaults on Monte La Difensa and Monte La Remetanea. It also fought at Anzio and then in the drive to Rome, where

it was the first Allied formation to enter the city. The Special Service Force then advanced as far as the Tiber before being deployed in Europe for the invasion of southern France, where it spearheaded the landing force.

After seeing action on the Franco-Italian border, the joint force was disbanded and the Canadian element was separated. It, too, was then disbanded in December 1944, having fought well, earned ten battle honours and been given the nickname 'The Devil's Brigade'. (The motto of today's Special Service Brigade 'Osons' refers to its historical links with the 1st Special Service Force and means 'let us dare'.)

In April 1968 the 1st Airborne Battery RCA came into existence to provide organic support to the Canadian Airborne Regiment. It had six 105 mm pack howitzers and 12 81 mm mortars. In 1974 the Battery was in Cyprus in a defensive position around Nicosia airport. In 1977 the unit was disbanded but was then redesignated 'E' (Para) Bty of the 2nd RCHA – an airborne field squadron which came into existence at the same time as the Battery and was also disbanded in 1977.

The Canadian Airborne Regiment was

Above: Two men from the Special Service Force 'play dead' after their position has been overrun during a platoon attack.

Men of the Canadian Airborne Regiment give covering fire during a tactical exercise. The paras exercise in a variety of terrains and in 1985 took part in Exercise Border Star in the Texas desert.

formed at Edmonton, Alberta, in 1968. Its role was 'to provide a combat-ready, quick-reaction force in support of national security, North American defence and international peacekeeping'. It absorbed the traditions of the 1st Parachute Battalion and the unique USA-Canadian Special Service Force. It also took on some of the roles once exercised by the Airborne Brigade which had existed in 1948 and was made up of battalions of the Royal Canadian Regiment, Princess Patricia's Canadian Light Infantry and the Royal *22ème Regiment*. They did parachute and arctic-warfare training and exercises but, in 1958, were reduced to a cadre, the Defence of Canada Force.

The Airborne Regiment was first stationed at Griesbach Barracks, Edmonton, where the Canadian Airborne Centre and the Parachute Maintenance Depot are also located, but in 1977 moved to Petawawa. Since then it has taken part in a great many exercises, for example in the Arctic, in Jamaica, with the 82nd US Airborne Division at Fort Bragg and in the Californian desert. (The Airborne Centre consists of three wings: the Training Wing, the Aerial Delivery Training Wing and the Trials and Evaluation Section.)

In 1978 the Regiment was reorganized; its companies were reduced in size and 3 Airborne Commando was reconstituted to absorb 3 Mechanized Commando from the Canadian Brigade at Lars in West Germany. It now consists of 741 officers and soldiers who are all volunteers. There is the headquarters and signal squadron of 192 personnel, the 138-strong *1er Commando* (which is formed from members of the Royal *22ème Regiment* and is the only French-speaking unit outside the Province of Quebec), the 138 personnel of the 2nd Airborne Commando (from Princess Patricia's Canadian Light Infantry) and the 3rd AB Commando of the same strength. The whole is supported by the Airborne Service Commando.

The units are armed with TOW anti-tank missiles and with .50 calibre machine guns. Weapons training has high priority but other things which some of the troops are taught and practise include pathfinder and reconnaissance techniques, freefall parachuting, hand-to-hand combat, sniping, mountaineering, rapelling, SCUBA-diving and watermanship.

A typical annual training cycle would be: regimental skill-at-arms camp, brigade small-arms camp, sub-unit and commando-level exercises, regimental winter survival training and regimental training in arctic, jungle or desert conditions. This would be followed by a brigade exercise and then, possibly, by a divisional exercise.

In addition to all this, the Regiment participates in support tasks in Europe and the Middle East but its specific tasks are to: deploy as a deterrent force in times of crises; destroy any enemy lodgements on Canadian territory; recapture vital points; construct an airhead for larger conventional forces; carry out the above duties in North America; and deploy by air-landing anywhere within seven days for international peacekeeping. To do this a commando group is permanently on 12-hour notice to move to the airhead at Trenton, Ontario.

Once warning of impending action was received, a pathfinder group with freefall equipment could be airborne in 24 hours, to be followed by a commando group in 48 hours and the whole battle group within 72 hours. A peacekeeping force, with all its vehicles and support elements, could be in position in seven days from being asked for by the United Nations organization.

DENMARK

Denmark has one of the smallest populations of any NATO country but, because of its geographical position, is of great strategic importance. Denmark consists of a mainland peninsula and a number of large and small islands which stretch across the narrows of the Baltic Sea. Copenhagen, the capital, is situated on the island of Sjaelland, overlooking the Sound through which the Soviet Baltic Fleet would have to pass to reach the North Sea.

For its defence Denmark relies heavily on its army and maritime forces and has a total armed forces strength of about 31,000, of which just under one-third are conscripts doing their national service. The army has a total strength of 17,500 (including 6,500 conscripts) which can be quickly supplemented by an Augmentation Force of 6,000 reservists who are ready for immediate recall. In the longer term, this Force can be reinforced by the Field Army Reserve of 35,000 men, while the Regional Defence Force (24,000) and the Army Home Guard (60,400, including 8,500 women) are responsible for area and territorial defence. Denmark is, therefore, more than capable of defending itself, and regularly has exercises in which almost all its full-time and reserve forces take part.

The Danish Army has a number of independent reconnaissance battalions which are divided into companies to provide tactical intelligence for its five mechanized infantry brigades and five regimental combat teams (an additional seven on mobilization). In addition to these reconnaissance companies, the Danes have their own special forces unit which is known as the *Jaegerkorpset* or, more commonly, the *Jaegercorps*.

The first *Jaegercorps* units were formed in 1785 and were organized and used as traditional light infantry. The word '*Jaeger*' is used by a number of Western European countries and means 'hunter', but it is used to describe the light infantry or rangers. As lightly armed units, the original *Jaegers* would deploy in advance of conventional infantry and cavalry, carrying out reconnaissance, laying ambushes and sniping at the enemy, but as infantry tactics changed over the years, the need for this type of battalion has gradually diminished. Of the three original units, two were disbanded and the third assumed its special-warfare role in 1961 and subsequently became Denmark's Special Operations Company.

A Danish Army NCO fires a wartime German MG 42. In spite of being equipped with some weaponry which is outdated by most Western standards, the Danish armed forces are, nevertheless, considered very effective.

Although Denmark has no airborne units as such, parachute training for military purposes does exist and all *Jaegers* are para-qualified. As with most parachute units throughout the world, they are all volunteers. The *Jaegerkorpset* recruit from all branches of the armed forces including the navy and the air force. Any man up to the rank of captain may volunteer to join.

Selection for this elite special forces unit is particularly difficult and lengthy. After passing a number of initial selection tests, the volunteer must undergo a series of courses comprising all the usual special forces skills, such as communications and demolitions and also freefall parachuting. The *Jaegers* place great emphasis on patrolling skills and every man is LRRP (long-range recce patrol) – trained. Part of their initial training is devoted to acquiring these skills but, in addition, the volunteers must be able to march over long distances with a heavy load and survive undetected in a hostile environment for up to two weeks. In addition to this, each is a qualified scout-swimmer, an important skill taking into account Denmark's geography. Surface swimming using a wet or dry suit is a common method of infiltration. Boat handling is also taught, using different types of inflatable boats.

Jaeger training lasts a total of two years and it is only at the end of this long period that the volunteer becomes qualified and joins one of their five-man LRRPs. He may then wear the *Jaeger*-bugle badge, with parachute wings and a red beret.

Apart from their normal training, *Jaegers* are constantly involved in NATO exercises both in and outside Denmark. There is close liaison between them and other NATO special forces, including Britain's 21st Special Air Service Regiment and the Royal Marines Commandos.

As well as training its own personnel, the *Jaegercorps* runs a number of annual training courses for the Danish Army, including parachute and patrolling courses. One interesting feature about these courses is that they must be passed by all army officer candidates before they are commissioned into their own units. Not only does this ensure fit tough officers but it also spreads para and specialist patrolling skills throughout the army.

The Danes take the defence of their country very seriously, partly because of their renowned characteristic of individualism and partly because many remember what it was like to be occupied by a foreign power. Much time and effort is spent in training and preparation, and Denmark's armed forces, and in particular units like the *Jaegerkorpset*, are certainly capable of standing up to any attempted aggression and of fighting back.

GERMANY, FEDERAL REPUBLIC

AIRBORNE FORCES

West Germany's *Fallschirmjäger* are among the most highly trained of NATO's airborne forces. In the event of an East/West conflict, German paratroopers would be a vital element in NATO's strategic reserve, capable of quick-reaction counterstrikes against enemy armoured thrusts.

Germany was one of the first countries to recognize the value of airborne forces and was the first to employ paratroops successfully in war. Germany's airborne tradition dates back to the early Blitzkrieg days of the Second World War when the *Fallschirmjäger*, then part of the Luftwaffe, made a number of strategic strikes against enemy defensive positions which were well forward of their advancing armour and infantry. German paratroops were used in the invasions of Czeckoslovakia, Poland, Denmark and Norway, but it was during the invasion of the Low Countries that their full potential was realized.

The German officer corps had long been considered an elite, pursuing the established traditions of the Prussian Army of the nineteenth century and owing much of its strategic and tactical thinking to the teach-

ings of Clausewitz. Among the German High Command there were a number of brilliant tacticians who believed in the Blitzkrieg or 'lighting-war' concept whereby fast, hard-hitting columns of armour and mobile infantry, heavily supported by artillery and ground-attack aircraft, would smash through the enemy's defences, striking especially between corps, army or international boundaries. Having thus created a wedge into which the main body of their forces would follow, they would drive deep into enemy territory. Airborne troops would be used to capture vulnerable points such as airfields and bridges, secure vital river and canal crossing points before the enemy could destroy them and ensure, by capturing airfields, that air-landed reinforcements and resupply would be quickly available.

Although used in a ground-infantry role during the latter stages of the Second World War, German paratroops remained a force with which to be reckoned. This group was captured during the savage battle of Monte Casino.

Right: Kraka cross-country vehicles are deployed from the rear of a CH-53. Each aircraft can carry five of these vehicles when folded, or three which are ready for immediate use.

Below: CH-53 helicopters on their final approach during heliborne assault. The CH-53 is capable of carrying up to 55 fully equipped troops and is the prime mover of West Germany's airborne units.

Before the German advance into Belgium and the Netherlands, paratroops landed before first light on 10 May 1940 and had, by daylight, succeeded in capturing the bridges around the Hague and Rotterdam, which were vital to the defence of the Netherlands. Having secured those bridges the *Fallschirmjäger* then captured a number of airfields, while those still held by the Dutch came under intensive aerial bombardment from the Luftwaffe. By late afternoon on the same day the Dutch Air Force had been destroyed and German reinforcements were being flown into the airfields held by the paratroops. The Dutch were unable to defend the entire 320 km (200 miles) of their borders and initially tried to defend the shorter Grebbe-Peel Line but were unsuccessful. Unable to prevent the German XVIII Army from pushing west towards the coast on a line parallel to the River Maas, the Dutch broke the dykes and flooded the eastern lowlands. This had some effect in slowing the German advance but the final outcome was inevitable; after the bombing of Rotterdam (which killed 980 civilians and wounded a further 29,000), the Dutch had no option but to surrender.

At the time of the invasion of the Netherlands, the Germans only had a total of

4,500 trained parachutists. Of the 4,000 of these employed during the invasion, only 180 became casualties, a remarkably small number considering the part played by the airborne troops in the operation.

The attack on Belgium was almost simultaneous and the main attack on the Belgian defences along the Meuse and the Albert Canal also began on 10 May. The day after the German VI Army moved into Belgium, German airborne troops landed by glider on top of the Belgium fortress of Eben Emael which overlooked the junction between the river and the canal. Within a few hours it was in German hands. Other airborne units landed to the west of the canal, securing bridges vital to the German advance. As the British and French armies moved up to counterattack, they reduced the strength of their flank and committed their most mobile forces in support of the Belgian armies. This move allowed the Germans to launch their major thrust through the Ardennes and towards the Channel coast.

The successes achieved by this relatively small airborne force during the early part of the war were out of all proportion with the number of troops involved. As Germany continued to increase its airborne and gliderborne forces, both the British and Americans began to train paratroops which evolved into airborne operations.

In 1941 the Germans launched a massive airborne assault on the island of Crete, in what was one of the most ambitious invasions of the Second World War. Having had to withdraw from Greece after a short three-week battle, the Allies were holding Crete with a combined Greek, British and New Zealand force numbering nearly 74,000 troops. General Kurt Student assembled a force of some 500 transport planes and 70 gliders and after a period of intense aerial bombardment parachuted and air-landed his airborne force of 22,500 men. Although the Allied defenders fought bravely and stubbornly, they were soon overcome by the smaller but tactically superior German force. After capturing the island's only airfield at Maleme on the second day of the invasion, the Germans were able to bring in reinforcements almost at will and, with complete control of the air, the invaders severely hampered the withdrawal of remaining Allied forces by sea. The Royal Navy lost a total of nine warships during the evacuation and a further 17 were damaged.

The campaign on the Greek mainland and the island of Crete lasted for a total of 56 days and on 31 May 1941, one week after the Greek government capitulated, the last Allied troops left the island. Crete's defence had cost the Commonwealth forces 26,000 men killed, captured or missing.

The capture of Crete was a bad turning point for Germany's airborne forces due to the large number of casualties incurred.

Airborne troops for cover after leaving a UH-1D Huey. These helicopters, flown by army pilots, are invaluable for small-unit heliborne operations.

Right: Each FallschirmPanzerAbwehr company is equipped with Krakas, armed with either MILAN missile launchers or a 20 mm anti-armour gun.

Out of the 22,500 men involved in the invasion, 30 per cent became casualties, including more than 4,000 paratroops. Although the operation was a success, it was the last one of its kind mounted by the Germans for the remainder of the war. From 1942 onwards, the *Fallschirmjäger* fought as conventional ground troops, their exceptionally high standard of training enabling them to carry out a number of well-fought defensive battles toward the latter stages of the war.

The West Germans had no standing army between the end of the Second World War and 1955, when they were invited to join the North Atlantic Treaty Organization and formed the Bundeswehr. There were a number of senior officers who had experience in airborne operations or had served with the *Fallschirmjäger* during the war, and it was these officers who helped to organize and train the new elite.

The Bundeswehr now have three airborne brigades. Known as *Luftlandebrigade*, one is attached to each of the three German army corps. The 25th Brigade is based at Schwarswald, the 26th at Saarlouis and the 27th at Lippstadt.

Each corps has its own area of responsibility within NATO's Central European Region and the primary role of the *Fallschirmjäger* brigades is to act as the corps' rapid-deployment reserve. Each airborne brigade consists of a headquarters and three *Fallschirmjäger* battalions, each of which have two airborne infantry (*Fallschirmjäger*) and two airmobile anti-tank (*FallschirmPanzerAbwehr*) companies. Both the infantry and anti-tank companies are capable of rapid aerial deployment from either C-160 Transal aircraft or CH-53 helicopters. Smaller units, such as infantry sections, are carried in UH-1D Hueys.

In the corps' airmobile reserve role the tactics employed by the *Fallschirmjäger* against an enemy armoured threat would vary depending on a number of factors, but typically their deployment could follow this pattern: airborne infantry would either parachute or deploy by helicopter into an area in the line or path of the enemy advance and secure a landing zone (LZ) for anti-tank troops, who would be airlanded by CH-53 helicopters. Armed with TOW anti-tank missiles and 20 mm Feldkanone, both mounted on small Kraka cross-country vehicles, these troops would then rapidly deploy into position. They would be able effectively to engage a variety of targets – including T-72 main battle tanks and low-flying aircraft such as *Hind* helicopters – while being protected from infantry and light armour attack by their own airborne infantry.

Tactics such as these have been developed over the years and, during exercises, have proved to be highly effective. The days of large airborne combat deployments have passed, and apart from parachuting in strategic reinforcements or small groups for special missions, most *Fallschirmjäger* deployments will in future be carried out by helicopter.

Training The West German Army, like all but two of its NATO Allies, Britain and the United States, is composed largely of conscript soldiers undergoing national service. In Germany it is known as *mannschaften* and, although it is compulsory, nearly all the conscripts feel it their duty to be able to defend their country from attempted Soviet aggression. All conscript paratroopers serving in *Luftlandebrigade* must be volunteers. About two-thirds of the total strength of each brigade are conscripts, the rest are either short- or long-service regulars.

Volunteers who wish to join the airborne forces must first pass stringent physical and psychological tests. Physical fitness is highly stressed in the Bundeswehr as a whole but it is especially emphasized in the *Fallschirmjäger*. Volunteers must be able to sprint 100 m (330 ft) in 13.4 seconds, run 5,000 m (16,400 ft) in under 23 minutes, long-jump over 4 m, (13 ft), throw a shot-put 8 m (26 ft) and swim 200 m (660 ft). On satisfactory completion of these tests, recruits are then posted to a brigade, where they undergo basic military training.

Each brigade is responsible for its own training. Recruits are formed into a platoon within a training company and spend the next three months under the instruction of regular NCOs and officers. They learn military skills such as fieldcraft, battle drills, weapons handling and marksmanship. Much emphasis is placed on shooting skills in the Bundeswehr and each infantry section has its own sniper, equipped with a Heckler and Koch G3 rifle fitted with a telescopic sight. Training throughout the 12-week period is intense and particular attention is placed on physical fitness, with runs every morning and sport every afternoon. By the time recruits finish their basic training, they are in peak physical condition as well as being highly efficient in basic military skills.

After passing-out from the brigade's training school, the recruits are sent to the German Army Parachute Training Centre at Altenstadt in Bavaria where they spend the next four weeks under the instruction of NCOs from the 1st Airborne Division. There is a very intense level of instruction at Altenstadt, with the average student-to-instructor ratio being 8:1. The recruits spend the first two and half weeks of their parachute course doing ground training such as learning how to control the para-

chute in flight, how to correct malfunctions and how to execute a correct parachute landing fall. Techniques learned during this phase are then tested with the aid of a standard jumping tower. Recruits who do not come up to standard are sent to another unit. During the third week, the recruits make a total of 15 controlled descents from the tower, practise exit drills on the ground and 'hook-up' drills in a C-160 Transal flying over the DZ. During the fourth week, the recruits complete at least five parachute jumps from a C-160: the first and second are from 400 m (1,300 ft) without equipment, the third is with equipment, the fourth is a night jump and the fifth and final is a standard day jump with full equipment. On successful completion of the last jump the recruits are awarded their 'wings', which are worn on their chests, and become qualified paratroopers.

Fallschirmjäger are among the best paid troops in the German Army. In 1985 the average conscript earned a total of 180 DM per month untaxed, with food and accommodation paid for by the government. Paratroopers also receive an extra 150 DM per month 'jump' pay, which, in the case of a conscript, almost doubles his monthly income.

Once qualified, the paratrooper returns to his brigade, where he joins either an airborne infantry or an anti-tank company

Left: 'Digging in' is still a part of the life of a Fallschirmjäger in the field. Here paratroopers prepare a hide for a Kraka.

Overleaf: Marksmanship is considered an important skill in the Fallschirmjäger and two men in each section are equipped with a G3 rifle fitted with a telescopic sight.

Below: Paratroopers practise with their section weapons at Sennelager Training Area. The paras spend an average of one day per week firing their weapons.

Above: West German paratroops board a C-160 Transal for one of their many training jumps. The Transal is West Germany's medium-range, tactical-transport aircraft.

Right: An army jumpmaster stands in the exit doorway during the aircraft's final approach to the DZ.

in one of the battalions. There, he will spend the next ten to 12 months learning how to use the weapons and equipment of his section in a series of exercises ranging from platoon to corps levels. At least one day per week will be spent on the ranges practising firing personal and platoon weapons. Fitness training remains a priority; the Germans and the British have the fittest armies in NATO. The *Fallschirmjäger* have three company 5-km (3-mile) runs per week and once every two weeks there is a platoon 13-km (8-mile) run with full equipment.

The regular soldiers serving with Germany's airborne forces are either temporary career volunteers who have enlisted for between five to 15 years, or non-commissioned and commissioned officers who are serving for 20 or more years. These men do continuation training at the Airborne Training Centre at Schoengau in Bavaria. Known as the *Luftlande und Luftransport Schule*, the Centre offers a wide variety of courses, including military freefall (both low and high altitude opening), combat and aircrew survival courses and a number of specialist junior-NCO courses.

One of the 31 separate courses at Schoengau is the four-week Ranger course. This is designed to teach Ranger tactics and techniques to junior NCOs and officers and is a shorter version of the eight-week course run by the *Infantrie Schule* at Hammelborg. The four-week Ranger course must be passed by all those wishing to become platoon leaders in the infantry, including para and mountain troops. Each course is commanded by an experienced captain who heads a training team of four NCO instructors. The emphasis of the course is placed on personal military skills and, throughout it, students are assessed on four main subjects: leadership, tactical fieldcraft, individual survival and unarmed combat. Of these, leadership qualities are considered to be most important and anyone failing in this area would never be allowed to command combat troops in the field. Tactical fieldcraft includes night navigation, obstacle-crossing and camouflage and concealment. By the end of the course, the student should be capable of leading his men to safety through enemy-held territory. Throughout the course, each man is given the chance to lead other students in a number of different situations. Combat survival techniques include trapping and fire-lighting skills, the building of shelters and astral navigation. The unarmed combat taught is a general mixture of jujitsu and karate, with emphasis on the silent kill.

During the Ranger course, the students

learn how to abseil down cliffs, infiltrate through enemy positions, conduct raids for intelligence purposes, carry out ambushes and live off the land. They are constantly under pressure, having to plan raids and give orders when almost totally exhausted while, at the same time, knowing that they are under evaluation by their instructors. The students live 'in the field' for days at a time, usually with very little food and even less sleep. There are tests every week and, at the end of the course, a final exercise is conducted by the students, during which they are assessed as to whether they have attained the high standards needed to qualify as 'Ranger-trained'.

Only around 50 per cent pass the course first time around, which is a small figure, considering the high standard of training and fitness already possessed by the students. Those who have passed all but one subject are allowed to return for the final

Above: A paratrooper prepares to jump. The standard rate of exit is three men every two seconds from each of the two exit doors.

Above: The
Fallschirmjäger *spend much of their time in the field but, unlike many of their NATO counterparts, they are relatively lightly equipped.*

exercise alone; all others, except those who have failed in leadership, are given one more chance to complete the whole course.

The Ranger course is just one of a number available to regular paratroopers. Many go on to learn military freefall parachuting and join the brigade's pathfinder platoon. Others go on to train in heliborne operations, or become air despatchers or parachute-jumping instructors.

One aspect of training and deployment that the *Fallschimjäger* do not share with their NATO colleagues, except perhaps with the British, is their ability to fight within an urban environment. The West Germans have long realized the importance of fighting in built-up areas, or FIBUA as it is known, and intensive urban warfare is expected during any East versus West conflict. Airborne companies regularly train for this role in disused factories and other buildings, specially fitted out for the purpose. Drawing on their own experi-

ences of street fighting in Stalingrad and those of the British paras at Arnhem, the *Fallschirmjäger* train in small five-man teams. Two of these teams operate together, one providing covering fire as the other moves forward. Various methods of entering buildings are practised – through roofs, windows, walls, sewers and, on occasion, through doors.

Equipment Weapons and equipment in West Germany's airborne forces are basically the same as those issued to the rest of the army. The Heckler and Koch 7.62 mm G3 rifle is the standard-issue weapon except that the airborne version differs slightly by having a telescopic instead of a rigid butt. The G3 rifle is accurate and capable of fully automatic fire, an important consideration when used by lightly armed paratroops who often need to call upon instant firepower. Each eight-man section also has two G3 rifles fitted with telescopic sights for use by snipers, one *Panzerfaust* anti-armour weapon, one

Above: Paratroopers make a dash from one building to another during a FIBUA (fighting in built-up areas) exercise.

Left: A gun group provides covering fire during a building assault. By remaining in the centre of the room they present less of a target to the 'enemy'.

7.62 mm belt-fed machine gun (MG 3) and one 9 mm Uzi submachine gun. Each airborne infantry platoon also has one MILAN anti-tank missile launcher, a most effective high-kill probability weapon, which can engage armour up to a range of 2,000 m (6,560 ft).

The *FallschirmPanzerAbwehr* airmobile anti-tank companies are equipped with TOW anti-tank missile systems and Rheinmetall 20 mm guns. These are mounted on the small Kraka cross-country vehicles (which are like moon-buggies) and provide the *Fallschirmjäger* with a flexible, highly-manoeuvrable anti-armour asset.

Helicopters play a vital role in West German airborne operations. The UH-1D Huey or 'Slick' is the standard airborne section carrier, while the much larger CH-53 will carry two fully equipped infantry platoons or three or four Krakas. These helicopters are flown by army crews and are tasked by division in support of the airborne brigade. The *Fallschirmjäger* also use C-160 Transals for parachute operations. These can carry over 80 fully equipped paratroops and are flown by airforce pilots but have *Fallschirmjäger* jumpmasters and air despatchers.

The *Fallschirmjäger* have standard

German Army vehicles including VW jeeps, which together with the Krakas are used for operational mobility and are air-portable using CH-53 helicopters. In 1985 the Bundeswehr reintroduced camouflage for their vehicles and the *Luftlandebrigade* were the first units to try out a new three-colour scheme. Whereas in most armies, camouflage is applied at random, in the Bundeswehr the optimum markings have been decided with the aid of 'computer-assisted design' and are identical on all vehicles of the same type. There are also plans to reintroduce camouflaged combat uniforms to the Bundeswehr.

The West German airborne brigades are among the best trained in NATO. The conscripts who manage to become para-troopers are all volunteers who undergo the same rigorous training as their regular counterparts, and they have some of the most experienced officers and NCOs in the Bundeswehr. The airborne companies can be rapidly deployed by air, complete with their own anti-armour element cap-able of countering enemy flanking attacks, or they can be deployed in smaller groups to 'take out' enemy strong-points, head-quarters and other important targets. Tac-tics are constantly reviewed and updated.

Above: The Kraka provides the Fallschirmjäger *with a high degree of mobility allowing them to carry larger support weapons than most of their NATO Allies.*

Overleaf: One of the few problems with the Kraka is that when fully laden it does occasionally become bogged-down. 'Fully laden' often means 'overloaded'.

New, specially designed equipment is being produced for the airborne soldiers, including a new Weasel armoured vehicle. Capable of air-delivery, the Weasel is a small, tracked vehicle which will be replacing the now outdated Kraka and will afford Germany's airborne elite with the mobility and firepower it deserves.

OTHER SPECIAL FORCES

Apart from the *Fallschirmjäger*, the Bundeswehr has two other elite units, known as LRRP Companies and *Fernspäy* Companies. LRRPs are long-range reconnaissance patrols and consist of specially trained infantry troops which are capable of carrying out deep-penetration for intelligence-gathering purposes. The British Special Air Service run a LRRP school at Weingarten in Bavaria, and the West Germans have their own school nearby at Hammelborg. Both schools instruct in the 'art' of small reconnaissance patrols, which would, in wartime, provide invaluable information on the enemy's disposition, strength and movements.

Each of the three West German Corps have one LRRP Company, which is divided into six-man patrols. Operating behind the enemy's line of advance, these patrols would provide tactical and strategic intelligence direct to their Corps Headquarters. This would then be interpreted to give an overall view of the enemy's position as well as some indication of his future intentions.

The other Special Force units, the 'Fernspäy' Companies, are also attached to each of the Corps Headquarters. They are divided into a number of four-man patrols which operate behind enemy lines but, in addition to having an intelligence role, are also tasked with the destruction of vital points such as bridges and railway lines, and with conducting strategic raids on targets, such as enemy headquarters, supply depots and refuelling points. Members of *Fernspäy* Companies have usually been to the LRRP school and have passed the Ranger course. All are parachute-trained, usually in high-altitude, high-opening techniques, a method by which they can literally 'fly' themselves up to 48 km (30 miles) from their 'drop-off' position. By parachuting into enemy-held territory at night, *Fernspäy* patrols could move undetected into position before carrying out their mission.

In addition to the airborne brigades and the special forces companies, the Bundeswehr have one other special unit that should be mentioned: the *Gebirgsjäger* Division, based at Garmisch-Partenkirchen near the borders of Austria and Switzerland. This Division has three mountain-trained brigades: the 22nd Panzer-Grenadier at Murnau, the 23rd Mountain Infantry at Bad Reichenhall and the 24th Panzer at Mittenwald.

The Bavarian *Gebirgsjäger* are known throughout the Bundeswehr for their ability to operate in the German Alps in all weather. The majority of the troops come from the locale in which they serve and are used to living with months of snow during the winter. Furthermore many of them have been able to ski since they were four or five years old, but there is one particular custom that sets them apart from the rest of the Bundeswehr: the men of the Bavarian brigades are the only troops in the West German armed forces who are permitted to drink alcohol during their lunchtime mealbreak. Apparently they start drinking beer shortly after they learn how to ski, which is another reason why they are considered tough troops even within the Bundeswehr itself.

Sniping is one of GSG 9's various skills and one of the many practical methods they can employ to secure the release of hostages in a siege.

GSG 9

Although not part of the Bundeswehr, the *Grenzschutzgruppe 9* is a special counter-terrorist warfare unit. Known as *GSG 9* (a literal translation of the unit's name is Border Marksman Group Number Nine), it is part of the *Bundesgrenzschutz*, West Germany's border police, and comes under the direct control of the Federal Ministry of the Interior.

GSG 9 was formed after the massacre of Israeli athletes by Arab terrorists at the Munich Olympics in 1972. The West German government realized the need for a small counter-terrorist force capable of reacting to a similar type of situation and it was decided that the border police was the best structure on which to base such a unit.

Volunteers for *GSG 9* come from within the ranks of the *Bundesgrenzschutz*, which itself is an armed para-military organization. After passing a series of interviews and physical and physchological selection procedures, the volunteer must then undergo an intensive 22-week training course. During the initial 13-week phase the volunteer is tested on his basic and advanced police skills and receives further instruction in weapons' handling and unarmed combat. Although the volunteer must know the law as a policeman, it is also important that he must be very fit, and much emphasis is placed on physical skills.

If the volunteer passes the first phase, he goes on to study all aspects of terrorism and counter-terrorism in great detail. Lessons are learned from the experiences of other similar units and there is much study made of the various international terrorist organizations and the tactics they employ. While on the course, the volunteer must also learn the tactics employed in the countering of terrorism. Training is based on the taking of hostages, which is simulated: assaults are carried out on vehicles, trains, aircraft, ships and buildings.

Only around 20 per cent of applicants pass the selection and training course. Once qualified, the man becomes a provisional member of one of *GSG 9*'s four assault squads, one of which is permanently on standby in case its services should be needed. Training is a continuous process, as a high standard must constantly be maintained. *GSG 9* personnel are also responsible for training some senior government officials in such techniques as anti-ambush drills and defensive driving, and occasionally act as bodyguards for visiting VIPs.

A number of different weapons are used by the *Bundesgrenzschutz* and *GSG 9*. These include Heckler and Koch 9 mm P7 pistols and MP5 series submachine guns

(including the silenced version). A variety of rifles with high definition telescopic sights are used by the unit's specialist marksman section. Highly sophisticated electronic equipment, such as directional eavesdropping devices and cameras, is used by another section within *GSG 9*. All this specialized equipment is made up into 'packages' which, together with the operators, can be combined to take part in a variety of missions to counter any foreseeable threat.

In October 1972 members of *GSG 9* stormed a Lufthansa Boeing 737 which had been hijacked while on a flight from Palma in the Mediterranean to West Germany. After five unscheduled stops the jet ended up in Mogadishu, where the *GSG 9* successfully assaulted the aircraft. The hostages were released without loss of life,

Men of GSG 9, West Germany's counter-terrorist unit, deploy from a Bundesgrenzschutz UH-1D helicopter during a training exercise. They are armed with the Heckler and Koch MP5 9 mm submachine gun (SMG), a weapon that has found favour with many of the West's special forces in recent years.

while three of the four terrorists were killed and the other captured.

Since then the men of *GSG 9* have been involved in a number of smaller scale operations, but because of the sensitive nature of their work, they shun publicity and little information has been released. Much of their efforts go into the prevention of terrorist action within Federal German territory and, together with other internal government anti-terrorist organizations, they have been successful.

The *GSG 9* reputation for short, sharp and successful action is an effective deterrent against any would-be hijacker or terrorist who wishes to use German territory or people as a means to obtain his or her own political ends.

ITALY

Italy has a number of airborne and amphibious special forces units and, because of its geographical location, places much emphasis on its mountain-warfare troops. At present, the Italian Army has five *Alpini* brigades, in addition to one airborne brigade and one marine brigade. The San Marco Marines Battalion and elements of the *Alpini* are also parachute-trained.

AIRBORNE FORCES

During the Second World War, the Italians had two small airborne divisions. Although Italy had been one of the first nations to see the full military implications of the parachute and had, by 1928, trained more than a company of airborne troops, during the Second World War her airborne divisions were only used in the ground role.

In 1939 two parachute battalions, each consisting of 250 men, had been deployed to Libya. In 1940 a third battalion of about 300 men was raised at Castel Benito. In 1942 the *Folgore* Airborne Division was formed, comprising these three battalions plus other elements. After Italy's surrender to the Allies in 1943 a number of these men formed what was known as 'F' Squadron of the British 8th Army.

In addition to the *Folgore* Division, there were a number of smaller units in the Air Force and Marines who were also airborne-trained. In 1943 these, with other units, became Italy's second airborne division, the *Nembo* Division. These units carried out a few small sabotage raids during the war.

When the war was over, the Italians retained some of their airborne troops and, in 1946, reformed the Parachute Training School at Tarquinia. In 1952 a Parachute Brigade was created which, in 1978, became the Airborne Brigade, equipped with fixed-wing transport aircraft and helicopters and capable of both parachute and airmobile operations. Today's *Folgore* Brigade has its own integral airborne *Alpini* and commando troops, who, together with the airborne infantry and other specialists, maintain Italy's proud tradition of parachute forces.

ALPINE UNITS

As part of NATO, Italy is responsible, together with some of her Allies, for the defence of the European Southern Flank. This strategically important region, as well as Italy's own national borders to the north and north-east of the country, is made up of extremely mountainous terrain, and it is for this reason that Italy has long retained her elite mountain troops – the *Alpini*.

Paratroopers from the Alpini Para Company take part in a field training exercise in the Italian Alps.

At present Italy has five brigades of *Alpini*: the *Cadore*, *Julia*, *Orobica*, *Taurinese* and *Tridentia*. These *Brigata Alpini* are divided among the three Italian Corps responsible for the defence of the area around the Brenner Pass and the borders between Austria and Yugoslavia. There is also one battalion permanently assigned to NATO's Mobile Force, which is responsible for the defence of the Northern Flank and regularly takes part in the annual winter deployment in Norway.

Each of the five *Alpini* brigades consists of three or four mountain infantry battalions, supported by three mountain artillery battalions and an independent motorized company, equipped with armoured personnel carriers. These units are commanded by a brigade headquarters element, attached to which is a logistic regiment, an engineer company, a signals company, a *carabinieri* platoon and a

para-ski platoon. In addition to these units, each brigade also has a Fortress battalion which is specially trained to fight from pre-prepared defensive positions.

One of the most important elements of each brigade is the logistic regiment which provides the brigade with its transport and relies heavily on pack animals – mules. Another important asset to the brigade headquarters is the para-ski platoon which acts as the brigade's tactical reconnaissance and raiding force. Its personnel are capable of being parachuted into mountainous terrain.

Alpini brigades are largely made up of conscripts who are doing their 12-month national service. All complete the three-month basic training course run by the 2nd Alpini Regiment before undergoing mountain warfare training with the brigade to which they are then posted. Training is very intense, with much emphasis placed on

After Italy's capitulation during the Second World War, a number of units, including the Folgore Division, *joined the Allied cause. Many soldiers, such as this Italian Army major, led partisans in guerrilla attacks against the occupying German forces.*

physical fitness, a factor of obvious importance to mountain troops. A number of men go on for further training as gunners, sappers or radio operators, but the majority serve most of their conscription as infantrymen.

The obvious drawback of such a short period of conscription is to a certain degree balanced by the large number of men trained who, in the event of war, could be rapidly called up. This task is made easier because many of the men live in the same area as their 'regular' brigade.

The *Alpini* are equipped, in the main, as light infantry. Their role and the terrain in which they operate mean that weapons must be easily man-portable — or at least able to be transported by mule. The exceptions, of course, are the 155 mm guns of the artillery battalions. The standard-issue personal weapon is the 7.62 mm Beretta BM59 *Truppe Alpini* rifle. This is a special adaption of the US M1 Garand, with a folding butt, a cut-down stock and a pistol grip. The paratroop version is almost identical but has a removable flash-hider and grenade-launcher. Some men are issued with the 9 mm Beretta 38/49 submachine gun instead of the rifle, a more modern version of the 38/42 model which was one of the best wartime designs. The standard infantry support weapon is the 7.62 mm MG 42/59 machine gun, manufactured by Beretta under licence from Rheinmetall.

The MILAN anti-tank missile launcher is Italy's standard anti-armour weapon, as it is for most of her NATO Allies. The heaviest and most unusual item in the *Alpini* inventory is the 105 mm M56 pack howitzer. Of Italian design, this remarkable weapon can be broken down into 11 separate sections and transported by the

Right: A member of the Alpini Para Company. These troops have the same weapons and equipment as other Alpini units.

Opposite: A paratrooper, belonging to the 9th Col Moschin Assault Paratroop Battalion which is part of the Folgore Division. He is armed with a FAL BM59 Beretta assault rifle.

brigade logistic regiment's mules.

The Italians are proud of their *Alpini* troops and place much faith in their ability to defend Italy's borders. The *Alpini* mountaineer's felt hat with its black eagle feather and red pompom is an easily recognizable symbol of Italy's elite mountain troops, and a badge often seen in the remote mountain villages where the *Alpini* is in his element.

SAN MARCO MARINES

The San Marco Marines Battalion is the combat spearhead of Italy's naval and amphibious forces. Because of Italy's long coastline and strategic position in the Mediterranean, amphibious forces have long been considered another vital element of Italy's armed services. The San Marco Battalion has a total strength of around 1,000 Marines divided into three groups: operations, training and logistics. The operational element is divided into four companies which are organized along the lines of their army counterparts. These Marine companies are capable of conducting a variety of missions, including amphibious assaults and strategic raids. In addition to this, the San Marco Battalion is parachute-trained and capable of mounting offensive airborne operations.

A fully integrated sea, air and land force, the Battalion is equipped with two landing ship tanks (LSTs), which provide logistical shipping support and are capable of carrying over 500 troops, in addition to their armoured vehicles. These vessels, the *Grado* and the *Caorle*, are both former United States Navy LSTs and are now old. The planned introduction of a new purpose-built landing platform dock (LPD) in the late 1980s will greatly improve the Battalion's amphibious shipping capability. With its roll-on roll-off facility, the LPD will allow the San Marco Battalion to embark helicopters for operations and to carry and launch both large and small landing craft.

In addition to a number of small Italian-built landing craft, the Battalion has ten LVTP-7s (landing vehicle, tracked, personnel). These useful amphibious vehicles have greatly improved the Battalion's capability for beach assault, since each LVPT-7 can carry 25 fully equipped Marines or up to 4,550 kg (10,000 lb) of cargo. Capable of landing through running surf as high as 3 m (10 ft), these armoured amphibians have a land speed of 64 km/h (40 mph) and are armed with a turret-housed heavy machine gun. The standard M113 armoured personnel car-

riers, built under licence in Italy, are gradually being replaced by the VCC-1s.

With a few exceptions, the personal weapons and equipment used by the San Marco Marines are essentially the same as those used by the rest of Italy's land forces. The Marines were among the first to receive the new 5.56 mm rifles which are gradually replacing the 7.62 mm Beretta BM-59. The new rifle, known as the AR-70, is lighter and of improved design, capable of firing either single shots or automatically at a rate of 700 rounds per minute.

The San Marco Marines are among Italy's best trained troops, capable of conducting a wide variety of amphibious operations as well as being airborne-trained. They represent a small but significant contribution to NATO's Southern Flank. Between 1982 and 1984 they were deployed in the Lebanon as part of the Multi-national Peacekeeping Force, and their black berets with a lion badge became a well-known sight to the Italian

Above: Men of COMSUBIN train in cliff-assaults near the base at Varignano. During operations climbs such as this would be carried out at night.

Opposite: A mortar team of the San Marco Battalion, equipped with the 81 mm Brandt mortar. The Battalion's standard personal weapon is the Beretta SC70 assault rifle.

An Incursore *during an underwater training exercise. The* Incursore *combine the skills of paratrooper, mountaineer and frogman.*

stallations. A number of successful attacks were carried out by Italian underwater swimmers, including sabotage missions at Alexandria, Gibraltar and Malta. Italian combat swimmers pioneered a number of techniques of modern warfare in their particular fields: small submersibles and human torpedoes.

Today, *Incursori* combat swimmers are still a part of the Italian Navy and undergo an exhausting ten-month training programme, similar to that carried out by the US Navy's Underwater Demolition Teams (UDTs). Much of the training is carried out at La Spezia, and includes navigation, communications, demolitions and medicine. Emphasis is placed on physical fitness and swimming ability and all men are trained in the use of open- and closed-circuit SCUBA techniques. All then go on to become Ranger-trained and, in addition, become para-qualified.

On completion of their training, combat swimmers are assigned to the headquarters of one of the naval operational commands. Under the direct control of the commander-in-chief, they provide a number of services, including beach reconnaissance for the amphibious landings conducted by the San Marco Battalion.

There are a number of international terrorist organizations operating within Italy's borders, one of which, in particular — the Red Brigade — has been responsible for a series of assassinations and kidnappings. Among the Red Brigade's prime targets have been Italian government officials and businessmen. To counter this threat, Italy has established a specialist anti-terrorist group along the lines of West Germany's GSG 9. Known as the *Nucleo Operativo Centrale di Sicurezza*, or *NOCS*, this unit has a strength of about 50 specially trained personnel, many of whom are drawn from the *Carabinieri* Parachute Battalion. The *Carabinieri* are Italy's national para-military police force but also act as military police to the armed forces, with elements serving with the *Alpini* brigades as well as the *Folgore* Division.

The *NOCS* unit operates closely with other Western European counter-terrorist organizations and police forces and, in January 1982, was responsible for the release of US Army General James Dozier, who was being held hostage by Red Brigade terrorists at a flat in Verona. Since then they have carried out a number of successful operations, including the recovery of large amounts of weapons, ammunition and explosives from terrorist caches, and have arrested many terrorists. *NOCS* is the smallest and most recently formed of Italy's specialist units but one of its most active.

public at home, assuring this small force a future in Italy's armed forces, despite major cutbacks in other areas.

OTHER SPECIAL FORCES

Italy has long had a tradition of clandestine naval operations. During the Second World War, combat swimmers from naval assault units proved themselves by destroying Allied shipping and harbour in-

THE NETHERLANDS

THE ROYAL NETHERLANDS MARINE CORPS

The Royal Netherlands Marine Corps (RNLMC) is part of the combined NATO amphibious forces and is capable of conducting operations worldwide, wherever the need should arise. In addition to the Corps' NATO commitment, it is also ready to conduct peacekeeping duties for the UN on 24-hour standby and is also responsible for the security of the Netherlands Antilles. Because of its long historical links with the nation's seaborne forces, it is tasked with the military, ceremonial and physical training of the Royal Netherlands Navy. The motto of the RNLMC is 'Quo Patet Orbis' which, translated, means 'wherever the world extends'.

The Corps' battle honours of Kijkduin, Chatham, Atjeh, Rotterdam, Java and New Guinea illustrate the wide variety of operations it has undertaken during the past 300 years.

The Corps is the oldest unit in the Netherlands armed forces, having been raised in 1665 to take part in the war with England during a period said to be the 'most exciting and glorious in Dutch maritime history'. With its strong seafaring tradition, the Netherlands needed an elite force which could pursue its overseas policies – and this the RNLMC has done, as far afield as the East Indies and China.

During the Second World War the Dutch Marines defeated the Germans initial attempts to advance across the Maas bridges, objectives vital to the success of their offensive in May 1940. The Corps later fought in the defence of Rotterdam before the government's surrender. A number of Dutch servicemen contrived to escape across the Channel to England after their country was occupied and formed the Princess Irene Brigade, which included a detachment of Marines. The Brigade took part in the Allied invasion of Normandy in June 1944 and from then on fought throughout north-west Europe. Since the end of the war, the size of the

An NCO of the RNLMC working with a British Gunner (RA) commando. The Dutch and British Marines enjoy a mutual co-operative relationship unique within NATO.

Dutch marines land from an LCA (landing craft, assault) during an amphibious assault. RNLMC training is both tough and realistic.

RNLMC has increased dramatically and it has seen action in various campaigns in East Java.

The Corps' present strength is 2,800 men, including 170 officers and 800 NCOs. Only around ten per cent of the Corps' total strength is made up of conscripts doing their national service, and nearly all its officers and NCOs are regulars. The initial term of service for officers is seven years; for non-commissioned officers, the minimum is four years. This means there is a high proportion of highly trained troops within the Corps plus a number of reserves that can be called up quickly should the need arise.

The Royal Netherlands Navy provides much of the logistic support for the RNLMC, including medical officers, cooks and clerks, thus relieving the Marines of these tasks and permitting them to maintain a very high ratio of 'teeth-arm' troops. The small percentage of national servicemen are involved in all aspects of the Corps' activities and, at the end of their service, have the option to extend or go onto the reserve list. A small number are selected to become officers or NCOs.

The RNLMC comes under the command of the commander-in-chief of the Royal Netherlands Navy. There are three operational commands, each with their Marine elements. These are Home Command, which is responsible for the defence of the Netherlands; Corps Command, which includes the headquarters and is responsible for operations and training; and Antilles Command, which is responsible for the defence of that region.

The Corps Headquarters is in Rotterdam and provides the intelligence, operations and training sections, which are under the command of the Corps Commandant. Basic training of recruits is done at van Braam Hochgeest Barracks at Doorn. Here, recruits are taught weapons' handling, fieldcraft and climbing, spending much of their time in the combat-training areas. Doorn is the Corps' largest shore establishment and houses the Physical Training and Sports Centre, whose facilities are much used. Recruits also learn amphibious-force techniques while at Doorn and practise the handling of inflatable boats and landing craft. On the island of Texel there is an amphibious training area based at the Joost Dourlein Barracks, where recruits practise their new skills and also heliborne assaults, which play an increasingly important part in the Corps' role. Recruit training is intense and varied and a very high standard of proficiency must be achieved before the men go on to join a combat unit.

The Marines have two main combat groups, the 1st and 2nd Amphibious

Above: Dutch marines ski-march across the frozen wastes of northern Norway. A number of men from the RNLMC are highly skilled in arctic warfare, and some undergo the arduous mountain leader 2 course with the Royal Marines Mountain and Arctic Warfare Cadre.

Right: Members of the BBE/Counter-terrorist unit are winched aboard a Dutch Navy Lynx helicopter during an exercise.

Combat Groups. The former, 1st ACG, is based at the van Braam Hochgeest Barracks and is tasked with two operational priorities: to support NATO's defence of its Northern Flank and to maintain two 'Quo Patet Orbis' contingents, which can be deployed anywhere in the world at 24-hours' notice in support of the UN's peacekeeping role. It may also be used as a rapid deployment force by the Netherlands government.

Each year 1st ACG deploys to Norway for winter warfare exercises which last for three months. While there, it comes under command of 3 (British) Commando Brigade Royal Marines — a relationship between the two separate national forces which is unique in NATO. Command is

delegated by the Corps Commandant to the Commander of 3 Brigade and the Group becomes an integral part of the British Brigade.

The 2nd ACG comes under command of the Flag Officer Royal Netherlands Antilles. It is partly based on the islands of Curacao and Pinta. Marines arriving there are given continuation training in jungle warfare.

Regular soldiers may serve in either of the two ACGs and may, therefore, became experts in both arctic- and jungle-warfare techniques. The ACGs are, however, organized to operate independently. Each has a total strength of 700 men, divided into three companies of three platoons, plus a supporting arms company

and a service support company. The supporting arms company is armed with 81 mm mortars, Dragon anti-tank missiles and Stinger anti-aircraft weapon systems. Infantry weapons include the 9 mm Uzi submachine gun and the Heckler and Koch G3 rifle. Both ACGs conduct frequent exercises with other NATO units, especially British and US Marines, the Belgian Para-Commandos and French units based in the Caribbean.

For about five months of each year one independent unit, Whisky Company, is a permanently intregral part of Britain's 45 Commando Royal Marines. Since 1973, the Company, with a strength of about 150 men, has trained with 45 Commando at its base at Arbroath in Scotland, and also in Norway. In Scotland units can train in snowy and mountainous conditions and yet may still be within 'quick reaction' distance from Norway. Nearly all members of Whisky Company are para-trained. A number of men also do the exhaustive mountain leader 2 (ML2) course with the Mountain and Arctic Warfare Cadre of the Royal Marines. Once trained, former members of the Company are responsible for training other Dutch units such as the ACGs, the Dutch Special Boat Section and the Company Boat Group in arctic-warfare techniques.

The Company Boat Group, another independent unit, is integrated with 539 Assault Squadron RM, which specializes in amphibious operations in the Arctic. There, temperatures may drop as low as −70°C (−94°F), including a windchill factor.

Dutch LCAs (landing craft, assault) of the RNLMC cross one of Norway's many fjords. Britain's 539 Assault Squadron Royal Marines includes a Dutch detachment during its annual winter deployment in Norway.

Equipped with specially converted (landing craft, assault) LCAs and small raiding craft (rigid raiders and Geminis), the Company Boat Group is capable of landing small parties of men in the most adverse weather.

The RNLMC also has its own Special Boat Section, which trains alongside its British counterpart. Known as 7(NL) SBS, it is based on board HMS *Thetis* in Den Oever (near Den Helder) but spends much of its time deployed in the field. The training of these swimmer-canoeists is most arduous and includes a diving course at the Mine Counter-Measures Centre at Den Oever, where they learn to use various types of underwater breathing apparatus and become proficient at underwater demolitions. They also attend the Naval Communications School in Amsterdam, where they are taught how to operate sophisticated radio equipment and learn Morse Code and cryptography. In addition, they are para-trained and are integrated into 3 Commando Brigade's long-range reconnaissance units.

Apart from their primary role of underwater, amphibious and reconnaissance operations in the Arctic, 7(NL) SBS is also responsible for the security of Dutch oil rigs in the North Sea, and is trained in counter-terrorist techniques, operating in that role with the Close Combat Unit at Doorn.

The RNLMC are among the best-trained of all NATO amphibious units. They provide NATO with rapidly deployable forces with a great variety of skills which can be used 'wherever the world extends'.

A member of 7 (NL) Special Boat Section in a pose characteristic of many of the world's amphibious special forces. Apart from their primary SBS role, these men are also in charge of the security of Dutch oil rigs in the North Sea.

four million spread over 386,974 sq km (149,411 sq miles) of mainland area. The largest number are centred in the south of the country, while the north is mostly uninhabited — and it is in the far north that Norway shares 196 km (123 miles) of common border with the Soviet Union.

In order to prevent any surprise attack, Norway has a permanent cadre of 13,500 regular personnel plus between 28,000 and 29,000 conscripts, but it also has the highest comparative proportion of reservists to regulars in NATO: 87 per cent compared to the average of 50 per cent.

Above: All members of the Norwegian Army receive training in guerrilla warfare. Capable of operating in small groups with the minimum amount of support, such groups would severely hamper the advance of any would-be invader.

NORWAY

Norway, like its neighbour Denmark, is of vital strategic importance to NATO. Not only can it, in peacetime, monitor Soviet movements and intentions, but it is also the wartime anchor for NATO's Northern Flank.

Norway is fully committed to her own defence, subscribing to the total defence concept whereby the largest, best-equipped forces possible are combined with an extensive civil defence organization.

The nation has a population of just over

In the event of mobilization, the standing force would be massively reinforced by a reserve element of 235,000 men, backed up by a large Home Guard, or *Heimevernet*.

Much of Norway's defence policy stems from the lessons learned from the German invasion in 1940 and the subsequent occupation. Before the invasion Norway had a neutral, anti-militarist defence policy; mobilization orders for the reservists were actually sent by mail when the alert was given — with disastrous consequences. In spite of this, however, the Germans were hard-pushed to improve on their initial advantage and had to fight countless battles of increasing intensity as they tried to move further into the mountains, where a small, lightly armed force could hold up an army.

Today, the Norwegian Army has a standing force of 24,000 men, including 18,000 conscripts serving their 12-month national service. Conscripts spend between three and eight months undergoing specialist training and the remainder with one of the active units. On completion of their service, they are transferred to the

Overleaf: Norwegian troops in position during an exercise.

Below: Norwegian soldiers leave their armoured personnel carrier to take up position during one of their numerous winter warfare exercises.

The Norwegian Army as a whole, and their special forces in particular, make extensive use of the fjords. Small craft such as this would be used to outflank the enemy in the event of a conflict.

reserve forces, where they spend up to 21 days a year undergoing refresher training.

A unique aspect of the Norwegian Army is that it is the only one in the world entirely mountain- and arctic-warfare trained. Warfare in arctic conditions is probably the most arduous in the world. Survival during the winter months, when temperatures drop well below freezing, is difficult enough but to be able to operate in such weather takes a great deal of experience, something that Norwegians get at an early age. This, coupled with their military training, makes them among the best arctic-warfare troops in the world.

Like the Danish armed forces, the Norwegians have their own company-sized Special Force unit. All its men are parachute-trained and, with the exception of a small regular cadre, serve up to two years with the unit. In addition to their para-training, they become combat swimmers and LRRP experts, the emphasis being on mountain and arctic warfare. Their primary task is strategic and tactical reconnaissance, with the ability to conduct small-group strategic strikes. For them, demolitions and ambushing are two important skills; Norway has one main road running from north to south and any enemy advance could be halted in a number of places. The same applies to other vulnerable points, such as the railway system and bridges.

The Norwegian Special Force trains with British and American special forces deployed in Norway for three months each winter, and is closely associated with the Royal Marines Mountain and Arctic Warfare Cadre.

Together with the rest of the Norwegian armed forces, the Special Force is geared towards a defensive war during which it must rely to a great extent on external reinforcement. Because of this vital need, NATO has the equivalent of four brigades ready to reinforce its Northern Flank: the British 3 Commando Brigade, the multi-national NATO ACE Mobile Force (Land), the Canadian Air-Sea Transportable (CAST) Group and a US Marine Amphibious Brigade. Much of their heavy equipment — including vehicles, heavy weapons, ammunition, medical supplies and fuel — is stored in various locations around Norway.

During the war many Norwegians escaped to Britain and fought for the Allies while those left behind formed one of the strongest resistance movements in occupied Europe. It is on these resistance traditions that the *Heimevernet* is based. Today, the Reservists and Home Guards keep their personal weapons at home, and most of their heavier equipment is kept nearby. They, together with the standing army, would mobilize in the event of an enemy attack, would operate on their own initiative, and, if surrounded, bypassed or overrun, would aim to continue to fight even if the government fell. This, in itself, is a formidable deterrent to any would-be aggressor.

In the event of a surprise attack, and before the arrival of external help, the Norwegians would reinforce their standing army with their large reserve force and mobilize their Home Guard. The latter, apart from defending local depots and other vulnerable points, would also assist the regular forces by carrying out reconnaissance and scouting missions. It has a total strength of 90,000 men and women with an average age of 30 and can be mobilized within four hours, complete with uniforms, weapons and equipment. They are all trained in guerrilla warfare in a country they know intimately and, together with Norway's other defence assets, would be a decisive factor in its ultimate victory against any invader.

OTHER NATO COUNTRIES

Greece One Para-Commando Brigade is part of Greece's Army, and is well-trained and equipped, mainly with French and US airborne equipment. Unlike most conscript armies, the Greeks have a long period of national service, 24 months at the present time. This allows the training cadre of regular officers and NCOs to maintain a high standard. The Army's three aviation battalions and the Air Force's transport and helicopter squadrons are more than capable of carrying the Para-Commandos on either heliborne or airborne assaults.

Portugal The Portuguese armed forces have three small commando units: marine commandos who are part of the Portuguese Navy and whose role is conducting amphibious raids; Army commandos who occasionally have been employed in the airborne role, but are more often used as elite infantry; and airborne commandos who are part of the Air Force and would most likely be used in preference, should a task require airborne delivery.

Spain The youngest but most rapidly expanding airborne force within NATO is Spain's. Formed in the late 1950s, the airborne force has now reached brigade-size and is fully operational. Together with one air-portable brigade, the airborne force is capable of rapid deployment to protect affiliated territories such as Spanish Morocco.

FRANCE

FRENCH FOREIGN LEGION

The French Foreign Legion is a legendary unit which is shrouded in mystery. Most people, when asked, will have vague ideas about PC Wren, brave deeds and heroic deaths, but few know anything more. This is partly due to the fact that the Legion gained its reputation because it attracted some men who, quite often, had run away from their problems or crimes and had something to hide and, therefore, welcomed its anonymity. In return, the Legion maintained secrecy about them and itself and, as time passed, came to be considered a tough, sometimes brutal, organization which harboured the scum of the earth but was, nevertheless, a very formidable fighting machine.

That used to be the case but now Interpol computers screen out hardened criminals and only petty offenders who are thought to be capable of reform make it into the Legion. It is no longer a safe haven for drop-outs. Many men are rejected during the first interview. Many cannot take the physical and mental pressures and quit during the first few weeks of training. Even after six-months' service and having qualified as a fully trained recruit, the Legion reserves the right to reject men it considers to be unsuitable.

Until the 1960s, anyone with an almost suicidal desire to forget the past was quite likely to be killed in action before his five-year contract had ended, but this is not the case any more. The chances of seeing active service with the Foreign Legion are rare today but, even so, are better than in most armies, which is why the Legion still

The old image of the Legion manning isolated outposts in the middle of the desert has faded. Today's Legion works and lives in modern accommodation when not deployed on active service.

Legionnaires during the marchpast on Bastille Day in Paris. This is one of the few occasions when the Legion parades in front of the public.

attracts many more recruits than it needs — only one-third gain admission. But the main reason for volunteering is still the fact that the Legion offers a chance to start life again, with honour, that it is tough — and therefore elitist — and that, once enlisted, a man belongs to a family which protects him.

Two of the more specialized units of the Legion are the *1èr Régiment Etranger de Cavalrie* and the *2ème Régiment Etranger de Parachutistes*.

1ER REGIMENT ETRANGER DE CAVALRIE

The *1èr REC* was formed in 1921 in Tunisia and was recruited from three sources: from the 2nd Legion Regiment of Infantry, from French Army cavalry regiments, and from

a group of Russian emigres who had been obliged to leave their country after the revolution, many of whom had fought with the White Army against the Reds. The 1st was soon to prove itself in two dramatic actions which are still, perhaps, the most famous in its valorous history.

Posted to Syria to pacify a Druze insurrection, the Landrail Squadron found itself under attack in the town of Messifre, the last defendable position before Damascus. The enemy managed to kill nearly all the Squadron's horses while they were hobbled at their pickets and then launched a series of violent assaults on the Legionnaires during 16 and 17 September 1925. Although vastly outnumbered, the Squadron held out until relief came, thus denying passage to Damascus and saving the political situation. This action earned the Regiment its first citation to be followed by a second soon after when the same

Squadron came under siege in the town of Rachaya to the west of the Djebel Mountains. Once again many horses where slain at their pickets, but this time the Legionnaires were under constant attack for four days. On the evening of the third day, 23 November, Captain Landriau sent off his last carrier pigeon with news that the situation was critical in the extreme, ammunition was being rationed and they could not hold out much longer. Fortunately, there was a quick response and the town, now almost totally destroyed, was relieved by the 6th Regiment of Spahis.

For the next 13 years the *1èr REC* took part in the pacification of Morocco and Algeria, fighting bands of rebels and conducting security patrols along the developing Saharan highways. From 1939 until the French Armistice of 1940, the Regiment together with a newly formed 2nd Regiment, fought on French soil as part of the 97th Divisional Reconnaissance Group. Then, in 1943, the survivors of bitter battles against Hitler's armies fought, first of all, in Tunisia and, then in 1944, landed in southern France as part of the liberating forces. The *1èr REC* led French armoured units into Germany as the war came to an end and, after a short interval, was posted to Indo-China.

There, it fought a long campaign against the secessionist Viet Minh troops of General Giap. It was given an amphibious section equipped with Alligators (amphibious APCs) and M29C cargo carriers, known as Crabs. These had been designed for arctic warfare but were equally suitable for use in paddy fields or in sub-tropical swamps. From 1956 to 1963 the Regiment saw action in Algeria until, when that conflict was resolved, it was stationed for the first time on French soil, at Orange. In

A French Foreign Legion outpost at Ait Alli Iko in French Morocco.

1983 the Regiment became, for a short time, part of the peacekeeping force in the Lebanon.

Today the 1st Regiment of Legion Cavalry is part of the 6th Division of the French Army in the newly formed *Force d'Action Rapide*, equipped with AMX 10 RC armoured cars which have 105 mm main armament.

2EME REGIMENT ETRANGER DE PARACHUTISTES

Over the years the bravery and superb professionalism of the *2ème REP* has gained it an international reputation. An in-depth study of its history would not be possible in a book of this length but perhaps an account of two of its most famous battles will give some indication of the validity of that reputation.

The Regiment was created on 2 October 1948 in Morocco at Sidi-bel-Abbes, the home of the Legion, in order to meet the needs of the war in Indo-China. This conflict had started as a result of the declaration of an independent republic by Ho Chi Minh on 2 September 1945.

When the Japanese withdrew from Indo-China after the capitulation, the nation, which had been a French colony before the Second World War, was left without leaders or administration. Ho Chi Minh, who was a devout Communist and had spent some years in Moscow, took the opportunity to declare the country as a republic and himself as head of state. Serving as his military leader he had General Ngo Giap, who, before the war, had been a schoolmaster. The French refused to accept the situation, sought a compromise at a conference at Fontainebleau and, when that failed, set out to retake their former colony by military force. They found the Communists most entrenched in the north, based around the old capital of Hanoi. After their arrival and the imposition of the old rule, the French seemed

Men of the Gourms Arab mounted cavalry in French Morocco. The Legion has often operated in conjunction with locally raised forces.

superficially to have all the advantages and be in the ascendant. However, they were, in fact, faced with a problem of increasing difficulty, one which was, in the end and many years later, to see the defeat of the United States. The vast majority of the population were against them, racially and ideologically. The indigenous populations were stoic and stubborn and could accept defeats and harsh living conditions that would break the will of people of a different nature, and they were almost impossible to grasp and contain in the jungle regions into which they retreated to build up their organization and strength.

As time passed the Viet Minh, although very unprofessional in appearance in comparison with the armies of the West, became well-equipped with modern weapons, disciplined and responsive to Giap's command. Above all, they got by on an absolute minimum of logistic support. They achieved this transformation from a loosely organized mass of illiterate peasantry with help from the USSR (and, initially, until the split developed between the two biggest Communist powers in the world, from the Chinese as well). The French, on their side, received financial and material aid from the USA, marking the beginning of the latter's long, costly and humiliating involvement in this theatre.

It seemed that parachute troops would be able not only to reach Viet Minh bases which ground forces could not but also to inject an element of surprise into military operations which were usually compromised by the jungle telegraph within hours of their commencement. The *2ème Régiment* was, therefore, hardly formed before it was posted to the Indo-Chinese theatre of war.

In the autumn of 1950, Giap inflicted a major defeat on the French forces, killing nearly 5,000 men. And then, for the next four years, he kept up the pressure. By 1954 public opinion in France was beginning to go against the conduct of the war and it was vital to achieve a major French-induced victory and show that the end, and victory, was in sight. General Navarre decided to establish a major military base in the valley at Dien Bien Phu in the Thai Highlands. From here his troops could

Although considered by many people to be an infantry-based organization the French Foreign Legion has for a long time been supported by its own engineers, artillery and cavalry.

dominate the area, undermine the influence of the Viet Minh (which, like all such organizations, asserted its influence by intimidation of the local population) and then win the 'hearts and minds' of the people. That was the theory but, in the event, Giap encircled Dien Bien Phu with five divisions backed by ground and anti-aircraft artillery.

Within a short time Navarre's men were unable to hold the heights and had to retreat into a compound. Cut off, they had to rely on air supply, at first by air-landing but then, as the situation got worse, by air-drop. On 13 March 1954 Giap's troops began the battle to annihilate their enemies. (By far the majority of the French forces were not Frenchmen; they were Vietnamese — analogous to the South Korean and South Vietnamese troops who fought alongside the Americans — or were Legionnaires from many countries.) From concealed positions the Viet Minh artillery pounded the French, who retreated into trench warfare as a defence against the constant barrage of shells. In particular, the airstrip came under fire, making casualty evacuation and resupply perilous, even if the planes managed to run the gauntlet of anti-aircraft fire on their way in.

As the situation worsened, the 2ème REP was parachuted into Dien Bien Phu on 10 April. From then until the end, on 7 May, the Legionnaires fought with fantastic bravery and determination, making one counterattack after another in order to regain so-called trenches, which had collapsed into mud holes under the incessant monsoon rains. However, despite their incredible efforts — and the parachuting in of 384 Legionnaires of the 2nd Regiment of Infantry who had never parachuted before and knew they were going to almost certain death — the Viet Minh closed in inexorably and, with half the base in enemy hands, the French had to accept defeat. Nearly 10,000 men went into captivity, of whom most were never seen again. Of the 2ème REP, only some 50 survived. During the confrontation, the Regiment had endured horrific casualties, fighting a battle which was of no direct concern to most of the soldiers but was seen through to the bitter end for the honour of the Legion. In all, during the course of the war, the Legion lost 7,000 men. Later in the year Vietnam was partitioned.

Reconstituted, the 2ème REP went on to fight in Algeria until 1962. In 1963 it

Legionnaires moving position during their defence of Dien Bien Phu. In spite of reinforcements being airlifted in, the besieged garrision was eventually lost.

became a para-commando unit, capable of fighting under any conditions of terrain. Its 1,300 men were trained to be snipers, to climb mountains, to make beach assaults from the sea, to survive in all conditions and to fight by night. Today its six companies specialize in specific roles: in night and urban combat; in mountain and arduous combat; in amphibious warfare; and in behind-the-lines operations, demolitions and sniping. They carry the FAMAS 5.56 mm calibre rifle and the FRFI 7.5 mm or the FML 7.5 mm machine gun.

In 1969 and 1970 the *2ème Régiment* saw action against rebel troops in Chad and, in 1976, were sent to Djibouti to free hostages who were being held by Somali terrorists. Then came the second major battle to capture world headlines and add to their reputation.

On 17 May 1978 the *Régiment* was put on full alert to fly from Corsica, the new home of the Legion after the French withdrawal from North Africa, to Kolwezi, a mining town in the south of Zaire, formerly the Belgian Congo. Units of the Congolese National Liberation Front had captured the town and begun a systematic series of atrocities, at first against the local population but, as they got out of control and could see nothing to stop them, against the two thousand or so white people who had been living and working in the area. The local Zaire army was unable to intervene and the Belgians, who had retained some residual interest in the country because of the activity of their huge mining company, Union Miniere, found themselves able to offer help only in what they termed 'a humanitarian role'.

In this dire situation, the *Régiment* was flown to Kinshasha in Zaire in five DC-8s, arriving within 25 hours of having been alerted. There, three rifle companies and part of the Headquarters Company were issued with American parachutes, which did not properly fit their harnesses, and packed into four C-130 Hercules (five were needed) and one C-160, which was to be used by the Pathfinder Company to mark an unreconnoitred DZ. At midday on 19 May they took off for Kolwezi on a flight which took four hours and gave the Legionnaires the opportunity for a short rest after having had no sleep for two nights. During the late afternoon, they parachuted onto the DZ, which was co-vered with long elephant grass and ant hills several feet high.

After sorting out their equipment and regrouping, the three companies of the *2ème* split up and moved off, against sporadic resistance, to take over the key places in the town. However, during the night they were heavily counterattacked. At dawn the next morning, the fourth company jumped onto a second DZ to the east of the town, were immediately pinned down by rebel fire and were eventually extricated after a fierce fire-fight by another company. The support platoons and the remainder of the Headquarters Company jumped onto the original DZ and then linked up with the rest of the *Régiment,* who had, by then, rescued many of the hostages and made them congregate in a central place. During the day these people were flown out of the airport under the care of the Belgian Para-Commandos who had been sent in a defensive role. Ten days later the *Régiment* was back in Corsica having cleared the area around Kolwezi of rebels and earned its seventh citation.

The *2ème REP* is now part of the *Force d'Action Rapide*, a newly constituted group of French troops formed to carry out a great variety of roles.

A Legionnaire stands watch over his section's personal equipment before its deployment to Chad. The Legion has been involved in numerous conflicts since the end of the war in Algeria.

FORCE D'ACTION RAPIDE

The spread of international terrorism, the continuing unrest in the Middle East and Africa, the possibility of limited war in the defence of French interests in various parts of the world and the long-standing threat of a European war leading to nuclear exchange have convinced the French government of the need to be able to respond quickly to counter all these possibilities and stop them from escalating. To this end they have developed a massive rapid reaction capability of up to five divisions, in all some 47,000 troops, which can be committed to battle either as an immediate response to conventional brush-fire wars or, at the other end of the spectrum, as the first deployment of force in response to an overt threat in Europe. Small, specially trained elements can also be used in anti-terrorist operations.

Equipped with the latest weapons and the most advanced communications systems, all or parts of the *Force D'Action Rapide* (*FAR*), commensurate with the scale of the threat, can go anywhere in the world and be capable of fighting under most conditions. Two of its divisions have a preponderance of anti-armour capability and are most likely to be used in central Europe, while the others have specialized roles to meet almost any eventuality. Each of the five divisions is carefully structured to be able to react specifically to the immediate threat but may also be reinforced should the first containment not succeed.

4EME DIVISION AERMOBILE

This force has a strength of 6,400 and is composed of one regiment of command and support helicopters, one regiment of airmobile infantry and three regiments of combat helicopters. In all, there are 214 helicopters (90 anti-tank, 30 support, 84 transport and 10 light recce) in the *Division* which carry more than 400 missile launchers plus soldiers equipped with 48 MILAN anti-tank missile launchers. Thus, due to the exploitation of the latest developments in missile and helicopter technology, the *4ème Division Aermobile* (*DAM*) has enormous anti-armour capability. Units can deploy swiftly, take on an armoured column and then move on to inflict damage elsewhere. They can pick their time and place of attack and mount it with a great element of surprise. Using information relayed back by reconnais-

sance helicopters, the attack planes (90 helicopters anti-'char' — HAC) can deliver accurate but short-lived ground-hugging attacks with great mobility and then, after delivering the punch, can be beyond reprisal before the enemy has had time to react. Where suitable, other anti-armour attacks will be made by infantry deployed on the ground by the support helicopters and using the MILAN ATGW. The *DAM* is not designed, or expected to, hold ground.

6EME DIVISION LEGERE BLINDEE

This *Division* has 7,500 men in two regiments of armoured cars, two regiments of infantry in wheeled APCs, one regiment of artillery, one of engineers and one which provides command and logistic support. In all, the *Division* has 72 AMX 10RCs with 105 mm main armament, 24 APCs with HOT missiles, 340 troop-carrying APCs, 36 artillery and mortar pieces and 48 MILANs.

This *Division* was formed specially for the *FAR* in 1984 to meet a new concept of combining armour and mechanized infantry in highly mobile, fast-moving columns. With its guns and missiles it can speedily bring a very impressive amount of anti-tank firepower to bear on the enemy even though, because of its composition, it can also carry out the more conventional roles of reconnaissance, vanguard, escort and rearguard actions.

9EME DIVISION D'INFANTRIE MARINE

This *Division* has 8,000 men in three regiments of mechanized infantry, one armoured regiment, an artillery and an engineer regiment and a command and support regiment. It has more than 500 APCs, 36 AMX 10RCs, 48 artillery and mortar pieces and no less than 120 MILAN ATGW.

All units are trained in amphibious warfare and combined operations. In the future it is planned to equip the AMX armoured cars with image-intensifier sights, fit MIRA thermal image-intensifiers to the MILANs and introduce the SATCP-Mistral surface-to-air missile system into the mechanized infantry, artillery and engineer regiments. The system has a target

acquisition radar, a thermal-imaging camera for night firing and six missiles, which can take on low-flying targets moving at up to Mach 1.2.

11EME DIVISION PARACHUTISTE

This *Division*, with 13,000 men, is the biggest of all in the *FAR* and consists of six regiments of paratroops, one of light cavalry, one of artillery, one of engineers and two command and logistic support regiments. One of three re-roled *Divisions* now assigned to the *FAR*, it was created in 1971 as a rapid-reaction force – indeed, it was the kernel around which the rest of the *FAR* has been built. Equipped with 168 MILAN firing points, it could take on an armoured thrust but its parachuting capability also gives it great flexibility of employment. In addition, it could conduct small commando-type operations for reconnaissance or to destroy key installations, possibly behind the enemy lines. The *2ème REP*, in particular, is trained to specialize in that role, as is another component of the *Division*, the *1èr Régiment Parachutiste d'Infantrie de Marine*, the *1èr RPI Ma*, which is similar in concept to the British SAS.

27EME DIVISION ALPINE

This *Division* specializes in mountain and arctic warfare. With 9,000 men in six infantry regiments supported by one regiment of wheeled armoured vehicles, it, too, has a high number of MILAN launchers (108). Its troops are trained to operate under the most arduous conditions but can also take on conventional tasks alongside other *Divisions* of the *FAR*.

The *Force d'Action Rapide* has an Aeromechanized Echelon composed of the 4th Helicopter-borne Division, the 6th Division, with its armour and mechanized infantry, and a command and logistic support element. This combines the most mobile units of the *FAR* into a unique anti-armour strike force which has the capability of delivering a tremendous assault on an enemy tank column and then withdrawing before a counterattack.

With the APILAS 112mm anti-tank launcher (one of the most powerful yet developed) now being issued to some units, the *FAR* must possess one of the most potent anti-armour capabilities in the world and also be one of the most flexible in employment.

Legion paratroopers on duty with the United Nations Peacekeeping Force in the Lebanon. Like many countries within NATO, France regularly provides the UN with troops for peacekeeping duties.

EUROPE

SWEDEN

Sweden's defence policy is based on non-alignment in peacetime and is aimed at neutrality in time of war, but Swedish defence is an important factor in the overall security of the Nordic area. Situated to the east of Norway, the north-east of Denmark and the south-west of Finland, Sweden is well-known for its active foreign policy aimed at reducing tension between the two power blocs of Europe. Both Denmark and Norway are members of NATO but do not allow foreign troops or nuclear weapons to be based on their territories during peacetime, while Finland, despite its friendship and mutual assistance pact with the Soviet Union, has a policy of neutrality and military non-co-operation with the Warsaw Pact countries.

The total land area of Sweden is equal to the combined areas of West Germany, Switzerland, Austria, Belgium and the Netherlands but it has a population of only 8.5 million. Sweden supports a total war defence concept similar to those of its neighbours, and its armed forces are based on the rapid deployment of all trained conscripts, supplemented by civil and economic defence. All able-bodied men between 18 and 47 years of age receive basic military training lasting between 7.5 and 15 months; most conscripts between the ages of 30 and 35 serve with local defence units such as the static defence units safeguarding airfields, harbours or border areas. Sweden's only regular full-time servicemen belong to its 20,000-strong officer corps, which consists of NCOs, warrant officers and officers of all three services. These are supplemented by 13,000 reserve officers who, together with the standing force and reserve elements, comprise a total defence force 850,000-strong.

Included in the armed forces are several special operations companies, both army and navy in their wartime organization. The army unit is a Parachute Ranger Company known as the *Fallskärmsjägere* and consists of para-trained 'Rangers' who operate in small five/six-man patrols. All the men are LRRP-trained at the *Fallskärmsjägrskolan* and capable of living off the land for long periods and conducting a number of SF missions, including strategic reconnaissance and target attacks. The second special forces unit is the Coastal Ranger Company. Coastal Rangers are part of the Naval Coast Artillery and are specially trained at the *Kustjärgarskolan* to conduct combat and surveillance missions for their parent brigade. Like the *Fallskärmjägere*, the Coastal Rangers can be quickly committed to a vitally strategic area to carry out reconnaissance, and are also trained to counterattack enemy-held positions by either landing craft or helicopter. The Coastal Rangers can paddle silently among the off-shore islands, swim underwater to scout or carry out surprise attacks on enemy forces. The third unit consists of naval divers. In the naval forces there are four types of light diver, including the attack divers, who are specially trained for reconnaissance and surprise attack in the archipelago terrain. They employ a closed-circuit system and breathe pure oxygen. The apparatus does not give off

Attack divers of the Swedish Navy and Coastal Artillery surface before carrying out a target attack on one of the many coastal islands. The Swedish coastline borders on the area in which the Soviet Baltic Fleet operates, and these highly trained attack divers regularly take part in counter-insurgency exercises.

tell-tale bubbles, so the diver can carry out his mission unnoticed, but because of the danger of oxygen poisoning, these divers do not operate below about 7 m (23 ft). Diving training is conducted at Hårsfjärden near Stockholm and is also available to Coastal Rangers.

All three of these special forces groups represent an important asset to Sweden's defence policy and are part of the overall deterrent. It would require great resources and a great deal of time to make an attack on Sweden.

OTHER EUROPEAN COUNTRIES

Austria Like the Swiss, the Austrian Army is well-trained in mountain warfare techniques and has a number of alpine units. Many alpine troops attend the Austrian 'Ranger' school and go on to become para-trained. These troops are capable of operating in small groups and, by using terrain they know well to their (and its) best advantage, they are more than able to engage much larger forces.

Switzerland Probably the best known of the neutral, non-aligned countries, Switzerland, like a number of them, bases its defence on the total war concept. The Swiss have one special forces company of Para-Grenadiers who, like the rest of the armed forces, are trained to fight a defensive war inside their own country, where the raiding and sabotage skills of the Para-Grenadiers would pose a serious threat to any invader.

Yugoslavia Guerrilla warfare is a speciality of Yugoslavia's army. This is particularly true of the Yugoslavian mountain brigades, which, in addition to being mountain- and arctic-warfare trained, are capable of operating in small groups behind enemy lines, carrying out raids and ambushes.

THE MIDDLE EAST

No other region of the world has such a large number of special warfare units, most of which have seen active service. With a few exceptions, units are trained as airborne commandos, equipped as light infantry and, in addition, have guerrilla, sabotage and reconnaissance roles. Organized as companies and battalions, they have the primary task of functioning as assault commandos within a battle group, capturing and holding strategic targets, undertaking short-range reconnaissance and deploying raiding parties. In peacetime they act as counter-revolutionary warfare/internal security units with an additional intelligence-gathering role.

JORDAN

A parachute company, formed in 1963, was the nucleus of today's special forces. There are three airborne-commando battalions, consisting of 500 men each, which are subdivided into three companies. All recruits are volunteers who must be Bedouins with strong tribal links to the King and the Jordanian throne. There is a rigorous selection course before training commences, including instruction in guerrilla

and counter-guerrilla warfare. After service in one of the battalions, officers and men may be selected for the counter-insurgency brigade which is composed of special security groups (SSGs).

The loyalty of these units was tested in September 1970 when the SSGs and elements of the 4th Mechanized Division crushed the Palestinian Liberation Organization (PLO) in camps along the Salt-Aman highway while, at the same time, blocking a Syrian invasion from the north. Another SSG mission against the PLO guerrillas took place in 1976 when they recaptured the Inter-Continental Hotel, releasing a group of hostages.

The three battalions are equipped with American uniforms and small arms — including the M16 rifle and M60 machine gun — the Dragon ATGW, 106 mm recoilless rifles and mortars. Troops wear a maroon beret and US camouflage suits, with a winged sword surmounted by the Hashemite crown on the right shoulder. The force is ground and airmobile, employing Alouette III and S76 helicopters and C-130 and Aviocar parachuting aircraft.

SYRIA

Syria's first special force was a parachute battalion raised in 1958. It now has both para and commando battalions, each composed of three companies. Independent and airmobile, they are trained to operate in small groups which are capable of assault commando and security duties. Commandos are taken into action by helicopter.

The battalions are equipped with Soviet AKS-74 automatic rifles, the Dragunov

A C-130 Hercules transport aircraft of the Sultan of Oman's armed forces. The Sultan's army is one of the best-equipped and best-trained in the Middle East.

239

7.62 mm semi-automatic rifles and P-6 pistols. They also have MILAN and *Sagger* ATGW.

Syrian commando and para units have seen action continuously since the Yom Kippur War, during which a mixed force took the Israeli electronic observation post on Mount Harmon. Counterattacks were repelled until the Israelis retook the position at the end of the war. Since 1976 the units have been involved in the civil war in the Lebanon, fighting against Christian militia, the PLO and the Israeli Army. They fought in Beirut, Tripoli and Sidon in 1976 and, since then, in Beirut, Tripoli, Haleh and Homs.

EGYPT

Egypt's first parachute unit became operational in 1959 and saw service in the United Arab Republic Army before it was reorganized as a para-commando unit and sent to the Yemen. There, in 1965, they seized key positions in Sanaa, the capital. They were in action against loyalist troops throughout the following year, with mixed success. By the end of the decade, the special forces had been expanded, often at the expense of quality. They then consisted of two Independent Parachute Brigades, one Marine Assault Brigade, two Air Assault Brigades and seven Commando Groups. In more recent times a commando force of between 500 and 700 men, codenamed 'Thunderbolt', has been trained in West Germany by *GSG-9* for counter-revolutionary duties. It, too, has met with mixed success.

The units are ground and airmobile and are equipped with a mixture of Western and Soviet weapons and technology.

Originally, the commandos were trained to spearhead crossings of the Suez Canal but later, during the 1967 War, naval combat swimmers and helicopter-borne commando teams were inserted behind the Israeli lines to attack command and communications centres. Larger commando groups met with less success and were detected and eliminated by Israeli heliborne hunter-killer groups. Egyptian and Israeli special forces encountered each other on the battlefield in the light-infantry role with much mutual destruction. At the end of the war, elements of the 182nd Egyptian Brigade, defending the west bank of the Suez Canal, were engaged by Israeli paratroops with heavy losses on both sides, indicating that special warfare units should not be used in set-piece battles. Although the Thunderbolt force, *Sa'Aga*, has been trained by US Special Forces especially for use in counter-revolutionary warfare, including the termination of sieges, it has shown a lack of

subtlety in its actions. In 1978, for example, after the authorities at Nicosia had negotiated the surrender of terrorists who had hijacked a plane, the Egyptian unit exchanged fire with Cypriot National Guardsmen, losing 16 dead. Although more successful in 1975 at Luxor where they rescued all the passengers from a hijacked Boeing 737, in November 1985, at Luqa in Malta, 59 passengers were killed during the attempt to free 98 people. (Ironically, the same 737 was involved at Luxor and Luqa.)

ISRAEL

Israeli special forces could be said to have their origins in the joint Allied/Haganah operations in Eastern Europe and North Africa during the Second World War. After the state of Israel was created in 1948, one of the first acts of the new administration was to create a parachute unit which was,

Opposite: An Egyptian paratrooper wearing his parachuting gear during recent exercises with the US 82nd Airborne Division in Egypt.

Below: Israeli Commandos during a field training exercise. The Israeli armed forces are equipped with some of the most sophisticated weaponry available.

in time, to form the bases of the elite Parachute Army. Today, this consists of five brigades – two at full strength, one at half strength and two in the reserve. Selection and training is very rigorous and concentrates on demolitions, covert operations and internal security duties. Many soldiers specialize in field medicine, HALO parachuting and combat swimming techniques.

Israeli airborne units use a variety of captured Soviet weapons in addition to their own Uzi submachine guns and the new Galil SAR 5.56mm rifle. They also have a variety of Western heavy machine guns and ATGW. Airborne forces wear the standard uniform with a maroon beret and silver para wings on the left breast.

Other Special Forces There are known to be naval and marine commandos trained for small-scale raids and intelligence gathering. There is also a counter-revolutionary warfare group which draws most of its recruits from the paras. This unit, designated 269, specializes in situations where hostages have been taken and was formed from the paras and Golan infantry who provided the troops for the raid on Entebbe (Operation Jonathan.) The elite infantry brigades, the Golan and the Givati, contain four reconnaissance units: *Sayeret* Almond operates under Southern Command and specializes in long-range desert patrols using jeeps and light trucks; *Sayeret* Carob operates within Central Command against infiltrators in the Judean and Sumerian Hills; *Sayeret* Egoz

is deployed in Northern Command as a mountain unit; *Sayeret* Matkal is specially trained to operate anywhere in the world in all forms of combat and its troops are taught HALO, survival, languages and how to use foreign weapons. These units are believed to have provided intelligence before all major commando operations.

Israel has perfected the skill of striking at targets deep inside enemy territory. In the late 1960s, two raiding parties of paratroops, deployed and extricated by helicopter, destroyed the Naga Hamady transformer station and a series of bridges over the Nile, 250 km (160 miles) north of the Aswan Dam, under cover of darkness. A fortified anti-aircraft position at the mouth of the Suez Canal was destroyed by paras and marine commandos, landed from small raiding craft, despite a continuous barrage of fire from Egyptian artillery. During another classic raiding operation, heliborne paratroopers captured Beirut airport on 28 December 1968 and destroyed all Arab civilian planes in response to PLO attacks on El Al aircraft in Greece and Europe. In a daring raid deep inside Egypt, which echoed that on Bruneval during the Second World War, paratroops landed from helicopters, captured and dismantled an advanced radar system installed by the Soviets and lifted out the secret parts with Sikorsky CH53D helos.

Between 1968 and 1970 small groups of PLO guerrillas infiltrated across the Jordan River to attack civilian targets. Paras and *Sayeret* troops were deployed to counter

Soldiers of the 41st Infantry Battalion, SW African Army. There are a number of locally raised units operating in southern Africa, the most notable being the Portuguese-speaking 32nd Battalion which is credited with many of the SADF's successes in Angola.

South African paras pack their equipment during their basic parachute-training course. This is the same course as that undertaken by the Recce Commandos.

these forays in search-and-destroy operations. Although losses were high on both sides, in the end the PLO were convinced that it would be less costly to seek targets outside Israel. The new strategy was to concentrate on Jewish airlines and the hijacking of airliners.

One of the most successful airborne operations of all times was the drop on the Mitla Pass during the short-lived Suez operation of 1956. A battalion of the 202nd Airborne Brigade parachuted 300 km (190 miles) behind the enemy lines to be joined overland by the remainder of the Brigade 24 hours later. Advancing through the pass, the paras were ambushed by Egyptians dug-in on a mountainside and were harassed by concentrated artillery and air support. After bitter, close-quarter fighting, the 202nd dislodged their attackers and cleared the way through. The elan and fighting ability of this Brigade was demonstrated again in 1967 when they took the old city of Jerusalem against fanatical resistance.

AFRICA

Special forces used in Africa since the Second World War range from small groups of mercenaries to instructors from Britain, France, China, the Warsaw Pact group and Cuba to specialized regular troops, employed in anti-guerrilla operations by Rhodesia, South Africa and Portugal to the deployment of full-scale multi-unit groups such as the French Foreign Legion in Chad and the UN troops in the Congo. The whole gamut of operations has been seen since the middle of the century and continues to this day.

SOUTH AFRICA

The descendants of the Boers who formed guerrilla forces to fight the British at the beginning of the twentieth century are to be found serving in home defence units. Within the 80,000-strong regular Army there is a variety of special forces, for example, a parachute brigade based at Bloemfontein and a para-commando based at Kroonstat. The 1st Special Forces Brigade, also at Bloemfontein, contains most of the 'reccondo' units, including the Recce Commandos and a battalion of Angolan mercenaries who are trained in covert operations. The Recce Commandos also employ blacks for up-country operations on the north-east border.

Of them all, the Recce Commandos are regarded as the most elite, with their selection and training based on that of the British SAS. A proportion of the units are ex-Rhodesian SAS who have even closer links with the British equivalent. Their pre-selection is designed to ensure a high degree of intelligence and political motivation as well as to eliminate those who are not up-to-par physically. After basic training, recruits do continuation training in survival techniques, languages, the use of foreign weapons, tracking and scouting,

A member of the SADF special forces refills his water-bottles during operations. In some areas lack of water is a determining factor in the planning of patrols and it is not unusual to see soldiers carrying up to six water-bottles.

and demolitions. Some go on to become HALO and combat-swimming experts.

Most units saw service in Rhodesia until South Africa's disengagement in 1975. All have been deployed in the Angolan theatre. Operationally, these troops do long-range recce patrols to gather intelligence, often spending long periods within hostile territory. They may also be tasked with the destruction of strategic targets and communications.

The standard khaki battle dress with high boots and jungle hat are worn on 'ops'. The majority of personal equipment is carried in a double-sided backpack which is modified to permit a parachute to be fitted. Standard Western small arms are used, together with captured Chinese and Soviet weapons.

RHODESIA/ ZIMBABWE

The first Rhodesian special force was raised in response to a recruiting campaign for the Malayan Emergency and was to become 'C' Squadron of the Malayan Scouts and subsequently the reconstituted SAS. When that task ended the squadron of 250, all ranks, was based at Ndola in Northern Rhodesia as part of the armed forces of Rhodesia and Nyasaland but when the federation collapsed was reduced to a cadre. However, it later grew again in response to the threat posed by the guerrilla wars in Angola and Mozam-

bique. Joint operations with the Portuguese took men of the unit into combat and the Squadron saw continuous action from 1967 until Rhodesia became Zimbabwe in 1980. In 1978 C Squadron was redesignated the Rhodesian SAS and its all-white troops became the cadres for squadrons.

Uniform was optional when the unit was on operations and the distinguishing features of the SAS were not worn. Men carried AK-47 automatic rifles or the SVD Dragunov plus the 12.7 mm Soviet heavy machine gun, or the usual Western weaponry.

The Selous Scouts were undoubtedly the most effective of the many special forces which have been used in Africa. Raised by Reid-Daly, an ex-Rhodesian SAS officer, the ideals of that regiment were the basis upon which he developed a unit specially tailored for the terrain and type of action it encountered and endowed it with special skills such as tracking. It was multi-racial so its members were able to pose as Zipla or Zanla guerrillas on both sides of its borders and thus identify the guerrilla's structure, composition and supply systems. Guerrilla squads were then manoeuvred into contact with conventional troops. Because of the entangled nature of their operations with, at times, each side posing as the other, there were cases of atrocities being perpetrated by both sides, although the Scouts certainly did not deserve the infamous reputation they got as a result of enemy propaganda.

The 17-day selection of the Scouts was similar to that of the SAS with recruits being watched for 'the real individual' who would emerge after starvation, hardship and exhaustion, the latter being ensured by speed-marches of 32 km (20 miles), of which the last 12 km (7.5 miles) had to be done in two and a half hours while carrying a sand bag. The dedicated few who passed this test were then examined for a blend of gregariousness and self-sufficiency. Their emblem was a silver-winged Osprey badge worn on a brown beret.

On operations there was much overlap between Scouts and SAS, although the former tended to work mostly in the tribal lands on foot while the SAS tended to do those operations involving HALO or small-boat raids (for the purpose of intelligence gathering across borders) and attacks on guerrilla bases in conjunction with the Rhodesian Light Infantry (RLI).

Together these three elite fighting units, the Rhodesian SAS, the Selous Scouts and the Rhodesian Light Infantry Commandos saw some of the fiercest action of the counter-terrorist war. Between them they were responsible for more enemy dead per man than any other military unit.

Since the end of the war in 1980, these units have been disbanded, but many of their former members are serving with other armies, either in South Africa or elsewhere, where their skills and experience are being put to use in similar conflicts.

South African paratroopers during basic training, exercising with stone blocks to improve their upper body strength. Training in the SADF is rigorous by any standards.

INDO-PACIFIC REGION

This region has experienced continuous guerrilla war and insurrection since the end of the Second World War, as a result of which many special forces have been formed in order to protect ruling governments from internal subversion and national borders from external threats.

THAILAND

Thailand exemplifies the security problems of the region. Communist guerrillas fighting in Malaya have been based in Thailand for decades and pose a grave internal threat to the nation. Externally, Thailand is confronted by the armed forces of Burma and of Kampuchea (Cambodia), the latter being backed by the Vietnamese Army.

An American-type Ranger battalion has been part of the Thai army since the 1950s and became the 1st Airborne Special Forces Group in 1963. Since then three other such groups have been raised and redesignated as regiments. In the American tradition, they are primarily concerned with anti-guerrilla warfare, intelligence gathering and psychological operations, but in addition, they are tasked with training the population in counter-insurgency and local defence.

Volunteers for the Special Forces will have completed Ranger and Airborne training before undergoing selection. This takes the form of endurance marches, survival techniques, camouflage, jungle navigation and escape and evasion. During these phases of selection, volunteers operate as individuals and later graduate for integration into 'A' Teams with signals, medical, engineering and demolition specializations. All of them are trained to a high proficiency in the martial arts, usually Thai boxing.

American weapons and equipment are used but soldiers are also taught how to handle foreign weapons. They wear a two-piece camouflage uniform or a black *ninja* suit for night operations. Their distinguishing mark is a red beret with a gold cloth national army badge.

INDIA

The first Indian special forces units were parachute battalions raised during the Second World War; in 1944 Gurkha, Indian and British battalions were integrated into the 44th Indian Parachute Division. After Partition in 1947, the Indian Brigade was split between India and Pakistan. The reformed 50th Indian Parachute Brigade saw action against Pakistan in Kashmir between 1947 and 1949.

As a response to continual border clashes with Pakistan, para-commando units were formed from the existing Army Commandos (a short-lived unit) and the 9th Parachute Battalion. These are independent of the two Parachute Brigades (50th and 51st) which, between them, have eight battalions plus supporting arms.

India manufactures versions of all the foreign weapons used by its army, including the British Sterling submachine gun, the Belgian FN 7.62 mm FAL rifle and the British L4A4 7.62 mm conversion of the Bren gun. The troops wear green denim trousers, a 'Dennison' smock, DMS boots and puttees. A silver-winged parachute with an upright bayonet is worn on a maroon beret except by para-commandos, who wear a winged sword on the beret. Entrants undergo a 30-day selection course before a five-jump parachute course, which is done at Agra. Indian para-commandos trained Iraq's special forces which are now engaged in the Gulf War.

KOREA

The South The cease-fire after the Korean War left the Communist North armed and close to the South Korean capital city, Seoul, a strategic advantage which was capitalized upon by a massive expansion of the North Korean Army, much of which is deployed along the border. To counter this threat, the United States has maintained a large military presence in the South — the 8th Army's 2nd Infantry Division, supporting arms and services and a complete Wing of the US Air Force. In consequence, South Korean forces are largely equipped by the Americans.

South Korea has seven Special Forces Brigades organized in the same way as US Special Force Groups but without the distinction which the Americans make between Special Force and Ranger roles. The South Korean units are attached to different Army Corps and may be deployed in the assault commando (Ranger) role or in the anti-guerrilla/reconnaissance (US Special Forces) role. Elements of the Korean force are further trained in advanced parachuting or sea- or air-landing techniques. Capable of striking at tactical targets should the North Koreans cross the border, they would also be able to fight behind the lines as guerrillas.

Trainees get the same basic training as their US equivalents, with suitable volun-

teers graduating to advanced training. All are well versed in navigation and survival and are expected to qualify to Black Belt level in *Tae Kwon Do* (Korean karate). Their survival course has an extra and unusual element: the killing of a highly venomous snake with a karate blow and then eating it raw! Some units are trained in combat swimming and small-boat warfare, in mountain warfare and in HALO and low-opening parachute techniques.

South Korean Special Forces wear whatever uniforms are suitable for their specialized tasks: night suits, white camouflage and so on. They possess the M3A1 0.45 submachine gun, the M16 rifle and the M60 heavy machine gun. They served in Vietnam in specialist advisory roles, particularly in unarmed combat. Some may have operated in CIA- or Korean CIA-mounted operations.

The North Little is known about North Korea's special forces although estimates of their strength suggest that there are 22 special force brigades spread between the eight North Korean corps.

In common with all Soviet Bloc nations, North Korea's military philosophy is orientated to offensive and not defensive strategy. They are, therefore, likely to use their special forces to disorganize, confuse and weaken South Korean defences before the assault of conventional formations, to perform acts of sabotage, capture key civil and military sites before major airborne assault and to seek intelligence information. However, unlike special force units in Western-oriented countries, they would not be expected to show initiative and independence of thought. They would function as a small part of an overall battle plan and would be expected to stay behind enemy lines for days rather than weeks or months.

TAIWAN

In 1949, at the end of the Chinese civil war, Chiang Kai-Shek's Nationalist Army retreated to the island of Taiwan. After two unsuccessful attempts to invade offshore islands which remained under Taiwanese

A strong US and western European influence can be found in the armies of many South-East Asian countries. This mobile anti-tank team is armed with a MILAN missile system, mounted on a US-type jeep.

control, the Communists have accepted the situation and the two regimes co-exist with a policy of armed diplomacy. Even so, it remains the publicly stated long-term aim of China to reunite Taiwan with the mainland, while Taiwan has declared its unrealistic aim of recapturing the mainland.

Taiwan has a well-trained and well-armed army, about a quarter of a million strong, which also defends the offshore islands of Quemoy and Matsu which are close enough to the mainland to be the setting for artillery duels. There are four special force groups, which include two para brigades in an assault-commando role, combat swimmers for sabotage and intelligence-gathering roles and recce-commandos for long-range patrols. There is a great deal of overlap in the training and deployment for these roles. All are para-trained, including the combat swimmers, who are also, together with the recce-commandos, trained in small-boat operations.

The Taiwanese are almost exclusively American armed, though the locally made Type 65 5.56 mm rifle has begun to replace the M16A1. They also have their own version of the M3A1 submachine gun. The Taiwanese have exchanged special forces on short-term attachments with South Africa and Israel and trained Singapore's under a defence agreement.

The recce-commandos and combat swimmers based on Quemoy regularly test the mainland defences by landing agents and carrying out intelligence gathering. In return, during their selection procedures, Communist special forces are, so it is said, required to get into Taiwan and bring back souvenirs, such as cinema tickets, as proof of their having successfully done so.

AUSTRALIA

The Australian Special Air Service was formed in 1957, as the 1st SAS Company at Perth, Western Australia, the place which had been the base for the Second World War's Force Z, a unit which was designed for Special Boat Service work. Initially raised for long-range recce, the SAS Company became part of the Royal Australian Regiment but, during the Borneo confrontation, was detached again and expanded to regimental size. It now has a headquarters squadron, three sabre squadrons, a support squadron and

Opposite: South Korean paratroopers on their way to a training jump. The Republic of Korea keeps its armed forces in a constant state of readiness and its special forces are among the most highly trained in that part of the world.

Below: A Klepper canoe is brought ashore by men of the SASR. The Australian SAS are also tasked with carrying out amphibious operations of the same nature as those conducted by Britain's Special Boat Squadron.

a signals squadron. Because it is based in Western Australia, a largely unoccupied state, it has the security to train freely but covertly in the state's deserts and tropical rainforests in all commando-type operations including maritime raiding.

Selection is based on the British SAS system of timed navigation marches and takes place in the dry and featureless bush country of north-west Australia. Among the usual hardships of hunger, exhaustion and thirst, the Australian volunteer has to encounter poisonous snakes and salt-water crocodiles (which are renowned for ambushing their victims with the same stealth and cunning as an SAS patrol). Having learned parachuting, tracking, patrolling and survival to get his badge, the successful recruit must then do courses in signals, demolitions (including underwater demolitions) and foreign weapons.

The Australian SAS has enjoyed a truly international impact, having trained with Americans in Vietnam in long-range recce patrol (LRRP) techniques and at the Jungle Warfare School in Malaya, where they handed over the skills they had learned in Vietnam. They have exchange postings with US Special Forces, British and New Zealand SAS and the Arctic and Mountain Warfare Cadre and the Special Boat Section of the Royal Marines Commandos.

They wear standard Australian uniform with the sand-coloured beret and the winged dagger badge. British SAS-type para wings are worn on the right sleeve. American weapons are used, including the M16A1 rifle, the M60 machine gun and the M68 fragmentation grenade. In addition, they have a number of foreign weapons such as the Heckler and Koch sub-machine gun and the Israeli Galil SAR rifle.

The Australians have recently created a small unit of Aboriginal trackers whose task is to patrol the northern coasts and identify illegal immigrants and drug smugglers. This involves LRRPs of five to six weeks' duration in a poorly mapped, featureless and hostile environment. After

A patrol from the Australian SAS Regiment moves through thick bush during an exercise. The SASR sabre squadrons are organized along the same lines as their British counterparts.

Above: Members of the Australian SAS Regiment practise freefall parachuting from a Royal Australian Air Force UH-1 Huey.

Left: Officers and men of the 3rd Battalion the Royal Australian Regiment change their green infantry berets for the 'red berets' of the airborne forces after qualifying as paratroopers. One of the most recent airborne units, 3rd RAR adopted the airborne role in December 1983.

contact has been made, patrol boats and aircraft are called up to apprehend suspects. Although not strictly a special forces unit, it has a special forces role.

There are two Commando Regiments within the Australian Citizen Military Force, their reserve army. They are located in the major cities of eastern Australia and are organized in three or four companies plus supporting elements. They are distinguished by a green beret with a badge showing a sword piercing a boomerang (it has a striking resemblance to the SAS winged dagger). All Commando personnel are para-trained, with emphasis on marine operations. During the Vietnam War, NCOs of the Regiments served with Special Forces Training Teams.

The first operational tour was that of the 1st SAS Squadron in Brunei, to be followed by the 2nd Squadron's tour in Borneo during the Borneo confrontation 1965–66. Simultaneously, the Australian SAS began operations in Vietnam, where its three squadrons toured in rotation from 1966 until 1971. The Squadrons were based in Phuoc Tuy province south-east of Saigon and did LRRPs to identify guerrilla bases and lines of communication.

The SAS has now been given a counter-revolutionary warfare role and, in consequence, may move from Perth to one of the eastern states.

NEW ZEALAND

The New Zealand SAS was formed in 1954 to fight with the British SAS and the Rhodesian SAS in the Malayan Scouts. Of the volunteers, 138 came from civilian life and 40 officers and NCOs from the regular army but, after final selection, the squadron had less than a hundred men. Parachute training was done in Malaya, together with jungle-warfare courses.

Operations centred on eliminating Communist groups, followed by the gathering of remote communities and re-housing them in protected villages, all part of the broad 'hearts and minds' approach of the British authorities.

After Malaya, the Regiment was disbanded, but was re-established again as a Company in 1958. A troop went to Korat in Thailand in 1962 in support of the South-East Asia Treaty Organization, where, together with US Special Forces, it trained soldiers and police in counter-guerrilla warfare.

In 1963 New Zealand commemorated the centenary of two units which had operated during the Maori Wars, the Forest and the Bush Rangers, by renaming the squadron, the 1st Ranger Squadron New Zealand SAS. Since then it has seen action in Malaysia and in Vietnam and is now stationed near Auckland. It consists of a headquarters troop and five sabre troops whose selection, training, weaponry and uniform is based on the Australian SAS.

OTHER INDO-PACIFIC COUNTRIES

China, People's Republic Loosely based on the Soviet organization but more lightly equipped, China has three complete airborne divisions. Trained to operate as guerrillas or in advance of their own ground troops, they can also act as a strategic reserve to be deployed quickly to counter a specific enemy attack. Uncommon to airborne forces nowadays, Chinese paratroops come under the command of the Air Force and not the Army.

Indonesia The two Airborne Infantry Brigades in Indonesia comprise a high percentage of its military strength, considering the overall size of the Indonesian Army. It is unlikely, however, that with the few transport aircraft they possess, mostly C-130 Hercules and Short Skyvans, that they would be able to deploy more than a few companies by parachute.

Japan The 1st Airborne Brigade is the only airborne brigade of Japan's Self-Defence Forces. Although the Brigade is para-trained, the emphasis is on heliborne rather than airborne operations. The Japanese also have a special Naval Landing Force which includes, within its ranks, a number of combat swimmers, trained along the lines of US Navy SEALs.

SOUTH AMERICA

Brazil The Brazilian Army is one of the best-trained and equipped in South America. It has one Independent Parachute Brigade with integral supporting elements. The US influence can be seen in its organization and equipment and, unlike a number of smaller countries, Brazil is capable of deploying the Brigade by air.

Chile Another South American country with a viable airborne force, Chile has a number of paratroops from the Chilean Airborne Brigade which also undergo special forces training. Chilean special forces have strong links with US Special Forces who are responsible for some of their training.

INDEX

Figures in italics refer to illustrations